P9-DDI-167

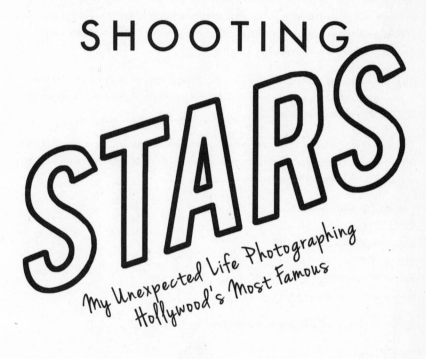

SHOOTING STARS

My Unexpected Life Photographing Hollywood's Most Famous

JENNIFER BUHL

sourcebooks

This book is a memoir. It reflects the author's present recollections of her experiences over a period of years. Some names and characteristics have been changed, some events have been compressed, and some dialogue has been re-created.

Published by Sourcebooks, Inc.

P.O. Box 4410

Naperville, Illinois 60567-4410

(630) 961-3900

Fax: (630) 961-2168

www.sourcebooks.com

Library of Congress Cataloging-in-Publication Data

Buhl, Jennifer.

  Shooting stars : my unexpected life photographing hollywood's most famous / Jennifer Buhl.

    pages cm

  (alk. paper)

  1. Buhl, Jennifer. 2. Paparazzi—United States—Biography. 3. Women photographers—United States—Biography. 4. Celebrities—California—Los Angeles—Miscellanea. I. Title.

  TR140.B845A3 2014

  070.4'9--dc23

2013046457

Printed and bound in the United States of America.

WOZ 10 9 8 7 6 5 4 3 2 1

To Rhe, Al, and Jo, who have never stopped believing in me.

Contents

Author's Note

*A*ll the events in this book are true to the best of my recollection. Celebrity names, appearances, and/or details have been represented as accurately as possible to the best of my recall.

To keep the nonfamous *nonfamous*, some names, distinguishing characteristics, and other details of noncelebrities, events, and individuals have been changed to protect identities.

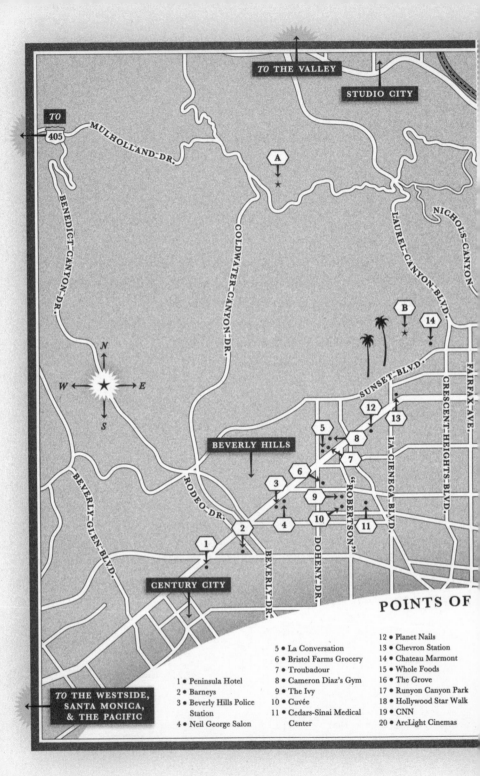

TO THE VALLEY

STUDIO CITY

TO 405

MULHOLLAND-DR.

A
★

STUDIO CITY

LAUREL-CANYON-BLVD.

NICHOLS-CANYON

BENEDICT-CANYON-DR.

COLDWATER-CANYON-DR.

N
W — E
S

B
★

14

SUNSET-BLVD.

CRESCENT-HEIGHTS-BLVD.

FAIRFAX-AVE.

BEVERLY HILLS

12

13

5

8

7

LA-CIENEGA-BLVD.

BEVERLY-GLEN-BLVD.

RODEO-DR.

6

3

9

4

10

"ROBERTSON"

11

BEVERLY-DR.

DOHENY-DR.

2

1

CENTURY CITY

TO THE WESTSIDE, SANTA MONICA, & THE PACIFIC

POINTS OF

1 • Peninsula Hotel
2 • Barneys
3 • Beverly Hills Police Station
4 • Neil George Salon

5 • La Conversation
6 • Bristol Farms Grocery
7 • Troubadour
8 • Cameron Diaz's Gym
9 • The Ivy
10 • Cuvée
11 • Cedars-Sinai Medical Center

12 • Planet Nails
13 • Chevron Station
14 • Chateau Marmont
15 • Whole Foods
16 • The Grove
17 • Runyon Canyon Park
18 • Hollywood Star Walk
19 • CNN
20 • ArcLight Cinemas

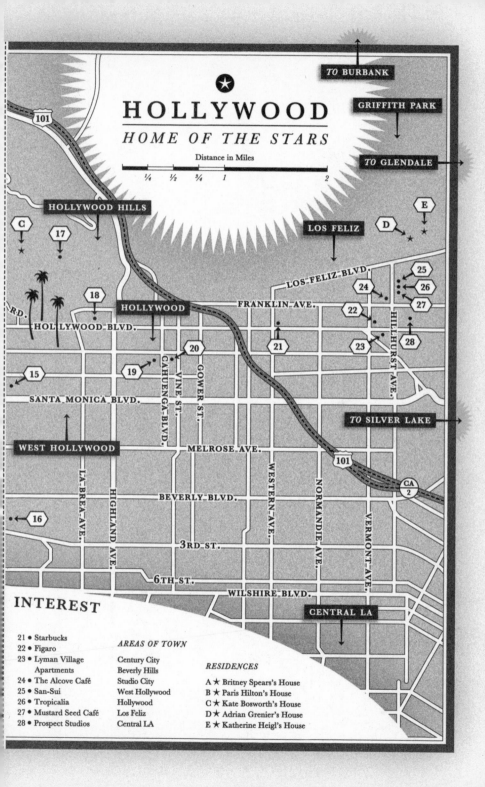

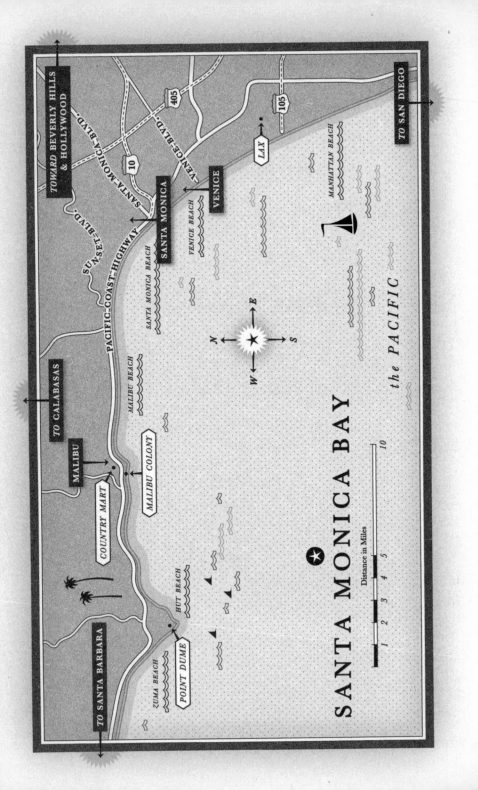

pa·pa·raz·zo *noun*, plural -raz·zi

a photographer who pursues celebrities to get candid pictures for publication.

in slang, paparazzi is used as singular—a successful paparazzi.

paparazza is the singular feminine; possibly a word I made up.

Origin: Italian. The last name of a news photographer in Federico Fellini's *La Dolce Vita* (1959), which was the name of a restaurant owner—Coriolano Paparazzo—in George Gissing's *By the Ionian Sea* (1901), a book read by Fellini at the time of the movie's production.

An alternate and contested origin of the word states that it originated from the Italian word *pappataci*, which describes a small, buzzing mosquito-like insect.

Introduction

*M*y lunch shift at Tropicalia, the Brazilian restaurant up the street from my apartment, has just ended. I'm sitting on the restaurant's patio drinking coffee and reading the newspaper. I didn't come to L.A. to be a waitress, but I'm thankful for the job.

I hear tires skid on the pavement and look up. Eight blacked-out SUVs have come to a screeching halt in front of White Trash Charms, the boutique across the street. I watch as seven guys jump out of their vehicles and a beautiful, skinny blond gets out of hers. It could be a mugging or robbery, or possibly gang violence.

No. It's Paris Hilton. Shopping.

I've never seen paparazzi in action before. For ten minutes, the guys press their cameras against the store window, bursts of flash going off every few seconds. When a meter maid walks up to write Paris's car a ticket, one of the paparazzi tries to negotiate on her behalf. Unsuccessful, he instead captures the ticket-writing moment. When Paris exits, the men crouch in front of her, moving backward while taking her picture. It's very physical, but oddly friendly somehow. The men thunder about loudly and intrusively, yet Paris remains untouched in a small bubble of space. And keeps smiling.

She drives off in her Range Rover, followed by a chain of similarly sized vehicles. But I notice one nice-looking Latino paparazzo has stayed behind and is sorting through pictures on his camera. I'm curious about the whole spectacle—and a little starstruck too—so I amble over and strike up a conversation with the first question that comes to mind: "How much do you make on a picture?"

"Oh, at least five hundred," he says.

Holy snap. Right then and there, it's like God whacks me over the head. I have $50 in my pocket and less than a thousand in my bank account; my life is lackluster and I want more. I just haven't figured out how to make "more" happen.

"Do y'all ever hire girls?"

★ ★ ★

One week later, Richard (the nice-looking Latino paparazzo) has agreed to let me ride along. From the passenger seat of his SUV, I witness the year's No. 1 out-of-control celebrity: Britney Spears.

At least twenty guys swarm her car like bees around a hive. *They ought to call this a* gangbang, I think. Later I find out they do.[1] I see bursts of light amid thick, burly men. Britney is the only woman. I hear her name:

"Britney, can I get a smile?"

"How you today, Brit?"

"Brit, here!"

"Here!"

"Here!"

Five minutes prior, we were midway in the caravan, eight or nine cars back, when Britney's car turned into a parking lot and abruptly stopped. Richard followed, slammed into park, left the engine running, and took off sprinting. No way could I ever move that fast.

Immediately I lose track of him in the mass of men. Britney is the one to watch though. She is the passenger and has her door open with one leg hanging out. After about thirty seconds, her driver, Sam Lutfi, a guy who will later have a restraining order slapped on him by Britney's dad, starts to pull away with her door still ajar and her leg still hanging out. Slowly though, lest he run someone over. Or lest the Brit fall out...

Some of the men run alongside the vehicle as it begins to move through

---

1. Refer to the Glossary of Paparazzi Terms in the back of the book.

the deserted parking lot. Perhaps they think she'll stop again and get out. Others run back to their cars so they don't miss what is apparently called *the follow*.

Richard startles me when he opens the car door and jumps back in. Carelessly, he tosses his gargantuan camera, flash, and handful of tangled cords off to the side, and thousands of dollars' worth of equipment thuds to the floorboard where he leaves it. His car lurches when he pulls into drive, and we play no-touch bumper cars with the others, inching forward little by little until we fall into line. The race restarts.

This seemingly purposeless pass through an office park is our first stop, ten miles out from Britney Spears's Malibu home. According to Richard, she does this frequently—stopping haphazardly, sometimes getting out, sometimes not. "She likes to see us run," he says.

Why, I wonder, *would anyone participate in something like this? Does she have a choice? Is this what happens to all the stars?*

Now we're headed up Sunset Boulevard, toward town, into Beverly Hills. Though it's rush hour, we move fairly fast in our seamless convoy. Nobody stops at lights: it's as if we were strewn together like one long beaded necklace.

When we first left Britney's, Richard called in backup on his walkie-talkie and it has now arrived: Jean-Luc, a well-dressed Frenchman wearing dress pants, not jeans like everyone else, and an ironed shirt, joins us on the *chase*. He's on a motorcycle, and another guy is sitting behind him recording video. Richard says that's stupid: "Does he want to kill himself? Lunatic Frenchie."

We are mostly large SUVs, about twenty or twenty-five of us at this point plus the Brit-mobile, and more keep coming. Richard jockeys for position, in and out, missing other cars by centimeters as he tries to get closer to the elusive celeb. Apparently it's vital to be one car ahead—one car closer—in a line of two dozen.

Interestingly, no one looks to be endangering Britney. Everyone is behind her, going as slow or fast as she does, not crowding her. It's a stark contrast to the scene at the office park minutes earlier. It makes sense though: What would be the point of overtaking the car you are trying to follow? It's the paparazzi who own the jeopardy on the road, as well as unrelated drivers who happen to get in their way. The pedestrians could be at risk too. They gawk, confused as to what is going on as we edge curbs and ignore crosswalks hoping to gain ground against the competition.

We wind through Beverly Hills, into West Hollywood, and turn left off Sunset onto a narrow residential street, Kings Road.

"Holy shit, we're going to Paris's," Richard says. "Them two together are big." He informs me that Britney has been seen with the world's most famous socialite this week.

Our train inches up the steep, winding hill. *I think I can. I think I can…* Richard stands up and leans his body out the window while keeping his foot on the gas pedal and honking the horn. Cars ahead of us have stopped in the middle of the road. He cusses when he bumps the SUV in front of him (rather hard, I think), but it's another paparazzo so neither stops.

When we can't go any farther, Richard grabs his camera, jumps out, and like the others, leaves his car parked in the middle of the road. This time I get out too, running uphill a few feet behind him to a medium-sized stucco home covered in bougainvillea. It is situated on a small lot covered with vines and palm trees, and a low fence separates the property from its neighbors'. The environs remind me of Italy.

There are about twenty guys pacing in agitated circles. They are standing in the middle of the road in front of the house, their cameras dangling from their necks like wattles.

"Are we too late?" I ask. I might not be shooting, but I'm already starting to feel the desire: *I want the shot too.*

Soon I learn that this is Paris's house, but that Britney is not here. No one in the group knows where she went, or at least they're not letting on if they do. The road was too curvy, and Richard was too far back in the chain to do anything but follow the car directly ahead of him. Like the others, he figured she was going to Paris's.

Richard talks to the guy whose bumper he hit, and it sounds amicable. When we hear the noise of an approaching car, everyone moves to the side of the road, and the queen bee's GMC Yukon flies by, followed by a half dozen other ginormous vehicles. *And that's the reason it's important to be one car ahead: the closer you are to the celeb, the more likely you'll be able to keep up.*

But there is no race to the cars this time. Even I, a first-timer, can tell that we would never catch up: a giant parking lot of paparazzi SUVs sits on Kings Road, and too many vehicles block one another. She will be gone in a few seconds anyway.

It's dark now, and I ask Richard how late he works. The action was barely two hours, but the adrenaline that spiked through my system has left me exhausted. "As late as it goes," he shrugs. "But it's over today. Let's get your car."

We drive back to Malibu at a steady pace, but it still takes an hour. When we get back, my car is the only one remaining on the dirt road outside Britney's private seaside subdivision, the Malibu Colony, where Richard and I met for the ride-along ten hours earlier. I spent the morning making "contacts"—I need this to turn into an actual job—walking from car to car through two rows of paparazzi parked on either side of the road. I was the only female among the group of mostly Latino and British men. I wasn't surprised about the lack of women per se, but I did think it was odd that there were practically no Americans. The guys all seemed to leer at me in my short skirt and tall boots too. *What was I thinking, wearing that?* Most assumed I was a tabloid reporter and chuckled when I told them I was training to be paparazzi. One of them, the only American I met, showed me his new picture of Britney: a peek-a-boo of her shaved snatch, completely bald, folds and all, which I really didn't care to see. "It's all over the Internet," he said proudly, feathers puffed up like a mating rooster.

Apparently Britney had flashed the paparazzi when she'd gotten out of her car last week. *Who doesn't wear underwear with a short skirt when cameras are all around? Was that intentional?*

The fact was, at that point, I knew very little about any celebrity. I'd lived in L.A. for a year and a half but had seen just one, Brian Austin Green, and that was on a production assistant (PA) job I'd picked up for two days off Craigslist. And obviously, you can barely count Brian Austin Green as a celebrity.

I get out of Richard's car and am nearly run over when the Yukon barrels by me and into the private subdivision. The smaller procession, maybe five or six vehicles, is still trailing, and they again park on the shoulder of the road outside the Malibu Colony: Britney's back home.

But neither Richard nor I will wait around for a nighttime outing. I head east toward my home in Los Feliz, processing my day on the long drive. *Is it always this intense? Will I eventually be able to handle more…or start to crave more? Could it possibly kill me?*

The ultimate video game is what I equate it to: spying, celebrities, chases, shooting, loot—*Will there be loot? Please, let there be loot!*—everything is here. And more—it's reality.

Britney was the prize today; the one…devoured.

Could she possibly like it?

Richard says she loves it. So does he.

★ ★ ★

After watching the Paris and Britney gangbangs (as vulgar as that sounds to me, I will soon desensitize to the term), I was in. Now I needed to figure out how to get the job.

Paparazzi firms are news agencies. Celebrity news, albeit, but they are every bit as on-call as CNN. I phone a firm whose name I find online and get right through to the owner.

"Dylan Sheen," he answers.

"Hi Dylan," I begin. "My name is Jennifer. I'm an amateur photographer and would like to be a paparazzi." I use the plural since "paparazzo" doesn't seem like the right word.

"What's the difference between f4 and f10?" he asks aggressively.

"Ahhh,"—I haven't thought about that in a while—"well, f4 is a wider aperture, so you need less light. It also has a smaller depth of field."

"What's the aperture's correlation to the shutter speed?"

When I answer that correctly too, he changes tactics.

"Well, we don't just want a picture of Britney Spears. We want a picture of Britney without any underwear on. We want pictures of Britney Spears's PUSSY."

He makes sure to say that last word extra-loud with an emphasis on the "Pu." Then he pauses, sure he's gotten me.

Freak, I think. *Who says the P-word to someone they don't know?*

"OK," I say out loud.

He carries on a bit more about getting *the shot,* then suddenly has to go. "Call me back in an hour and we'll meet," he says and hangs up.

I *really* don't want to meet Dylan. Even more, I don't want to take pictures like that.

But why would I have to? Ethical boundaries exist in every profession. I've always respected mine. I still would.

Next I try Aaron, a Scottish guy from an agency called Celebrity X News (CXN).[2] I met Aaron on the street the day of the Britney chase and while, no joke, I couldn't understand more than two consecutive words he said to me, I'm pretty sure he told me to call him if I wanted a job. Aaron answers on the first ring and puts me in touch with his boss at CXN.

From the outset, the agency seems professional, possibly because both Aaron and his boss are British, and like most Americans, I'm a sucker for the accent. I schedule an interview, thrilled not to have to call Dylan back.

★ ★ ★

Five days later, I'm at CXN's office in Venice Beach. Right off, the space feels comfortable—there are no sterile cubicles, the kind that make my chest contract in suffocation; no boring-looking people in suits poring over their computers; no beige carpet, cream walls, or uniform furniture;

---

2. Unless noted, names of celebrity photo agencies have been changed.

no hushed voices. Everyone works in one open room with camera equipment and tabloid magazines strewn over a small floor space and large posters on the wall—blown-up pictures of celebrities in tabloids with CXN's credit line emblazoned on the bottom.

The staff introduces themselves. I meet one of the three owners, an American and former paparazzo who shot the O. J. freeway chase and used the cash he collected to start the business; two English editors, including Aaron's boss J.R.; and a secretary, also British, who says she brokers online sales.

J.R. is the staff coordinator and lead photo editor. He appears either mildly autistic or mildly drunk—at this point I'm not sure which—and takes me outside while he has a cigarette. He asks whether I'd like to work days or nights.

"Days, I guess." That sounded better to me.

"Days pay more," J.R. says. Lucky me.

When we get back inside, he asks if I have a sample of my work. I show him my backpacking-through-Asia photos which happen to be on my laptop: the Pushkar Festival with throngs of Indians selling camels; Ton Sai climbers hanging on rocks over the Indian Sea; Ko Phi Phi, the Thai island ravaged in the 2004 tsunami; naked Buddha statues; more naked Buddha statues.

"I don't get to see pictures like this very often," he says as he scrolls through. "They're nice."

He asks me one more interview question: "Have you ever been convicted of star-stalking?"

I laugh.

Pause. Pause. Pause. Pause. Like ten seconds here.

But it was a serious question. "I have to ask," he finally says when I don't respond.

"Uh, no. I've never really been that interested in the stars." I rarely read the tabloids and am the worst star-spotter out there. But I don't tell him that. I've always wanted to be a CIA agent too. I don't tell him that either.

J.R. has little faith in me beyond avoiding a restraining order, that much I can tell, but it's clear he's also fascinated by the prospect of hiring

me. I offer variety to the stale, mostly male paparazzi culture. Some soft-
ness. Womanness. At the moment, CXN doesn't have any female shooters. "Almost nobody does," he says. "You'd be freelance too, pay your own
expenses and find your own stories."

Apparently I was hired. Sort of.

And why not? The risk for him was minimal, and if I were as talented
as I was confident, his payoff could be big. An agency makes 40 percent
of every freelance picture it sells, and one sales guy can easily market
the photos of twenty or more photographers every day. The more photo
contributors CXN has, the more money they make.

From J.R. I request just one thing: equipment to borrow until I can
afford my own. J.R. rummages through a closet and finds a dusty camera,
the kind whose batteries last not quite twenty minutes of consecutively
being "on," and some other parts I'll need. He leans out the window and
takes a few test shots of a seagull on a telephone pole. "It seems to work,"
he says, and hands it over.

"When I was on the streets," J.R. offers, "my partner was a woman. She
made twice the money I did."

"Does she still work?" I ask.

"Nope. Decided to go have a baby."

I smile at the thought. J.R. doesn't care if I'm interested in the stars
and he doesn't care if I have experience. He only cares about one thing:
if I can make him money. I'm another camera on the street, and a pink
one to boot.

Year 1

Chapter 1

City of Angels is a false moniker. It's vampires, not angels, that run the town. Exquisite but bloodthirsty, Los Angeles was sucking the life out of me. I was losing vision, confidence, and most of all, hope. One swift bite would kill me. And I, with my cup half-full of self-assuredness and optimism, was one of the strong ones.

Like most, I had come to the city to pursue my dream of working in "the industry," the film and television business. I arrived eighteen months prior with a boatload of confidence and five years of solid production experience. Why wouldn't I get hired?

I applied for hundreds of positions. New postings appeared online every hour, and my résumé met many of them word for word. After a month of receiving no responses, my search broadened: waitress, coffee shop, sales girl, temp job, anything. I breathed easier when Priscilla's Coffee in Studio City hired me. But it wouldn't take care of the rent or other mounting expenses. I continued applying for production work and during the next six months received two responses to my inquiries. One resulted in the two-day Brian Austin Green gig; the other in an interview for work on a reality show, which I did not get. It seemed thousands of talented, experienced people were applying for the same jobs. Like available men in the city, there were just not enough to go around.

Eventually, I bagged the search for a TV job and spent all my free time working on my real dream: an undercover media project that I couldn't figure out how to film (and which if I told you about, I'd have to kill you). To pay the bills, I picked up odd jobs and continued working as a barista, then waitress. A year and a half later, I had almost gone through the $12,000 my brother had lent me when I first moved to the city and wasn't sure how I'd continue to make up the discrepancy between my meager paychecks and my expenses, nor how I'd ever pay my brother back.

Loneliness was setting in too. Besides money, I needed a man. I had hit the mid-thirties panic: still young enough to have kids (I want three!), but needing to start *now*. And my heart longed for a mate, not just a baby. Most guys I met, however, were like me: artist-types working at restaurants. But unlike me, these men gave priority to their dreams over their relationships. They didn't want wives; they especially didn't want babies; and they had endless things to do before they thought of settling down. I knew I needed to escape my hipster Los Feliz neighborhood and find manly men who were more concerned with women than their "art," but I didn't know how. The little I'd dabbled in Internet dating had left me feeling even more desperate.

Not only was I lonesome, I was bored, a curse like death for an extrovert like me. I had fantastic girlfriends, but socially, I longed for the male interaction and constant community I had had before moving to L.A., as a backpacker traipsing my way through parts of Europe, Southeast Asia, Australia, and New Zealand. I get my energy from others, and if I'm not around people—*a lot*—I start to fade. Serving lattes to customers at Priscilla's Coffee for eight hours didn't cut it.

And then, there was the "diving board." For years, I had been having this strange recurring vision: a picture of me on a high-dive board, bouncing. I interpreted it to mean that I was being prepared for something, and that I was bouncing to get ready—to get height, so that eventually I could jump. For some time, I had been asking God, *Can I please dive off already? Didn't you make me with a purpose in mind? Why is my life such a waste?*

I needed direction. I needed fuel. I needed money, a man, and motivation. My prayers to God had become fervent: if I didn't get help—quick—those bloodsucking beasts (destitution, loneliness, and purposelessness) would smell weak prey, and I would be taken. In other words, without a big break soon, my days in this city were numbered.

And that's when God whacked me over the head with *the paparazzi*.

★ ★ ★

The Monday after visiting CXN's offices, I start working. "It's official," I tell my friends. "I'm a pop...I mean, *pap*," I explain, stumbling over the funny nickname the paparazzi call themselves. (I realize that some of you will initially have a problem with this term and you will only be able to think of a gynecological procedure. Don't worry, that will pass.)

New pap training begins on "Robertson," a stretch of Robertson Boulevard between 3rd Street and Beverly Boulevard. Here, expensive shops and trendy restaurants line the sidewalk, and every day, the dining and shopping attract at least one famous person. Dozens of paparazzi loiter the pedestrian-friendly sidewalk waiting to spot that someone.

By the end of the week, I have shot one celebrity: Danny Bonaduce. I probably don't have to tell you how little the world cares about Danny Bonaduce. It's like a sports photographer going to a pro football game and shooting the water boy.

After five days on Robertson, it is crystal clear that I have no idea what I'm doing, and if I want to succeed at this job I'll need help. So, both by way of necessity and because he's charming, I choose Aaron—the unintelligible Scottish guy—as my mentor. He has no idea what he's in for.

★ ★ ★

On Saturday, my friend JoDeane and I are out for a neighborhood stroll. After my lackluster week on Robertson, I'm beginning to question my new career choice—perhaps I misinterpreted God's message—and Jo's talking me through it. We are a couple of blocks from my apartment when we see a classic convertible with the top down turning into the entrance of Prospect Studios.

"Do you know who that is?" JoDeane whispers as we walk past the studio driveway while the smoking-hot guy in the convertible whom I do not recognize in the slightest waits for us to cross in front of him.

"No. Is it someone famous?" I ask.

"Patrick Dempsey. Doctor McDreamy. Please don't stare, Jen."

I do anyway. I swear, had he even a dim resemblance to the gawky teenager in the old 1980s flick *Can't Buy Me Love,* I would have recognized him. Surely. The man in front of us, however, is neither skinny nor awkward. He is not youthful or gangly. He is not the least bit self-conscious. What he is is strikingly attractive—a strong-jawed, manly man with a thick mane of dark hair atop his head and a six-o'clock shadow any woman would want burning her body. He is possibly supernatural.

Let me be clear: JoDeane has a talent I now wish I had with my new gig. She *always* sees celebrities. She has this weird celebrity radar. As I mentioned, I've seen Brian Austin Green. And I needed someone to tell me it was Brian Austin Green, and then I needed him to tell me who the hell Brian Austin Green was. Of course, I've also now seen Paris and Britney. And let's not forget Danny Bonaduce. JoDeane, by comparison, has probably seen, like, twenty-five celebrities this year alone.

Later, when I tell J.R. about the Dempsey sighting, he agrees it's "worth a go" and assigns me to Aaron via an email. Aaron and I are to meet at 8:30 a.m. in front of Prospect Studios. My first official assignment—I am stoked!

★ ★ ★

"I didn't sleep the night before" is unfortunately not a cliché but a full-blown reality for me. The morning mirror disappoints—a lack of rest is harder to hide when you're thirty-five and a half.

I stick on a hat to cover what I can, throw on Hudsons—my only pair of designer jeans, which I wear most every day—a "Sweet and Toxic" T-shirt from Urban Outfitters, and the cowboy boots I've had since college. I skip out the door and walk down the street to meet Aaron at the studios.

"Hi!" he says, giving me a hug. I've noticed Aaron hugs like he never wants to let go. "How's the new pap?"

"Goooood," I say, suddenly shy.

After pleasantries, I describe Patrick's car as best as I can remember considering my pea-size regard for vehicles. "It was small. And blue. Possibly?" I show him where JoDeane and I walked, and exactly how the convertible pulled into the studio lot. I also tell him that I read that Patrick is a "family man" and deeply in love with his wife, a "regular" woman.

"That's not gonna help you spot him," Aaron says, rolling his deep blue eyes.

After briefly considering the rest of the information, Aaron moves his SUV to the lively four-way intersection near the entrance of the studio, pulls to the curb, and parks. "This'll do," he says. Apparently Aaron thinks the stop-sign intersection is the best place to watch for Dempsey's arrival to work, which later I realize makes sense: it's much easier to shoot into a nonmoving vehicle. Aaron grabs two packets of sunflower seeds from inside his car. "I'm *peckish*," he says, then hops out and onto the hood of his 4Runner.

I hesitate, not sure what to do.

"Right here, luv," he says, patting the metal beside him.

For the next three hours, we sit on Aaron's car, not looking out of place in L.A. where anything goes, and I play a role at which I'm adept: overeager student.

I'm still using the camera from J.R.'s closet. Aaron picks it up. "I don't understand it," he says after turning a few dials on the back. "It's a piece of shit," he decides.

"Well, what should I do?"

"Put it on automatic for now. Buy another. We'll rely on mine today." (Note: "Automatic" isn't really a setting on a professional SLR camera. The "Program" function, which automatically sets the f-stop and shutter speed, is what Aaron meant.)

Aaron's *Nextel*, a walkie-talkie, *chirps* on and off all morning with pap friends checking in. "Any action? Any action?" they always begin with.

"No action. No action," Aaron responds.

"You need to get a Nextel," he tells me.

Paps use Nextels more than their phones. "Especially on follows," Aaron says. "If you got a partner, you don't have time to dial and wait. Ring, ring. Pick up. When a follow's trying to lose you, ya gotta get to your mate, *now*."

Aaron's body jitters and his leg shakes when he talks. I don't mask my study of him: he's wearing well-worn designer jeans that hang loosely on his skinny frame, black Converse lace-ups with holes in them, and a vintage plaid button-down. His thick blond hair falls in his eyes and could use a trim, and he wears horn-rimmed glasses that make him look like he could be working on a PhD. *He's trendy*, I think. *Just like everybody in L.A.* I also notice that he has a mole on his cheek in the same spot as Cindy Crawford does. I don't know Aaron's age—haven't asked 'cause I don't want him to ask mine—but I imagine he's about thirty.

The morning passes. Aaron has gone through both packets of sunflower seeds plus yesterday's "leftovers" from his pocket. These seeds are his breakfast and lunch, I notice. He eats them like a bird—pops one into his mouth, cracks it between his teeth, digs the seed out with his tongue, then spits out the shell. "Dexterous tongue. Important," he mumbles at one point. Not sure how to reply, I say nothing.

By noon, Aaron's bored. "Let's go find someone," he says as he jumps down from the hood and chucks his very expensive camera on the front seat. "We're going to trawl. Get in."

"You mean *troll*?"

"No. I mean *trawl*."

"Trawling" or "trolling" is the equivalent of police "cruising," and according to Aaron, paps, like the cops, spend significantly more time trawling and waiting for celebrities to appear than being in action. *Trawl* is British for "troll."

So, we take off. On the way into town, Brian, another CXN pap with a sexy accent I can't yet place, beeps in on the Nextel and we make a plan to meet at "Halle's." Apparently, Halle Berry's house is in the heart of West Hollywood and a central place for paps to convene. Aaron says if you gotta meet up, you might as well do it at a celeb's house. "You're always keeping tabs on 'em. Gotta know who's in town, who's staying at home, who's shagging at their boyfriend's," he says.

With light traffic, it takes us about twenty minutes to get there. Just as we pull up, Brian's SUV is U-turning, and he circles his arm out the window and motions for Aaron to follow.

"Sweet. There's the vixen." Aaron points to the white SUV that's two cars in front of Brian's. "That's her."

"No way!" I squeal. The novelty of seeing a celebrity will not wear off for quite some time.

We follow Halle for barely a mile. Then she pulls into the parking lot of a veterinary office. Aaron whips his car into position, as does Brian, and the two hang out their windows taking pictures of her from about fifty feet away as she walks into the vet holding her dog.

The camera echoes a fast *chuh-chuh-chuh, chuh-chuh-chuh*. "You'll start to love that sound," Aaron says when he's done.

I agree. It is a lovely sound, like money coming out of a slot machine.

Brian pulls his SUV around next to us. "Think she saw us?" he says to Aaron.

"I think so. She obviously didn't care."

"We got it anyway."

"It's *nailed*," Aaron agrees. "Let's get outta here."

"I heard Gwen's at the Ivy."

"Yeah, me too. See ya there."

★ ★ ★

I know the Ivy. Everyone in L.A. knows the Ivy. It's a restaurant on Robertson where celebrities go to be photographed and other diners go to see celebrities. All lunch entrées are $28.50 and mediocre. I've eaten there once, and (obviously) didn't see anyone famous…or at least didn't recognize them. "It'll be a gangbang," Aaron warns, "but it's good practice for you."

That makes me nervous. I've only ever witnessed a gangbang, never joined one. As we drive past, I see a mass of bodies surrounding the restaurant. We find a metered spot a few blocks away, and Aaron gets out fast, fiddling with his camera. Since my camera has one functioning setting—Automatic—I don't have anything to fiddle with.

We walk briskly. When we are two blocks from the Ivy, Aaron looks up and points to a convertible sports car stopped at the light ahead. "Hey, is that the kind of car Dempsey drives?" he says.

"Yeah, it looked something like that."

I grab his arm. "Aaron, I think it's him."

"Run," he says without missing a beat.

"Huh?"

"Run," he says again and pushes me forward. "Go get it."

I'm thinking, if Aaron really believed Dempsey were in that car, he'd be running with me. But I run anyway, something I will get good at, and when I get to the intersection, the car is still waiting, and—you're not gonna believe this—the same smoking-hot guy is inside! The light changes and he wants to turn, but two girls are walking the crosswalk in front of him so he must wait. My camera is to my face now, and I call out, "Patrick!" He looks up, then back at the road like he doesn't see me. I snap five frames before he drives off.

I feel higher than I've felt in months as I walk, beaming, toward the gangbang. It's in this moment I realize I will succeed at this job.

Aaron stands tall and fair in the crowd of mostly Latino men. He's easy to spot outside the Ivy.

"It was him, Aaron! Can you believe it?"

"Did you get it?"

"I think so. I took five pictures."

"Let's see 'em."

"Remember, I gotta preserve the batteries. We shouldn't."

"Ahh, right. Well, I'm sure you got him. That's great, mate. Your first set. Congratulations." Aaron appears excited for me. He's told me this business is cutthroat and competitive, but he doesn't seem that way. How bad could it be?

"What should I do here?" I ask, ready for another hit of adrenaline. There doesn't look to be a way to move closer to the restaurant, and I can't see over the thirty-something paparazzi heads crowded up against the patio rail, much less shoot.

"Nuzzle up in there," he says, softly pushing me into the pack.

I wish to blend in, but know I do not. I feel like the new kid at a school where no one speaks my language. The pap crowd rocks like gentle waves, up and back, and eventually I make my way in and off to one side. I'm elbow-to-elbow with bunches of non-Beverly-Hills-looking guys wearing baseball caps and droopy gangsta-like trousers, all toting massive cameras. No one speaks to me and no one makes eye contact, but I can *feel* I am noticed furtively. Aaron, who stands with Brian on the other side of the heap, winks at me every once in a while.

We wait an hour. Just when Gwen Stefani is about to come out—and we know this because the Ivy's security team posts up on the patio like military guards—the paps hush and cameras move into position. Gwen walks out and down the steps leisurely, smiling, head held high. She's even lovelier in person than she is in the magazines—all eyes and lips on baby white skin. It's a shame though that her equally luscious husband, British singer Gavin Rossdale, isn't accompanying her. Gavin, like Dempsey, is another spectacular male who appears, from my occasional tabloid perusals, to be extremely in love with his wife. I shoot nonstop, and while my camera's faltered *chug-a-chug-chug* doesn't sound like Aaron's, I get shots—a few of which will end up in focus. Aaron and Brian get pictures from their angles, and we'll put them together in one set. Maybe we'll make nothing, or maybe we'll make a few hundred. "Gas money," Aaron says.

Big money, I think. I haven't made more than a hundred-a-day in years.

Gwen departs, and the paps scurry off in every direction, like ants after their hill has been stepped on. Except for Brian and Aaron. They stay on the sidewalk and keep chatting.

"Three sets *in the bag*," Aaron says referring to Halle's, Patrick's, and Gwen's pictures. "Let's just enjoy it." Then he scoops two more lint-flecked sunflower seeds out of his pocket and pops them into his mouth.

I stand at Aaron's side awkwardly, listening to him talk to Brian about work and celebrities but not being included in the conversation or knowing exactly how to join. Brian won't even look at me.

Aaron tells me later that when Brian first saw me, he remarked, "*She's* a pap? How's that gonna work?"

Aaron explains: "Don't get me wrong, Jen. We all think it's nice to have *birds* around [girls, he means]. We just aren't sure how to 'integrate' you."

I don't see this as an immediate concern. I mean, I've never had problems making friends before. But as one of approximately six female shooters among hundreds of Los Angeles paparazzi, I will soon discover how hard "integration" really is.

The respite outside the Ivy is short. Aaron's Nextel beeps. It's J.R. with a tip: Matthew Perry is at the ArcLight cinemas.

"Awesome! I love *Friends*!" I gush.

Aaron and Brian look at me like I have three heads. "He's worthless," Aaron says. "But there are worse ways to end the day."

I can tell that even if "Matthew is worthless," Aaron is still running high on Halle, Patrick, and Gwen-drenaline.

"You coming?" he says to Brian.

"Hell, yeah."

★ ★ ★

At the famous Hollywood theater off Sunset Boulevard, Brian takes an obscure hiding place on the second story of the parking deck, and Aaron and I position ourselves on the ground level. Even though I tell him, "I really want to see Matthew," he faces me twenty feet away from the theater's exit, toward him and his camera. Aaron plans to shoot—literally—through the crook of my elbow, and apparently if I face out, that will look strange to Matthew, and he will know subconsciously that something is off and may cover his face. "No celeb's ever gonna notice you with your back toward them," Aaron says.

We don't have to wait long. Matthew exits before the movie lets out, we take shots, and he never sees us. I get to see the back of his head once he passes.

"And that's how it's done," says Aaron.

Our shooting day is over. It was fruitful, but I shouldn't expect that every day, Aaron warns. We also still have a couple of hours of editing ahead of us, but that's OK with me. I'm falling in love. We go to Starbucks, and I watch Aaron knock out a preliminary cut and edit on his laptop. We probably have a hundred shots of Halle, Gwen, and Matthew altogether, but only edit and send in the best ten or so of each. Brian will do the same with his shots. I have just five of Dempsey and we send in two—two that are actually medium-sharp! The editors at the agency will combine the sets and take another crack at editing. "They like to feel useful," Aaron says, "so they usually make a few adjustments. Mostly they just resize though." By midnight, or sooner, the pictures will be posted to CXN's website and sent out via email to all major magazine and blog editors and to CXN's affiliate agents around the world. By eight the next morning, the pictures may end up on one or many blog sites—PerezHilton, TMZ, People.com—and magazine editors and TV producers will start calling if they want to buy any for their next hard copy issues or tabloid shows.

I never find out what our shots of Halle, Gwen, or Matthew went for. "They never tell you," Aaron explains. "You gotta look for it in your sales report in three months. By then you won't remember today." But the next day J.R. calls to congratulate me on my first sale, one of my Dempsey pictures. "A big one for a fourth-page," he says. "Fifteen hundred dollars to *Us Weekly*. Should be on the newsstands next week."

Aaron doesn't want his credit on that photo. "It was all you," he says. So after CXN takes its 40 percent, I'll make $900. Big money! And again I think, *I'm gonna succeed.*

I might not be into reading the tabloids, but at this price, obviously somebody is. And I recognize for the first time who is actually chasing the celebrities.

Chapter 2

*P*aps start the day *doorstepping*—they go to a celebrity's house, wait for the celebrity to leave, then follow him or her. It's been a week since we shot Halle. She's out of town now, and I know only two other celebrity addresses: Britney's and Paris's. Aaron tells me that Britney is way too hard for me right now, so if I want to doorstep, I should work Paris. "She's easy and nice," he says, "and *always* money." He also tells me that before her sex tape came out, she would sit outside the Ivy trying to get photographed but no one would take her picture because she didn't sell. "She had to take matters into her own hands."

I spend the morning with my neighbor, Donna, who lives in the unit under me at the Lyman Village Los Feliz apartments. Donna is new to L.A. and spent last week chumming around with me on Robertson looking for celebrities. This morning she announces, "I'm just gonna be your sidekick for a while. Cool?" Living off savings from a lucrative massage therapy career—the legitimate kind—Donna thinks paparazzi-ing is as much fun as I do. I'm thrilled to have the company.

Right now, we are sitting outside Paris's Tuscan-style villa on a warm December afternoon hoping for some daytime movement while trying to figure out if the starlet is hosting a Christmas party this evening. Of course, we wouldn't be invited guests, but J.R. says you often get lucky at Paris's parties with "debauchery on the front lawn."

Paris's pattern, we're told, is to go in and out all day, so although we may not know for sure if she is home, she's an all-day target. From nine to noon, however, we see no movement except for workers cleaning up empty vodka bottles (J.R. says she has a lot of parties), and paps who swing by every quarter hour only to leave a few minutes later.

After phoning J.R., we move off Paris and head to Robertson. At three o'clock, I spend an hour taking pictures of Tori Spelling strolling her miniature mutt Mimi LaRue around in a trolley. Tori is on Robertson filming her reality TV show and doesn't seem to mind that twenty-five paparazzi are tripping over her carriage and each other trying to get her photograph.

A gangbang of this style is comparable to shooting a red carpet event.[3] Each star walking a red carpet will stop in front of a row of photographers, smile and turn, reposition, smile and turn, etc., until presumably all the photographers have gotten a shot. Tori, on Robertson, does this. She walks slowly, patiently, constantly looking up and smiling, waiting for all of us to get shots. This paced shooting is gratifying in that even *I* get nice pictures. The financial reward, however, is questionable: *if* one is lucky enough to sell a frame when there are a dozen or more look-alikes, the large number of similar shots on the market destroy its value. The shot is worth pennies.

It will take me about a year to determine if gangbangs are cost-effective. "Pennies" actually means "one or two hundred dollars," which is a lot for me at the moment. Also, I find out later that there are exceptions. For instance, even in a gangbang, there could still be *the shot*, and you may get it. After about a year in the business, I end up deciding that if the total time (parking, waiting, and shooting) can be completed in under an hour, it's probably worth it. Otherwise, keep moving 'cause you may find something better.

★ ★ ★

By four, Donna and I are beat and we head for home. While inching along on slow-moving Sunset Boulevard, Donna pushes for a two-minute detour by Paris's house. "One more look?"

---

3. For the record, red carpet photographers are considered press and not paparazzi.

I reluctantly agree. Up the hill, round the curve to the mini-mansion…

"Oh my God! Oh my God!" screams Donna, pointing at a blond girl getting into the passenger side of a black Audi. "It's her. It's her. It's Paris. Hurry. Turn around. Go! Go!"

Adrenaline floods me. I turn *on*. I attempt a quick U-turn, a laborious effort on the narrow hill in the 1987 Mazda station wagon my brother gave me when I moved to L.A., and pull in behind her.

I don't see any other paps. I know what this means—"An exclusive, Donna! We have an exclusive!"

I follow Paris down Kings Road, and we head west on Sunset.

My crackling nerves need more than driving to release their tension. I bang on the dash. Donna keeps screaming: "Yes! Yes! Yes!" It's like we're in some hideously exhilarating *Bourne* chase but with real people—famous ones—real payoffs, and limited risk of death.

I call J.R. and attempt to sound cool and collected. "So, Paris just left, and Donna and I are behind her."

"Fabulous," he says in his "slurred" British accent. "Follow her."

And then what?! I've never followed anyone by myself. *Do I stay in my car and shoot? Get out? Where do I stand? Do I use a flash?* Excitement fills my blood, though common sense tells me it's highly unlikely I'm gonna pull this off. Of course, I don't want J.R. to think I can't do the job, so I don't ask any questions.

We turn left off Sunset, onto La Cienega, then head west again on Santa Monica Boulevard. When we hit Robertson, we take another left, south…heading straight toward "pap headquarters." Aaron says Paris always drives down Robertson to get paps to follow and photograph her. We pass the center of operations. We see the paps but they don't see us. Still exclusive.

Donna unplugs my camera battery from the cigarette lighter and puts it in my camera. It was dead after Tori, even though I'd turned it off each time she went into a store.

I call Aaron. "I don't think I can shoot," I say. "I'm shaking too much." He tells me that the rush is a good thing. "It's why we do the job." (I find this an interesting comment. Aaron doesn't say, "It's *how* we do the job"; rather he says, "It's *why* we do the job.") Then he explains what will happen. "Paris always takes a few seconds to get out of the car. She'll brush her hair or something. She wants you to be ready."

I won't be ready.

Aaron says he'll come and help, which makes me feel warm on a couple of levels, but he doubts he'll make it before she stops somewhere. "The entry shots are all you. You can do it," he counsels. At least I think that's what he says. I can still barely understand Aaron's "Scottish."

The girl who's driving Paris does two U-turns in horrid traffic on Beverly Boulevard (so, of course, I must too), then someone yells the vulgar C-word out their window—at me!

Dude. I'm just following!

I notice the passenger in the Audi light up. I call Aaron again. "Paris doesn't smoke, does she?"

Is it possible Donna and I both mistook a doppelgänger for the world's most recognizable star?

"*Fags* [i.e., cigarettes], no. Pot, yes," he says just as Donna and I get a big whiff of reefer in our windows.

And then…it happens. And it's just me. I'm petrified, but somehow I do it. Paris stops. I stop. I get out of my car, walk to the front of hers, and wait for her to move. A horn begins to honk, nonstop, because I left my car blocking the alley. I wait for Paris to finish primping in the car's mirror.

When she opens her door, she gets out leisurely, one leg at a time. I'm about twelve feet in front of her and take pictures until she reaches me. Then I step aside. Paris and her friend go into a small building. I don't know if I remember to say, "Paris, do you mind if I take a few frames?" Aaron told me to say that. It's more polite.

The horn is still blaring, and the guy in the blocked car is now aggressively swearing. I go move my station wagon. When Aaron pulls up, I'm shaking but can't quit smiling either. It's an insane rush. He was right.

"Another exclusive! Congrats!" he says as he gets out and gives me that same forever-hug. Then Aaron beeps J.R. to tell him what's just happened, as is protocol—CXN likes to know what pictures are coming in. J.R. responds by inviting both Donna and me to the company Christmas party scheduled for that evening. I don't think he forgot to do that before, like he says he did, but I don't care. Now *with my two exclusives* he's starting to notice me.

Donna takes my car to go get ready for the party, and I hop in Aaron's. He looks at my photos, says "they're soft," i.e., out of focus, and thinks we should stick around for her to exit. *No problem. I'll wait with you all night.*

After two hours, the sun's almost set and we'll still need to edit and change before the party. "We can't be bothered much longer," says Aaron.

"How long do you usually wait?"

"No specific time. Five minutes, five hours, more. Ya never know. Gotta figure out if they're worth it."

A door on the exterior of the building has been left ajar. Twice, we see Paris walk down the hall to the bathroom.

"I've got an idea," says Aaron. "Next time she hits the *loo*, we'll talk to her."

"You can do that?"

"Sure. Why not? It's Paris."

From our strategic position in his blacked-out 4Runner, we see her enter the bathroom for a third time. We get out, move inside the building, and stand next to the restroom door with our cameras in hand, but down. We hear her washing her hands. She exits. Aaron twinkles his blue eyes and says, "Hey luv, could we just take a few frames? Then we'll go and leave you alone."

Paris pauses. I'm not sure she can understand his accent. She says, "Is my driver here yet?" (The Audi girl left after she walked Paris inside.)

"Please, Paris. Just a couple of shots?" Aaron requests again.

"Not yet. I don't have my makeup on," Paris squeaks in a high voice that Aaron says is not typical (he says she's lovely in every way), then turns and walks back to the "Acting Studio" from where she came.

"Do you always give them an option?" I ask, perplexed.

"I try to, but usually I'm asking while I'm shooting."

So then they are generally not *given an option.*

Aaron explains that someone "hard to get," Jennifer Aniston for instance, is never asked. Then he tells me about the iconic picture of Britney when she had her baby in her lap in the front seat of her car. He says that Britney came out with the baby that day and asked the paparazzi not to take her picture. "I'm not in the mood," she said. So, they didn't shoot her. But then, when she got into the car like *that,* they of course had to.

I like hearing this from Aaron. It confirms what I've thought all along: while others may be vultures, at least some of us have discretion with the pictures we take.

We head back to the car to wait. It's completely dark when a large blacked-out Escalade pulls up. The car stays running with the driver inside. I wondered how we were going to know when Paris's driver was here. Aaron said he'd know. Now I know too.

He sends me to knock on the "Acting Studio" door. "Tell Paris her driver's here."

My brows V-down in protest. *Is this part of the job?*

"It's fine." He laughs. "Remember, it's not Brad Pitt. It's just Paris."

I *wish* it were Brad Pitt; though he might be less receptive of our inquiries.

I follow orders, knock, and crack open the studio door. Paris isn't in view, but I relay the news to the staff, who respond with confused faces and silence. *Is this how it works?* they wonder too.

I return outside, and Aaron and I flank the exterior door. He tells me to "just keep shooting" when she comes out, and shows me how she will walk from the door to the car. Though only because I ask. I don't think he's counting on me to get the shot.

Paris's driver is dressed in a dark suit and is now holding the vehicle's back door open in anticipation of her arrival. He doesn't seem fazed by our presence; maybe this isn't unusual. The SUV is so high he's put a small step down for her use. There's a streetlight illuminating the scene. I almost can hear the sound of the clapboard, "Take One," then some voice yelling, "Action," and then Shakespeare's famous words:

"All the world's a stage, and all the men and women merely players; they have their exits and their entrances."

Then, she enters. Paris keeps her chin held high and smiles—at Aaron. She seems to know exactly who's taking her picture. Her long blond extensions are pulled up in a bun and she wears a full-length dress with a slit down the cleavage to reveal that perfect skin covers her entire body, not just her face. She holds a stack of papers with an acting book facing outward. Though it's nighttime, she wears sunglasses.

It all happens in less than five seconds. I take three shots, then my camera jams, so with my own eyes I watch Paris climb into the Escalade while Aaron lights her up. There's no denying, she's spectacular.

★ ★ ★

A few hours later, Brian, Donna, Aaron, and I all ride together to the Christmas party. We enter a low-lit Venice Beach bar and see that the festivities have begun without us. J.R. immediately comes over to offer congratulations on the Paris set, sloshing his drink all over my top as he talks. His hands keep "falling" from my lower back to my *bum*, so I continually swerve to avoid their touch. Donna, all tatted up and down, looks like a '60s hippie in a flouncy rose dress and super high heels. Brian, with his full-sleeve tattoos and muscular build, very obviously *fancies* her and is stuck to her like glue.

Aaron leads me through the party, introducing me to everyone. Brian is a Kiwi, a New Zealander, but most everyone else is British—about ten "snappers," as photographers are called in the United Kingdom, and the half dozen office staff. I meet Simon, a Brit from a small village in Essex who will later become my closest pap confidant and partner. He has an appealing, weathered face and is about forty. I like him immediately. Simon's wearing a wife-beater T-shirt, jeans, and a Lakers hat, and when I ask him why he shaves his arms, he says, "Keep me whole body clean, mate. Shave all me hair." Interesting.

The night passes quickly and festively, no one missing out on free drinks.

And like every British or Commonwealth company I've ever worked with both in the United States and abroad, it appears perfectly acceptable to drink, party, and perform naked lap dances with your coworkers—and come Monday, expect no repercussions. All is forgiven, forgotten, or laughed about, and often repeated the next weekend.

At two when the bars close, J.R. is unable to stand and his staff carries him to a cab. Then Aaron and me, and Brian and Donna (holding hands at this point) drive back to Aaron's Hollywood apartment. We scramble eggs, open two cans of baked beans, and make tea. Sometime after four, Aaron wraps me in one of his bear hugs, and we fall asleep on the floor.

Chapter 3

*W*ith a stack of phone numbers from the company Christmas party, pestering my new coworkers for advice is a cinch. Even though the other CXN snappers are much more competitive than Aaron, they don't seem threatened by women and certainly not by my questions.

Paparazzi 101

Below, a few tips, though putting them into practice remains another matter:

1. It is often advantageous to establish fleeting eye contact with the celebrity. That way, he or she will know you are not a threat. Then *ka-boom*, pick up your camera and shoot. If, however, you are not careful with your eye contact and instead *eye-fuck* them (as we say), you will be busted: "PAP" is tattooed on your forehead.

2. If busted, don't *then* try to hide. This seems obvious, but truly it is not. You *always* feel like you want to hide. Once they know you're there, give them some space and wait for the shot. Often they'll *give it up* anyway.

3. Try to shoot from your car. Your car is your best hiding place. (Although this point is arguable in my case—no pap in L.A. drives a tint-free blue station wagon like mine.) Another technique you can try from your car is to honk your horn in an attempt to get the celeb to look up. "Don't holler their name,

though," advises Vince, a Brit who rarely leaves his car. "Then they'll know you're a pap. Just honk, or holler some random word." ("Fire"?)

4. Make 'em laugh. If you can do this, Aaron says, you're golden. No bad energy, everyone goes home happy, and most importantly you get a smiling shot, which is what the tabloids want. I find this last point odd. *Don't the mags want ugly, embarrassing, and scandalous?* That seems to be what's often in there. "Nope," advises Aaron. "Ultimately, they don't like to tarnish their stars. They're all in bed together."

5. Don't "get greedy," as Simon calls it, with your shots. This is a HUGE mistake for new paps because we don't yet know when we've nailed it. When you get greedy, you get into trouble. "Get the shot, and get out," says Simon. (Though "trouble," it seems, isn't usually *big* trouble. Just inconvenient and embarrassing.)

★ ★ ★

Six weeks into my new career, I'm ready for a big break. Having answered a casting call for extras, I am on the movie set of *The Invasion*, starring Nicole Kidman and Daniel Craig. Nicole's "good money" and "hard to get," and because I've done extra work before and know extras are usually in close proximity to the cast, I cautiously conjecture, *Have I found the secret to success? Why don't other paps do this?*

I have been hired for a two-day shoot and am on the set by seven each morning. To be clear, extra work is horrible. Besides an early start, you have no idea what time you'll get off, so you can't make plans for the evening. Then, your entire day involves sitting around with the other extras in a "holding area," like you're a herd of cows. For a ten-plus-hour day (at minimum wage), you spend approximately one hour on set. There, you will be required to move your lips and make appropriate hand gestures but not utter a word. No one keeps track of you while you're in the holding area, which is why I think maybe I'll be able to sneak away and shoot.

At around noontime on the second day, Daniel is off set, milling around. It takes me more than an hour to work up the courage to approach him.

"Hi, Daniel. Would you mind if I took your picture?" My small point-and-shoot camera is in my hand, not hidden, but not aimed at him either.

He shakes his head and appears disgusted that I've even dared to ask. I feel horribly gauche, but truly, Daniel doesn't know I'm anything more than a presumptuous fan. (In retrospect, I find his reaction arrogant.)

That evening, all the extras don evening attire and are called to the set. I am one of about a hundred in a dining room scene. Nicole is brought in last and is conveniently seated at the table adjacent to mine. I am now holding my camera, which I smuggled in in my beaded clutch, underneath my white dinner napkin. My finger is on the shutter. With the camera on Automatic/Flash Off, I attempt shots of Nicole via the make-a-hole-in-your-napkin-and-shoot-through-it trick. When the scene is over, I run to the bathroom in the studio warehouse and check my shots. I have fifteen of napkin blur.

No other opportunity presents itself. By eleven that night, I've more or less given up and am off set waiting for wrap. Suddenly, Nicole's husband, country music singer Keith Urban, walks up and embraces her. At the moment, rumors are circulating about problems in their new marriage and his need for rehab. Right now, Keith and Nicole are *big*. Mind you, I have no idea what "big" means in terms of money (same as I don't know what "good money" and "hard to get" mean), but that's what J.R. told me. I know I must try again.

Like a robber contemplating a holdup, I lurk. No one watching would mistake me for a professional paparazzi, however. My hands shake and I'm scared like a rat in a snake's cage. The feeling of adrenaline-overload sickens my gut and my over consumption of "craft services," the term used for gastronomic catering on film sets, moves upward from my stomach. Keith keeps looking my way, so I know they notice me.

I take shots, this time with the camera-hidden-in-a-scarf-hole trick. I take a lot of shots. And then some more. I don't stop to look at my pictures but think I must be getting something good. Keith and Nicole are holding pretty still, and I'm barely ten feet away.

Keith is attractive, but it's Nicole's beauty that's overwhelming. It would be hard not to stare at her even if I weren't taking pictures. She's at least five-foot-ten, but her limbs are narrow and long, and she looks highly breakable. Until she saw Keith, Nicole had not smiled in two days, and I wondered if she was sad. It's no secret Nicole is desperate for kids. She may be rich, famous, and exquisite, but she's still pushing forty and has the same biological clock tick-tick-ticking as the rest of us.[4]

I continue shooting. The two chat and embrace and are affectionate together. More shots. Still more. You can see where this is going. My mind starts to swirl, it blurs, and with gusto I completely disregard Pap Tip No. 5: Don't get greedy.

Oh, but I do get greedy. Very, *very* greedy. Why, I ask myself later, couldn't I have stopped after twenty shots?

Suddenly, the flash goes off.

Time stops. I am in a dim, quiet tunnel, and my catered dinner lying heavy in my stomach moves closer to my mouth. The feeling is not unlike stubbing one's toe—*nailing* one's toe—and waiting those few seconds before the pain crawls up to tell the head, "*Mother*—*r*, that hurt!"

I'm frozen with my head curled down when Keith grabs my arm. I don't look up, but I imagine his face leaves no question about his thoughts. In front of twenty-five extras and a production crew with whom I've been fairly friendly for two days now, he yells, "Let me see that. What are you doing?"

Keith knows full well what I'm doing.

"What are you taking pictures of? Huh? Huh?"

The only thing I can say—and I can only whisper—is, "I'm sorry. Just please don't embarrass me. I'm sorry."

He shows a tinge of sympathy and still holding me by the arm roughly escorts me outside and hands me over to his personal security guard, sort

---

4. It's worth mentioning here that, while at that specific point in time, Nicole did not have biological children, she *did*, in fact, have kids, a tidbit the media delicately ignored. When she and Tom Cruise were married, they had adopted Isabella and Connor.

of like he's throwing out the dog who just shat inside. I am most thankful though. Out of the studio, out of the limelight. I did not come to L.A. to be the star.

"She's taking pictures of me and Nic. Take care of her," he orders his guard. Then returns inside.

To my surprise, Mr. Security smiles and offers me a seat in the passenger side of his black leather sedan. Kindly, he explains that "everybody has to be careful these days because, you know, there are paparazzi out there."

Yes, I know. Visions of courts and prisons and criminal records explode in my head.

He tells me we'll work it out. "Don't worry," he says. "We just have to delete the photos."

As we're deleting, Keith comes out again—this time with "Nic"—and points, arm fully extended, at me. My car door is open, and I look into both their eyes: they deserve a mug.

They don't say anything, just stare at me for a few seconds, then turn and go back inside. A few minutes more and the production crew— apparently having convened and discussed my "invasion"—come to tell me that I will be immediately dismissed from set (good, it's almost midnight), and though they are sure that I'm more embarrassed than anything, they are still obligated to report the incident to the agency for which I am an extra.

Huh? That's it? You aren't gonna press charges and call the police?

Once everyone is sure the photos are deleted, I'm released from Mr. Security's car. I run to the holding area, quickly change out of my wardrobe, and haul myself off set before anyone can change their mind. The sight of the baby blue wagon in the dark parking lot is as comforting as seeing a lover at the airport after a long separation. She starts immediately, and her worn but reliable wheels lead me through the gate to safety. I audibly pray to never have to return to the scene of the crime, Warner Bros. Lot 5 in Burbank.

When I get home, I rummage through the bathroom cabinet collecting all the Western and Eastern sleep aids I can find, climb into bed, and pray to the sleep god to whisk me away to a far-off galaxy—one with no stars! My request is ignored and replaced with torment for the next eight hours: back to Lot 5, flash going off again and again, Keith grabbing my arm over and over…

★ ★ ★

"Good morning." J.R. calls at eight when I'm still in bed. "How'd it go last night?"

I feel groggier than he sounds, the clonazepam et al. still in my system. I fill him in, apologizing that I had to delete all my photos.

(Five seconds.) "Ahhhh," J.R. exhales. (Five seconds.) "That's no problem." (Five seconds.) "Ahhhh," he says again. (J.R. is the world's longest pauser.) "Just bring your card in and we'll recover them."

Do what? It wasn't all in vain?

When I get to the office, J.R. plugs in my memory card, pulls up a $30 Internet program, and in a few seconds images start popping up on the screen. They are dark and grainy, but undoubtedly of Keith and Nicole.

We will sell them, but not in the United States because I'm too scared I'll get sued. CXN isn't worried about this, but I'm smart enough to know they won't protect a freelancer. Besides, they didn't see how blazin' mad Keith and Nic were.

On my way back home, Ulysses Bartlet, the only one of CXN's three owners that I didn't meet at the company Christmas party, rings. ("Rings" is what my British coworkers say, instead of "calls" or "phones." I love it, so now I say it. It seriously annoys my American friends.)

Bartlet lives in New York, sells photos from his home office—"while naked," Simon thinks—and coordinates his undercover staff like the unseen boss on the speakerphone in *Charlie's Angels*. He introduces himself, then says, "You have more balls than any of my staff."

"I just don't know any better," I reply. And, we're off to a great start.

Early on, J.R.'s advice to me was, more or less, "Use your breasts to get tips." My breasts are small, but he made his point: people who give star spotting tips are much more receptive to harmless, non-thug-looking females. When I burn out looking for celebrities on a given day, I traipse through stores and restaurants giving out my card in hopes that someone will call me about a sighting. Today, my two-month anniversary on the job, this tactic finally pays off.

(Side note: My future protocol when someone does tip me off: I usually give them $50 to $100 depending on how much I make. I could make $20 or $200 or $2,000 or more. I generally don't pay the tipper—or "tipster," as they are more commonly called—if I don't get a shot. If Bartlet, the CXN boss who controls the money, is in a good mood, he'll pitch in for half of the tip money, which is only fair since he's taking a heavy cut.)

It's noon when J.R. calls. He's heard that Ashlee Simpson is moving into a new house. He knows the street, but not the exact house, and wants Aaron and me to go look for trucks or other signs of moving. We pick up sandwiches and head over. After a sweep with no sign of movers, we park at the bottom of the street, and I hop in Aaron's car to wait.

Aaron spends the next hour trying to teach me how to extract sunflower seeds out of their shell with just my tongue. I would never have imagined that watching Aaron's tongue maneuver in this intricate manner could be such a turn-on.

A call from Joey, a grocery stocker who works at Bristol Farms in West Hollywood, interrupts our tongue games. I met Joey one day when I was shopping and he was stocking. We started to chat, I told him what I did, and he took my card. Over the next couple of years, Joey will end up being my best, most consistent tipster. He is a good-natured American guy, not in it for the money, more for the fun, and he *gets it*—he understands what information I need to know and how to communicate it *fast*—which makes him easy to work with. When Joey calls today, he tells me that

Ashlee Simpson is there. The irony. During the twenty-minute speed-drive to Bristol Farms (I stay in Aaron's car), Joey texts the play-by-play:

> She's wearing a green hoodie. She's in the fruits and veggies. She's got a full cart. A girlfriend is with her. GET READY, she's on her way out!

With thirty seconds to spare, we get to the parking lot of Bristol Farms. Aaron spots Ashlee's car immediately (he knows most celebs' cars by sight) and rams his 4Runner into position. When he sees her exit the store, he drops his back window (the only vehicle I know of with this handy feature), circles his body around from the driver's seat, and *chuh-chuh-chuh, chuh-chuh-chuh*, Aaron nails it, fast and forcefully. I'm too slow to do anything but watch.

Ashlee never knows we're there. And now, relaxed and confident with shots in the bag, we follow her home to the street where we were parked earlier. Aaron lags so far behind I'm surprised we don't lose her, though his shrewd follow skills do get us there without being noticed. (I come to notice Aaron loses celebrities often. He doesn't seem bothered by this. "Part of the game," he says. He also says that I'm an awful follower because I get right up on the car's ass and the celeb knows I'm there. But at least I don't lose them.)

We catch up to Ashlee's Range Rover just as she pulls into her new driveway. But Aaron continues on, not wanting to alert her of our voyeur eyes. We circle back hoping she'll unload the groceries but more intent on not blowing our cover so we can use the address later, unnoticed. The garage door is down and the gate is closed, but from the street we can see into Ashlee's second-story bedroom. The curtains are up, the bay window thrown open, and she's unpacking.

Aaron doesn't reach for his camera. He tells me that we wouldn't be able to sell the shots anyway. Supposedly one of CXN's owners has pictures of Mischa Barton buck naked, but they're unsalable because they were taken through a bedroom window. "Celebs have privacy rights in a few places," Aaron explains. "In their homes, in their *back*yards (not their front), and in bathrooms."

It's worth noting here that the U.S. Constitution (and most other Western governments) give paparazzi their rights too. The Constitution allows a public person's privacy rights to be circumvented in the interest of the public's right-to-know, a sensible law with regard to political figures; an arguably unfortunate one for movie stars.

For now, we call it a day. Tomorrow, Aaron and I will start fresh on Ashlee. We assume we're the only ones with her new address, which we know will be a short-lived advantage. In the case of someone like Ashlee, who at the moment is riding the coattails of her sister's fame and is "out there" most every day, other paps are bound to spot her, follow her home as we did, and get the new address.

★ ★ ★

Who's Who

Paps are all over the world, but most live in Los Angeles, the city with the highest concentration of worldwide celebrities. To put that in perspective, probably three paps live in Stockholm, ten live in Sydney, one hundred live in New York, and five hundred live in L.A.

Most paparazzi are tied to an agency, either as staff or freelance. If a pap is not tied to an agency, he or she must find a way to get addresses, tips, and most critically, morale.

Each agency—and in L.A. there are five or six big ones and a handful of small ones—has its own "street culture." ZZP and West Coast Wing, two large agencies, are similar to CXN in that they are run by Brits and hire mostly their own kind. Much of CXN's staff was recruited and brought over with visas from the United Kingdom. The snappers are ex-news photogs, which Bartlet says is good paparazzi training, though I don't see why Americans couldn't do the job just as well. Besides its British staffers, West Coast Wing scoops up most of the stand-alone freelancers as contributors, though Rodeo2, a mostly Latino agency, beats it out in sheer street numbers. British paps seem to place blame on Rodeo2 for "ruining" the business with its copious numbers, but I view its existence as an inevitable by-product of the proliferation of the Internet (where everyone can now find lots of information on celebrities, including their whereabouts) and the emergence of digital photography (which has decreased the overall cost and skill level necessary for market entry). Anyway, the Rodeo-ers aren't so bad. They ignore me, but not with disrespect.

Where respect deteriorates is on the European side. It's too early in my career for me to understand why this is, but I will eventually figure out the problem. It's called "Tall Poppy Syndrome," and I was first introduced to this Commonwealth ailment three years ago while in New Zealand on my backpack adventure. Tall Poppy is the idea that if you rise above the norm, i.e., if you're a "tall poppy" in the community, then you should be cut down. Community members will make every effort to nip that success of yours in the bud. This is counterintuitive to our American culture, one that worships success from anyone regardless of how they came to it. The syndrome explains why many Brits from West Coast Wing and ZZP will not acknowledge me on the street. Aaron says they're disdainful of the fact that I'm not "institutionally trained" yet seem blatantly confident. Plus, I smile too much. JoDeane says it's because they realize I'm a threat. For some reason, all the British photogs at CXN like me—perhaps because I'm quick to admit I know nothing. Or maybe just because they like having "birds" around.

The tabloid magazines—the glossy ones in the United States at the moment being *People, Us Weekly, Star Magazine, Life & Style,* and *In Touch,* and on the seedier side, the *National Enquirer*—are dominated by Brits as well. Weekly, I sift through the issues at the newsstands exclaiming, "That's Simon's picture"; "There's Aaron's"; and occasionally, "There's mine!" We've already seen the pictures on CXN's private website, and after talking to our coworkers, often know the stories behind the shots. All the paps say seeing their pictures in print is still a rush. I'm guessing many stars feel the same.

Besides checking out our artwork, paps read the tabloids to glean information. For example, a photo may reveal which gym a celebrity frequents, what car a celebrity drives, or when and where a film is being shot. Plus, the mags' choice of photos tells us who's selling, reminding us whom we should target.

As Aaron said, the mainstream media primarily wants pictures of pretty, happy stars. I know this sounds surprising, but I will soon witness firsthand many instances of tabloids and blogs (besides the *National Enquirer* and *Star Magazine*) not printing unattractive photos of stars. There are three reasons for this: One, pretty pictures are, well, prettier to look at. Nobody wants to flip through an entire magazine of photos of celebs having bad hair days. Two, the mags want you to think that we—the celebs, the paps, and the mags—are one big happy family. This is because if it looks like the stars *want* to be photographed, then consumers feel no shame in looking at their pictures. The public can have all they want while not feeling the slightest bit guilty of contributing to supposed "stalking" (which you'll come to see, usually isn't nearly as stalker-ish as people think). And the third reason the tabloids print pretty, happy pictures is because they view the celebrities as their clients, and the last thing they want to do is piss off their clients (or their clients' studios) with too many bad photos. If they do that, they may get blacklisted from exclusive stories or other information. (I see this behavior within hard news too. Many papers and networks cater to their newsmakers—politicians, for instance—in the same way the tabloids cater to the celebrities.)

But the mags are *trashy*, you probably say.

When you think about it, however, what kind of trash are you really looking at? A celebrity's weight and wrinkles, celebrities without makeup, a *single* celebrity's dating life—those topics are always fair game and yes, they are trashy. But others—a star's sexual preference, marital infidelity,[5] nudity

---

5. If the celeb is actually married versus just bf-gf, the tabloids are much more wary of exposing a tryst.

(accidental or intentional), and drug abuse[6]—in other words, the *really* trashy items the paparazzi often discover on the job—are more often than not taboo, particularly if the celeb postures him- or herself as high-end or a family person. Under no circumstances will a tabloid "out" someone if he or she is gay. Even if there are pictures. Which there often are.

But, but, but...you might say. OK, there are noted exceptions. Specifically, two groups of people are often *not* afforded these "really trashy" exemptions. Those are the celebrities at the TOP of the ladder (the top 10 biggest celebrities, more or less), and the celebrities at the BOTTOM of the ladder (like reality show people). For example, some stars are *so big* that the tabloids will write just about anything to justify a cover story. Take Brad Pitt and Angelina Jolie: tabloids will pull something out of thin air because they know they'll never get an "exclusive" with Brangelina anyway. On the other hand, some stars are *so unimportant* that the tabloids will print anything ridiculous—or true—they hear about those stars because the repercussions are minimal. For example, they know that no matter what they say about the latest *Bachelorette* or one of the Kardashians, another interview with either is always an option. But besides the *top* and *bottom* celebrities (and perhaps the self-induced "train wrecks" too), most of the other thousands of movie stars are given a break.

The above is true for the *American* tabloids. The tabloids across the pond, however, like their news media, operate differently. They're self-admittedly rawer and meaner than their American counterparts, and they don't shy away from blasting their governments or their celebs. Without fail, British tabloids always pick the most unsightly celebrity pictures to print. They will, for example, in the future, pick the one unflattering shot of Heather Mills from a set that I will take during her ugly divorce with Paul McCartney (her mouth is at a funny angle) to use to blast her. And from then on, every time they talk about Heather "keeping her mouth

---

6. If a celeb has been to rehab and drug abuse is "official," then the tabloids will talk about it. Without rehab though, or a DUI, or something else "official," then it's usually shoved under the rug.

shut," they will reprint that picture. (Which will make me a bit sour because she had been so gracious as I'd photographed her.)

Another example of European versus American press: a CXN colleague shot Cameron Diaz and Drew Barrymore in Hawaii smoking what anyone who has ever smoked pot would say looks just like a joint, if it isn't one. (Google it. It's a great set.) The tropical photos blanketed Europe's tabloids, but in America there wasn't a mention of it. I could just hear CNN saying, "But how do we *know* it's marijuana?" Now, if the two were arrested on possession charges and *the police* reported it, then CNN would have been all over it. 'Cause if the police said it happened, by all means, it must have.

Bottom line, hardcore "trash" (adultery, nudity, drugs, and *very ugly pictures*) is generally printed only with a few unlucky celebs. (Homosexual orientation is *never* printed unless it's been press-released by the actor/actress themselves. And nudity, well that's an American puritanical thing, thus it's only barred from our media.) So while this may not be what stands out at you in the tabloids (and slowly, like in many things, America is inching toward the European way), it is what's really happening. And I know this because time and time again, throughout my career, I will witness it when consistently my own and my colleagues' "unbecoming" photos *do not print* (at least not in America).

So what does print? Generally, the tabloids want stories that are either completely subjective (fashion, for instance) or completely factual (a legal divorce, for instance). *For the most part,* Hollywood spends her time on love stories, babies, divorce, fashion, beauty, and failing beauty. She reports stars doing things that regular people might possibly do: falling in and out of love, buying houses, being stylish, being beautiful, combating aging, and battling weight. Tabloids show us what they think will keep us entertained, without taking too many legal risks and without including *too much* hard-core trash (so you won't feel guilty about what you're reading). And ultimately, that boils down to the paparazzi's bread-and-butter: pretty, happy pictures…much like *Us Weekly's* stars who are "Just like *Us*."

Chapter 4

The days flew by during those first few months. The job was fresh and exhilarating, but at the same time extremely challenging. Two things quickly became clear. One, I was nowhere near to becoming a professional photographer. (While I'd owned an SLR since I was sixteen, "action" photography—while hiding—was not something I'd ever honed in on.) My celebrity shots were, more often than not, out of focus, improperly exposed, or otherwise unusable. Usually they had an important body part (notably feet or forehead) missing. And two, I had absolutely ZERO abilities at *stealth*. If I was—miraculously—able to keep up with the targets all the way to their destination, every one of them, without exception, saw me once I was there. And since I had usually pulled up in the wrong position to get a clear shot, I would need to yell their name (or some "random word") in the hopes they would turn my way, which they usually didn't. Even if they did, I was rarely quick enough to get the shot before they turned back around again.

Sometimes, however, the lost shot was more than my beginner's incompetence. I simply did not have the proper equipment.

So I caved, went to Samy's Camera, and purchased equipment on credit. A bare minimum pap kit: a "semi-professional" camera body (the "body" of the camera is the camera without the lens), a *short* and a *long* lens (we never call them "wide-angle" and "telephoto" like other people do), a detachable flash, a small point-and-shoot (which I will use for "pretend to be a fan" shots, as well as video), and a few other odds and ends—set me back about four grand. No matter, I still hadn't gotten a shot all week—it was already Thursday—and I'd peed in a cup *twice*! Everyone said it would come to that: "Never leave your doorstep [i.e., your celebrity] to pee!" (because they could leave). But I didn't think it would happen so soon.

★ ★ ★

Armed with my new kit, this morning starts with my doorstep, Eva Longoria, leaving her house. (I know this sentence sounds strange, but that's how we say it. "She," Eva in this case, and "her doorstep," Eva again, are the same thing. Eva's doorstep is both *her* and *her house*.) Eva blows me at the first light she comes to. (Which, despite your first thought, is not as it sounds either. *Blow* is simply another British term the guys use to mean "to ditch.") Now I am left to troll. I'm terrible at trolling; I never see anyone despite the fact they're supposedly all around. The streets are not short of beautiful people though, ones I think *may* be famous, so I shoot them just in case. They never turn out to be celebrities.

Courteney Cox is on my newly mapped "troll route" because she lives in town and jogs. J.R. says she's not worth much. "A pretty face, but boring. And a bit old." (Courteney's forty-two at the moment.) I drive by her house anyway.

'Appy days!—as Simon (the pap who shaves his whole body) says when something goes his way—Courteney is jogging. I pass her as she heads down Loma Vista, a street perpendicular to hers. Skinny and straight with hair to match, Courteney looks just like she does on TV. Anyone would recognize her. Don't be impressed.

She must have just left her house. There's time to figure out what to do, but this scenario is foreign to me, and I have no experience from which to draw. *How do I photograph her without her seeing me? Or do I let her see me?*

I come up with three options:

1. Hide in my car and shoot her.
2. Get out of my car, hide in a bush, and shoot her.
3. Wave and say something like, "Hey Courteney, can I get a shot?"

I try to think about what Courteney will do. Best-case scenario, she won't see me, and I'll get into perfect position in front of her so that she's looking right *down the barrel* or slightly adjacent. She'll be running naturally into the setting sun and *chuh-chuh-chuh*, I'll *hose* her.

Working toward best-case scenario, first I look toward the sun. I'll need to get in between it and her. Even with my limited knowledge, I know that if the picture is backlit, i.e., the sun is shining *into* the frame, it won't be salable, especially in the case of a non-event like Courteney Cox jogging in all-black sweats. I don't know her jog route, and though I could follow her, I think that might be obvious. One thing I do presume: she will eventually run back to her house.

I decide it's safest to wait on her street where the sun's angle is not perfect, but acceptable. Now, where do I hide? Is there a full bush or a thick tree trunk? I haven't hidden in nature before, but paps say it's a reasonable tactic. I look around. Courteney's house is situated atop a steep hill with city views to the south. I contemplate ducking behind some shrubs in her neighbor's yard, then realize I'm wearing an orange top. I will learn to keep a change of clothes in my car. And a jacket. It's cold.

What about my car? Most paps have SUVs with vertical (not sloped), heavily tinted windows. The Mazda's windows are transparent, and the back window slopes significantly, which will distort my shots. And you should *never* shoot through the front window, everybody tells me—it won't work.

Maybe I'll be straightforward: I'll just ask her for a shot. It definitely takes the pressure off. According to Simon, who's been in the biz five years, asking used to work, but now with the "Mexican influence" (as he calls the large number of Latinos who have "taken over" the paparazzi business) the stars don't often comply. "No matter how lovely my British accent is to their ears, we have just become too many for them to cooperate anymore." Plus, if I want to use the "ask" method, I need to *know* my star, know that there will be a decent chance she'll say yes. Some stars always duck and hide—Demi Moore, Sandra Bullock, Leonardo DiCaprio. Some always comply—Paris. And some are fickle and it depends on their mood—Jessica Simpson, Reese Witherspoon. I don't know enough about Courteney to know what she will do. Simon would know; he used to be a painter and once painted her house. Plus, he's obsessed with cougars. But I don't think to call him now.

Courteney turns the corner and heads up her street. I have opted for No. 1 and am "hidden" in my car. My car is parked practically in front of her as she climbs the hill to her house, so I must lean my head, elbow, and camera out of the window. She can't miss me.

Before I take a shot, Courteney covers her face with her hand. I move to option No. 3, asking, "Hey Courteney. Could I have a shot?"

"This is my private time, and I don't look good now," she responds and keeps her hand in front of her face until she passes my car.

"OK, thanks," I say since I feel really boorish and don't know what else to say. I'm pretty sure I'm not thankful though.

An hour later, David Arquette, her husband at this time, goes for a jog. He also sees me, *covers*, and I get no shot.

Defeated and feeling like a nitwit, I give up for the day and head home. I call Donna, who couldn't join me today, and tell her what happened.

"I'm not worried, Jen." (She always says this.) "You can't learn if you don't fail."

"But I don't like failing."

"Which is why you won't."

★ ★ ★

As appreciative as I am for the new dose of testosterone surrounding my life, the hormones are so potent that I must take care to stay *a woman*. Thankfully I have "the girls": my four best friends, my BFFs, my besties. Several times a week, we meet at Figaro, our neighborhood French café, sit outside, something we can do any time of year thanks to the heat lamps they put out in the winter, and talk about every detail of each other's lives. At Fig, we are always flanked by overly beautiful people, smokers and diners wearing high-style hipster fashions. And lately Fig is becoming an *in* spot, so it's not unusual that there is an actor or actress sitting near us. (Usually my friends spot celebrities before I do. Then I often try to ignore them unless they're somebody really big, in which case I'll call a colleague with the tip. I can't be "on" all the time, especially in the evenings. Plus, I haven't mastered nighttime flash shooting.) My friends fit in perfectly in Los Angeles, each unmistakably gorgeous and stylish. They would say I'm their equal, but that's because they love me. I'm not gorgeous, not by Hollywood standards.

I met Georgia and JoDeane my first month here, and we've expanded our circle with two more handpicked members: Georgia's sister Alexandra and my roommate Amy.

Alexandra's in the city for music, her passion, and worries that I'm forsaking my dreams for money and adventure. I recently dragged her and Georgia to an evening shoot of Paris, but they both got bored and decided to wait in the car. Georgia's lack of interest in my job, however, doesn't diminish her support for me. "If I were famous," she told me (and it's no secret, Georgia would *love* to be famous), "I wouldn't mind being photographed as long as the paparazzi stayed far enough away." JoDeane, an avid tabloid reader and celebrity spotter extraordinaire, wishes I wouldn't impose on the lives of *people*, in particular the celebrities she likes, but she's coming around and has even started tipping me off. Amy, an actor (in L.A., females call themselves "actors" versus "actresses," which I assume has to do with equality), applauds anyone who can make money in this town and pompously proclaims my skills to all her thespian friends. She wishes she were pap-worthy and laughs with her gut when I tell her my stories. All us girls are in our late twenties to mid-thirties, me being the oldest, and live within walking distance of one another. We hang out several times a week usually at Figaro, which is not conducive to meeting boys but is our *local* (another British term), so we lack motivation to go anywhere else.

But that's a problem. As previously noted, I need to meet a man. And being around all that testosterone lately (especially Aaron's), this is becoming even more obvious.

Barring one short-lived romance, I haven't had a serious boyfriend in over four years. I date here and there, mostly there, and don't sleep around. None of us do. We think too highly of ourselves.

My friends and I were all raised the same. We developed high self-esteem and a sense of entitlement which assured us that we deserve greatness out of life and out of the partners we choose. Each of us wants it all: a fulfilling career, a wonderful family, health, happiness, and excitement. "Settle for nothing less," says Georgia.

But my eyes are a few years wiser, and more jaded. And I'm beginning to doubt my claim on "entitlement." I deserve as much as the next person, maybe even a little more (I mean, *damn* I've tried hard), but that doesn't mean it's gonna happen.

★ ★ ★

The contrast between my personal life, in which, dare I say, I like to think I could *be* one of the celebrities who live nearby, and my professional life, in which some would probably say I *stalk* them, is a bizarre juxtaposition. Without a doubt, I am beginning to struggle with the feeling of being "just like them" at home, but their slave, or worse, at work.

"I'm gonna bitchslap you."

"You're gonna *what*?" I splutter, stunned. I don't know exactly what "bitchslap" means, but I'm sure it's not nice.

"I said, I'm gonna bitchslap you," he says again. He doesn't say it loudly—others aren't far away—but he says it boldly, and he looks me dead in the eyes.

"Hang on a second. Why don't you say that for my video?"

I put down my camera, rummage through my back seat for my point-and-shoot, then turn it on video and start recording. By then, I'm noticeably unnerved and shaking. I point the camera at him.

"What did you say, *Seal?*" I think to use his name for sound-bite purposes. He doesn't say anything.

"Did you tell me that you were gonna bitchslap me?"

"No, I never said that."

"I think you did."

He moves away. I figure he realizes he doesn't want to be here, not with video. Seal's a monster of a guy—a dark, towering man with a cut-up face. No doubt he would knock me out with one bitchslap. But I know I'm in no danger now that I have a video camera.

He leaves and enters a building. I suddenly realize it's some kind of school. *Ahh, that's* the wrong I committed. I was trying to photograph him in front of his kids' school. And for a minute I feel a bit badly about that. It was a Saturday, and we had gone to an empty parking lot. I didn't realize it was a school lot—there were no kids around and no signs indicating it was a school, at least that I noticed. Since I've never worked him, I did what paps always do and followed the celebrity to where he parked.

Seal and Heidi, married at this juncture, are papped frequently and they don't seem to mind it—or at least they put up with it. But paps inform me later that Seal is a control freak, and his terms are that you can photograph him if you stand *off* school property shooting *onto* it, but you can't enter the lot. Actually, those terms are quite reasonable; I just didn't know them at the time. In my opinion, Seal could have just said, "You gotta leave—this is a school." Instead, he said, "I'm gonna bitchslap you."

I will come to find it infrequent that a celebrity gives me flack. They know the game (and are often in on it, as you'll come to realize). Besides, they prefer the police or the public do their dirty work. Seal's British though, and Aaron says that across the pond, the paps and the celebs hash it out on their own. He says there are plenty of brawls that never make the news.

Still, the Seal altercation was rather unusual. I will come to find that of celebrities, generally it will be *women* who give me a hard time. For any number of reasons, female celebrities seem to take out their frustration on their female paparazzi counterparts. Once, Hilary Duff—who loves it *most* of the time—berated only me with insults when a half dozen male paps are also shooting her. Another female pap, Carol, said she had Marcia Cross get in her face—right up to her nose, so as not to

43

be recorded on the nearby video—and whisper, "Fucking trashy bitch." The worst I ever heard about came out of Nicole Richie's mouth. She reportedly told a girl pap, "Your pussy stinks," when the pap came within earshot. *Ouch!*

But in this case, Seal, fully male, was the one to berate me.

In the end, I got the shot and the video, but nobody bought them. The tabloids didn't like the look in Seal's eyes, Bartlet told me, and they weren't interested in what he "may have" said to me.

But I know what he said, and I have made a point to never see Seal again. Paps are people too, and now I know one way that celebrities can get us to leave them alone: be really, really mean.

★ ★ ★

Speaking of mean, let me introduce you to the *heroes*.

"Heroes. Miserable rats," mutters Simon.

Heroes are what paps call people who should be minding their own business but mind yours instead. They are the people who believe they've made the world a better place because of their heroic acts. Heroes are the guys (and girls) who call us "bottom feeders," tell us to "get a real job" and to "leave the stars alone." They *block* for the celebrity even when the celebrity doesn't want to be blocked. Sometimes heroes are the valet guy and sometimes they are the security guard. Often, though, they're just a bystander.

Simon was on a Starbucks's patio getting heckled by a hero while he waited for Tori Spelling to exit. When she came out, she looked straight at the hero and said, "Shut up." Then she looked at Simon and said, "Thanks."

Everybody loves Tori.

Paris is the ultimate hero-buster. She flat-out tells security guards to get out of the way when they're blocking our shots. Whenever I need a confidence boost (often), I work Paris. She walks unhurriedly, doesn't have an unattractive angle, and drives an easy-to-spot, baby blue Bentley with no tint. The only problem with working Paris is that normally it turns into a gangbang. She really does *consistently* drive down Robertson *slowly* in her Bentley picking up paparazzi until she has a line of twenty cars following her. But Paris is a self-made star; she knows what she's doing. She leveraged her looks, money, her "Hilton" name, and *us* to get there. Frankly I'm in awe of her. She can do little wrong in my book.

★ ★ ★

To be clear, Hilary Duff is no Paris Hilton or Tori Spelling.

Actually, none of the paps are too sure what Hilary is doing these days, post–*Lizzie McGuire*, or why she still sells. Aaron says she might sing now. "She needs us and she knows it," he comments. He also tells me that she used to call the paps when she was going out, so not to feel sorry for her when she gets moody.

Her doorstep (i.e., "she") leaves early, and I am there. Hilary is being driven in her Range Rover by a security guard. In no way can my twenty-year-old station wagon keep up with the V-trillion engines most celebrities have; the guy blows me again and again.

I circle the neighborhood looking for the car, and by happenstance, not skill, continue running back into it. Hilary is apparently going somewhere nearby. After I re-find the Range for a third time, security gets frustrated, pulls over, picks up his phone, and calls the police. It's funny, I've never had anyone call the police on me, but I have no doubt that's what he's doing.

Instants later, one of L.A.'s finest shows up. This is my first of what will be *way too many* interactions with the Los Angeles police force. The officer blocks my car—"They love doing that," Aaron says—and starts in with the hassle: "Your registration is invalid." (*No, it isn't, or you would give me a ticket.*) "You have an outstanding citation." ("Really, for what?" I ask, honestly surprised. There is no response.) Eventually I realize he's trying to get me to admit to something, anything I might have hidden in my closet. Finally, he leaves with the threat, "I've written down your details." I'm pretty sure he can't do anything with "my details" and is just trying to intimidate me, but he's succeeded. I won't sleep tonight.

Chapter 5

After spending two years driving around the streets of L.A., I think it's unlikely the paparazzi will ever become as bountiful as the Los Angeles police force.

Still, we are too many.

According to Simon, the proliferation of paps, and in turn gangbangs, has occurred over the last four or five years. Simon started papping before the proliferation and has seen the business transition both in ethnicity—Europeans to Hispanics—and in numbers—from fifty to five hundred.

"I just don't like the way they're taking over the business," Simon says about the gangbangers. "Why can't they come in moderation? Fuck it, they pull in the cousins and the brothers and the uncles. They're like locusts, they are."

Although it sounds harsh, his harangue is told with a hint of love. Simon is the nicest guy in the business. Everyone says it. He never gets upset when his *job* is *jumped* or when someone blocks him out. "That's the game, luv. Gotta accept it," he tells me. Even when the police hassle him, Simon just says, "Cops got a job to do too. Let's move on."

But new paps, myself included, pose a problem for the veterans, or old-school paps as they like to call themselves. French and British "classically trained" newspaper photogs—Aaron, Simon, and most CXN paps—are considered old-school. Their predecessors came to the United States in the '80s and '90s and basically started the American paparazzi and tabloid industry. Many of them pulled in half a million dollars a year.

New-school paps—Latinos for the most part, mainly Mexican and

Brazilian[7]—started to shoot in the early 2000s. But they did not come with organized, cumbersome work visas like the British and French. Rather, they came in droves. These paps were just "here," ready to work. Then they recruited their families and their friends and their friends' families. New-school paps stole shots—and paychecks—from the Europeans and overall drove prices down by increasing the supply of pictures on the market. So when a celeb might have gotten shot once a month by an incognito pap before, now she was getting shot once a week, or more, and by several guys at once. As you can see, the increase in paparazzi has not been good for *anyone*, celebrity or paparazzi. (It is, however, good for you, the public. You now have much more to see. Free enterprise at its finest.)

The addition of new-school paps has also changed the rules. For example, Simon tells me that it used to be when you rocked up to a doorstep and someone else was already there, you'd leave. Staying would be considered jumping, and bad etiquette. But nowadays there are just too many paps and too few celebs for that to be practical, and jumping protocol has changed.

Today, "jumping" means moving in on a *story* when the celeb and paparazzi have *already left* the doorstep. The story—i.e., the celeb and accompanying pap (or paps)—is either on the road or at a location.

Most likely, a story will *not* get jumped if it is *not* in town—i.e., *not* in Beverly Hills, West Hollywood, or another area of high pap concentration. If a story gets jumped *outside* of town, then it is a pap's right to block other paps if he or she is able. On the other hand, if a story goes *to* town, or as it passes *through* town, jumping is a pap's biggest threat. The paparazzi blanket town, so if you and your story are spotted and jumped in town, there's not much you can do.

Once a pap is jumped by another pap, the risk of the story being jumped again goes up exponentially. The more paps on a story, the more likely it is that other paps will spot it, or call in their friends. Once jumping starts, it doesn't take long to accumulate a gangbang.

---

7. Americans, who make up about 10 percent of paps, would also fall into the new-school category.

Here's what it's like to run across a celebrity gangbang, which I will become quite familiar with in the ensuing months:

You're trolling. Neil George, a trendy Beverly Hills salon, is on your troll route. Kim Kardashian, Nicole Richie, Cameron Diaz, and other celebs get their hair done at Neil George. Every time you pass the salon, by instinct, you look for celebrities' cars that are parked or paps standing outside. If a celebrity's car is there, the paparazzi are going to notice. And if you spy paps, you know you've found a story.

You park, pay your meter, grab your *short-and-flash,* and walk over. No one says hello. No one looks at you. No one smiles. You see these people every day, but you'd prefer never to see most of them again.

You stand around (you never sit) for one, two, three hours (hair extensions, which the celebrities love, take forever). All the while you try to ignore the buzz from loudmouth paps cackling at one another's juvenile jokes.

Eventually, Bozo Bystander walks by. He *insists* on knowing who's inside.

"Who you waiting on?" he says. He addresses the group as a whole but tries to make eye contact with one of us.

Our first tactic: ignore him. We avert our gaze. No one wants to respond. A group of twenty acts as if they don't hear the guy.

He asks again, louder this time.

Again, we ignore.

Sometimes he leaves, which is good for all of us. But sometimes he persists. He repositions like a gnat, from one ear to another. "Who's inside?" he keeps saying.

Someone can't take it anymore. The pap who breaks responds with a made-up celebrity name: Kate Brando, he might say. Bozo is confused. *Should I know who that is? Maybe I'm the idiot?*

The reason we don't tell the pedestrian the truth—"Christina Applegate, Sandra Bullock, Natalie Portman"—is not because we're being obstinate; rather, it's because we're conditioned for Bozo Bystander's response. We know what he'll say. He'll call us either "losers," "bottom feeders," or "parasites." Or he will sneer, "Get a real job." And then, as we'd only hoped in the first place, he will leave, feeling he's done his good deed for the day by making us feel stupid.

The ground you stake at the gangbang is crucial, and you don't move around a lot. Like a lion, you're fully dialed in to where everyone is in relation to everyone else, and "the prey": *Where are the holes in the crowd? Where is the competition? Which way will the star walk?* A strong undercurrent is flowing, and everyone is taking it in. The reason you know this is because the minute you infringe upon someone else's space, you feel it. It might be subtle—a look, a growl—or it could be more—a shove—but one way or the other, you'll be told you're in another's territory.

By this time, the sun has moved a million miles over your head. You may have waited half a day already. You're exhausted.

Finally, the star exits. Everything goes down in about fifteen seconds. The guys closest to the star make themselves as dense and sticky as possible, blocking out anyone they can. They try to keep their bodies close together and between the star and the rest of the mass. They use ultra-wide-angle lenses (16mms), which have the ability to snap a full-length from about three feet away but often distort the image into a banana shape.

Once the star drives off, the paps take flight in a matter of seconds, getting on the follow or moving to another story. Rarely do I follow: the guys have had hours for the testosterone to build in their bodies, and it will be nasty.

When I look at my shots after this kind of gangbang, I may have twenty. All of them with at least one pap, or part of a pap, in them. If I have two clean headshots where I can crop out the pap/pap part and I haven't chopped off the top of the star's hair (which she's just had done), then I think *well done*.

Side note: On extended gangbangs when we, in mass, follow the celeb as she is shopping all over town, the celeb will usually engage us. After a period of time, she will ask something along the lines of: "Don't you guys have enough yet?"

A sensible question. If I were her, I'd wonder the same. But the fact is, no. We usually don't. What the celeb doesn't understand is that getting a full-length with all her eyes and teeth and feet and forehead in frame, and *without* other people, is no simple task. Melrose Avenue is not a red carpet, and we can't "go long" and form lines. By golly, *we're in the trenches!*

★ ★ ★

When I tell my mom my gangbang stories, she tells me to quit. "You aren't gonna meet any quality guys in this paparazzi business," she says. "Why don't you get a job as a secretary in a law firm?" In other words, why don't you leave the nasty paps to their nasty ways, and find an agreeable husband elsewhere? A nice thought, Ma, but not all that helpful.

The girls want me to quit too. They tell me I'm being *affected*: "You're so negative these days. You never used to be like that."

I get where they're coming from—my skin's not nearly as tough as it needs to be—but they don't quite get *me* either. Yes, I'm overwhelmed. Paparazzi-ing is arduous, intimidating work, and it's not easy being a female or a neophyte in this cutthroat industry. It's true, frequent failures and demoralizing lows engulf me, but the highs are insane. And the adrenaline nourishes me. Papping is giving me back an energy and excitement for life that I haven't felt in a long time. It's flat-out FUN! Besides, *I know I can do it*. And do it well.

The fact is, I need to live in the moment—I have always needed that—and right now, life is giving me "a moment." I identified at a young age that time is my most precious resource. If I waste time, I feel like I'm wasting life. That's why I don't have a nine-to-five structured career: I can't bear to waste eight hours a day if I don't love what I'm doing. I'd rather have no money. Don't get me wrong, my résumé is impressive. I've been quite successful professionally. I was once a CPA. I was a software consultant too. But those white-walled office jobs where I had to respect status quo were a dreadful fit for my personality. I got paid well, but what was the point if I thought I was wasting my life? When I quit the corporate world, I moved to Belgium with a boyfriend and went back to school for an MBA. Graduate school was not something I needed professionally; it was just a way to escape my previous reality, and at the time, not knowing anything other than white-collar professions, it seemed like a good choice. In retrospect, I wish I'd studied physical therapy or bartending or something I could have actually seen myself doing. Two years later I returned to the

States, split with the boyfriend, and started looking for a new career. CNN was based in Atlanta, where I was living, and looked like a fun place to work. Since my new criterion for a job was *it must be fun,* I set my sights on the network. It took me six months to get hired, and it was worth the wait. I *loved* it. I found my passion in media and journalism: creative work that was also a business. My jobs as a field and guest producer were challenging, rewarding, artistic, and editorial. But after three years, wanderlust got ahold of me again, so I quit CNN to travel. I backpacked through Turkey, India, and Thailand, and then made my way to New Zealand where I picked up freelance production jobs as I could find them while continuing to live as a traveler (i.e., in hostels). After a year in New Zealand, I went to Australia to work on a movie set before circling back through Asia and Europe and returning home two years later. That's when I landed in L.A.

No one would say I haven't done some cool stuff. The problem, however, is clear: I've done a lot, but I haven't stuck with anything. Not because I'm not driven but because I'm *overly* driven. When things get boring, I'm out. I have no tolerance for boring. And Hollywood—in all its layers of darkness and light, loneliness and romance—is anything but boring. *What's at the heart of this city, this melting pot of humanity?* I know there are demons in the City of Angels; there is good and there is evil. And I'm curious to catch a little of the battle.

Above any reasoning, however, I can't erase what's been put in front of me. I've got the passion, I've got the calling, so I've got to see this through. Every once in a while in life, the fog clears and you can see that you're in the right lane, even if it's dark.

★ ★ ★

The more I work with Simon, the more I want to work with him. He is precise and calculating as a pap, and patient and forthcoming as a mentor. He never tires of my questions, and his explanations are thorough and intelligent. I am increasingly in awe of his skills and enjoying his new friendship. Not to mention, he's *hilarious.*

Simon's shoot of Nicole Richie was like a ballet. She fluttered in and out of stores; Simon danced around her. He had *the instinct*—he knew where she'd move before she was there. When I was shooting Nicole's back, he was squatted three feet in front of her getting the full-length. Nicole had *the instinct* too. She didn't make it easy for Simon; she also didn't make it impossible. She just wanted him to work for it.

Have you ever paid attention to how someone exits a store? Or which way they face when they get in and out of a car? Or where the most natural route to walk is? You do these things yourself, *by instinct*, but they're not what you notice in others. Paparazzi, on the other hand, *do* notice. They *must* notice. They need to know how people will move *before they move*, and where they will go *before they get there*.

Nicole's photographs were beautiful. Movement flowed in the frames, giving the pictures a certain "tabloid" style, and one I am starting to appreciate for both its technical difficulty and its form. I notice that when a celeb is caught *in movement*, she is prettier (and most definitely *thinner*) than in real life. (I'm not exactly sure why this occurs. Maybe geometry could explain it, but I think it's the same reason the celebs stand with one foot in front of the other when on the red carpet. For some reason, it tricks the eye and elongates the body.) When the dance is over, both Nicole and Simon are satisfied. Watching them, I realize I have a long way to go.

★ ★ ★

Today, J.R. assigns Simon and me to track down Jodie Foster. I can tell that Simon isn't excited. I've learned that the tabloids don't have much interest in lesbians ("except for lipstick lesbians," Simon says, who according to him are "every man and woman's dream"). But I had gotten a tip from a friend that Jodie drops off her kids at eight every morning at a private school in West Hollywood, so J.R. deemed it "worth a go."

I arrive at 7:45 a.m. and pull to the beginning of the carpool line. Jodie is an easy spot in a silver Prius, and I *pick up* the follow (i.e., follow her) as she leaves the school. We go to a parking deck off Sunset and then on foot upstairs to a gym. Simon, who arrived too late for the follow (since he does not care about Jodie Foster), catches up with us there.

When he arrives, I have not yet attempted a photograph of Jodie. A shot with my long lens in the parking garage was impossible. I had no time to position myself the necessary number of meters in front of her, not knowing which direction she was going, and in the dimly lit garage my short-and-flash (versus my long lens/no flash) would have been necessary. Short-and-flash would have meant exposing myself, and "Jodie hates paps," per Simon, so she would have made that difficult. I was smart to hide and wait for his backup.

Of course, an inside-the-gym shot would make a great picture. *Jodie Foster climbs the Stairmaster just like Us* would sell, lipstick lesbian or not. "Should I go in for a tour?" I suggest.

"Uhh, if you want." Simon seems surprised that I'm making such an effort.

Jodie's not hard to find in the middle of a large room filled with people and machines. She is running on a treadmill directly in front of me but *what do I do now?* I suppose I could whip out my camera, take aim, and fire. I mean, what's the worst someone could do? Escort me out. Boo at me. Tell me to rot in hell. Throw spitballs, cups of water, smelly towels. Possibly clobber me over the head with a barbell. Obviously, this is why Simon did not come along. I pretend to get a text, cut the tour short, and leave.

Simon decides that though we can easily shoot Jodie as she exits the gym (we know she'll have to take a brief walk to the elevator), it's best to wait. "No need to blow our cover for a sweaty Jodie in a grey hoodie," he says. "Something better may happen."

This is a new tactic for me. I'm beginning to learn the ropes, but I'm still thrilled to just spot a celebrity. I have no experience waiting for a "better shot."

Simon goes to his car and situates himself by the parking deck's exit. He tells me to "lay low" and that he'll "pick up the follow."

"She may know your car by now," he says. "I'll call you in a few."

In a few, Simon beeps. (CXN has finally gotten me a Nextel.) "I lost her, mate. Sorry. Don't know what happened."

"Bummer," I respond casually. Inside, I am very annoyed. I have yet to develop "game" and my stealth follow was a big deal. *How did he lose her? She wasn't going fast. And why didn't he take a shot when it was a sure thing?*

Five minutes later, Simon beeps again. "Got her."

"What? How?"

"Weave your *web*, luv. They'll fly in."

Simon found Jodie's car parked outside a store a few miles from where he'd last seen it. This amazes me: in the clusterfuck of L.A., paps re-find people. It happens frequently. (With paps who have game that is. Like Simon. I take note.)

After Jodie's errands, none of which we are able to shoot (there was never a clear shot without being seen, and like the gym exit, the opportunities were too lackluster to *burn it*), she returns to the school and picks up her young son Kit. He looks to be about five. As we follow, Simon and I switch positions of lead car and, still undetected, follow Jodie to the Grove, the open-air shopping mall and movie theater in West Hollywood.

Even though she could valet, Jodie instead parks like a regular person in the deck. We park nearby and follow her and Kit on foot into the mall.

"Get out your cell," orders Simon. "I'll watch her."

Simon doesn't trust me not to make eye contact. Frankly, I don't either. As noted earlier, eye contact, or lack of, is one of the most important skills a pap develops. Once you make eye contact (unless it's the distracted, fleeting kind as previously discussed, versus the stare-down kind), you're done. In the car, on a follow, for instance, you often need to ID the driver, make sure it's the celeb you think it is. Sunglasses, side-view or rearview mirrors, and tinted windows all help conceal your interest, but you need to be able to recognize the celeb by the back of his or her head (which I can't do yet). A cell phone can help: while engrossed in a fake conversation, you're able to dart your eyes in an unfocused manner while putting the subject close enough to your periphery to identify him or her. This also works well when checking out restaurants and stores. The hostess or salesperson won't bother you if you're on your phone, and if you're actively chatting (to no one), it is an excellent way to stand still and look around for your next shot.

A celebrity's eye contact toward you is equally telling. If you're trying to figure out whether a star is on to you, Simon says, watch for his or her stare. Sometimes you'll notice a celeb trying to catch your eye in his or her side-view mirror. "Don't stare back," Simon says. "It's possible they aren't sure. Then, proceed with caution. You're a suspect."

Jodie and Kit sit at an outside table and order lunch. Simon and I shoot the meal from behind a hat kiosk about fifty meters away. We keep up a solid conversation about hats, and the salesgirl either doesn't notice or doesn't care. Simon switches out a lens just as Kit gets on his mom's lap, so we have to rely on me for that shot. (It ends up being the one they run in *Us Weekly* the following magazine cycle.) After lunch, Jodie and Kit ride the train around the mall. Their moments are affectionate and intimate, and there is no denying serious love between mama and son. My camera begins to feel like a violation of that love. At one point, I ask Simon if we can leave. "This isn't fun," I say.

He tries to reassure me. "These pictures are good for her. They show she's a good mum, and that's important for her career."

This is the first time I feel guilty doing what I do. But soon, I will understand more about the symbiotic relationship of celebrity and paparazzi, and the truth behind Simon's words will become clear, so today will also be the last time I feel guilty.

After the train ride, we "let" Jodie go. "We nailed it. It's exclusive," Simon says, and follows with his mantra, "Let's not get greedy." Getting greedy in this situation could result in being kicked out of the Grove by security or getting seen by Jodie. Nothing terrible, but no need to annoy anyone if we can help it. The chief risk, however, is getting jumped by other paparazzi. Paps trolling the Grove scan as much for other paps shooting as they do for the celebrities themselves, and since tabloids love celebrities with kids on their arms, we want to keep Jodie—and her son—exclusive.

Chapter 6

*O*n my desire to soak up information (and make money), I partner with CXN's staffers as much as J.R. will let me. Though my percentage is cut from 60 to 30 when I work with another photographer, 30 percent of something is better than 60 percent of nothing, which is more or less what I get when I work on my own right now. (A year from now, Simon and Bartlet nickname me "Jen-Full-Sixty" because I never want to work with anyone. They say it's because I want all the money for myself.)

I'm put with Aaron for most of the week. I like being with him. It's comfortable, and we have that elusive chemistry that makes breathing shallow and bodies warm. (Well, I have that chemistry for *him*. It's not clear whether it's reciprocal.)

Today J.R.'s assigned us to Hilary Duff. I've worked her only that one unfortunate time. But she doesn't worry me today, not with Aaron here. I'm starting to notice that when I work with a partner, anything seems possible.

Hilary lives in the eastern corner of the Valley in Studio City, an easy ten-minute drive from my house. I arrive at 8:30 a.m. Aaron comes a little later and brings the coffees. We park at the end of the street where we can see Hilary's *drive*, i.e., driveway (British), yet still attempt a stealth follow. Her neighborhood is full of curves and side streets, which will require us to keep a close tail or risk losing her. But the little or no traffic there makes it obvious there is one stubborn car always going her same direction. She won't have to be clever to suss us out.

I hop in Aaron's car, grab my coffee, and proudly unfold the "Hollywood

Stars Map" I bought the previous day on Sunset Boulevard, thinking it might give me a leg up.

Aaron nudges close to me on the seat and studies the map. "Celebs change their addresses as often as their *lippy* [lipstick]. They're all wrong. You wasted ten bucks."

An hour into the *sit*, an officious, heavyset man walks over from a nearby house. He approaches Aaron's car and knocks on his driver's side window. Aaron cracks it slightly.

"What are you doing?" the man asks.

"Not much. How about you?" Aaron says cheerfully, clearly not answering his question.

"I know what you're doing."

"What's that, mate?"

"If you don't leave, I'm gonna call the police."

"Cool," Aaron says like he's just ordered pizza, and rolls up the window. "Nosy fucking neighbor," he says to me. "Must be a bitch not being able to buy the street in front of your four-million-dollar mansion."

Aaron tells me a story. "Was on Jessica Simpson last week," he says. "The gatekeeper goes for a piss. Saw him leave, so went in with the next car. I'm sitting on her street for an hour, just down from her house, when some neighbor comes up and asks me what I'm doing."

When Aaron speaks, I still have to concentrate hard to understand his thick accent. I piece words together as best I can so I don't have to keep saying "what?" I've noticed that when I say "what?" too much, Aaron quits talking.

He continues. "I told him, 'It's a scavenger hunt, mate. I'm giving clues. Everyone's picking up maps from me to get to their next place.' The guy couldn't think of what to say. He just left me alone."

I love that Aaron does stuff like this. I mean, why are people so concerned with things that are not their business? If the guy had thought Aaron was a robber, OK then he should have called the police, but he didn't think that. Everyone in affluent L.A. neighborhoods knows that when a blacked-out SUV is sitting in front of a celebrity's house, it's a paparazzi. In fact, we probably *prevent* robbers from hitting up the richest people in town. We are better than a neighborhood security watch. Just get a celeb on your street and you're set.

The cops never show up at Hilary's, and at around 11 a.m., J.R. chirps. He's just seen a blog, and Hilary is in New York. We've been sitting on nothing.

It's too late to jump on another celeb's doorstep, so Aaron decides we'll head to town instead. On the way, Toby, a new "friend" (a loose term when speaking of acquaintances in this business) from a competing agency, Rodeo2, beeps me with a tip: "Brit's at the Chateau."

Many paps like to give tidbits of information and let you piece together the rest. It's part of the game for them.

I beep Toby back immediately—*How long has she been there? How big a gangbang?* I want to ask—but Toby's already on with someone else and I get the long, flat tone of his busy Nextel.

Aaron decides it's "worth a go," but we don't rush. We stop at McDonald's for another coffee. "If she's gone, no big loss," he remarks over the Nextel while pulling into the drive-through.

Aaron says this because everyone gets pictures of Britney—in fact, she's hard to avoid—but the Brazilians "own" her and they make most of the money. The Rodeo2 "Brazilian team"—that's what they call themselves—put in the time, sitting on her in rotating schedules all day, every day, and most of the night. Because of that, they are there for her "big events"—when she carried her baby in the front seat of the car, for example. Or the day she shaved her head or, later on, when a bald Brit beat the shit out of a Rodeo2 car with an umbrella for no apparent reason. (Afterward, she sent a handwritten apology note to Rodeo2, which the agency posted on its website. And later she explained it in *People* magazine by saying it was prep for a movie role, which to my knowledge never materialized.)

Britney's "BFF team" consists of about twelve Brazilians headed up by Mario, an older man who collects money bimonthly from Channing, Rodeo2's hands-on French owner, and then doles out the cash to his minions as he sees fit. With this sizable team, the Brazilians are some-times able to block other paps on a follow to keep Britney exclusive.

Britney is loyal to them too. (Except for that beating.) Sadly, she doesn't seem to have many friends right now, at least not ones who stick around, and it appears that she honestly looks at the Rodeo-ers as her friends. To this point, Donna and I worked her doorstep last week, arriving early at her Hollywood Hills home at around 10:30 a.m. (Britney never leaves until the afternoon, but if you arrive after eleven, all the parking places are gone.) At three, Britney's security team lead came out to the two dozen cars waiting on the shoulder of Mulholland and started asking around, "Who here's with Rodeo2?" Mario came forward for a private discus-sion, and over the next hour, Rodeo2 cars fell off the doorstep one by one like planes in an air show. When this happens—someone has inside information—everyone *not* in the know is left in a conundrum: *Stay and wait? Follow a Brazilian?* (Not that that's doable or allowable.) What we do know is that when no Brazilians are outside Britney's, she's probably not home. We found out the following day that Britney did come out but not in a car we knew, so we didn't follow. She gave an exclusive to her friends from Rodeo2—nothing salacious, just something inside a tanning salon, but solid worldwide money nonetheless. And bonus for Rodeo2, everyone else's day was shot, either waiting for nothing on Mulholland, or late-day *bottom feeding*, as Simon calls it, in the city.

And just so you know, Britney could do this—sneak out—any day. Instead, she usually comes out in her convertible with the top down or in one of her other well-known cars. If her security comes out in a car without her—to get gas, clean the car, etc.—the security will roll down all four windows as they pass us, letting us know that we do not need to follow. Make no mistake: Britney and company are in full control. OK, perhaps not of the starlet herself, but definitely of us. And as I'm learning, there's no question that paparazzi, security, and celebs—at least in Britney's camp—are all on the same team.[8]

---

8. During my years in this business, I came to learn that many celebrities, not just Britney, work extensively with the paparazzi. Celebrities call many of us, or our agents, and

When Aaron and I finally get to Chateau Marmont, a boutique hotel and restaurant in the center of Hollywood, Britney's already gone. I'm sure Toby's on the follow. After my fifth chirp, he picks up his Nextel, shouts out a Beverly Hills address, and hangs up. It's like I'm dealing with a twelve-year-old boy. I find the game exasperating, but Toby is my only non-CXN pap "friend" and I need him. He gives me lots of gangbang tips; in exchange, I listen to an hour each day of his personal *Jerry Springer*-ish relationship stories. We do this either in person, outside Britney's subdivision (where we first met—Toby never works anyone else), or if I'm working elsewhere, he calls (my preference so I can multi-task). I'm fascinated to discover people like him exist: Toby is a chubby American guy with a red face and a big heart who dates and desperately wants to marry his girlfriend, a professional phone-sex operator. ("I'm not jealous of her job," he notes. "I just get upset when she sees her kid's father.") People in this town never cease to amaze me.

Aaron and I arrive at the address Toby gives us, an apartment complex. Britney's just shaved her head, so she's even more tabloid-hot than usual, and a dozen paps are already here. Another fifteen roll in over the next few minutes, and we presume Toby tipped off half of those. Tipping off the competition seems counterintuitive, but Toby's motivation is that he'll get tipped back by any or all of us at some point. Besides, he shoots video and only calls in still photographers, so none of us are his direct competition. He just dilutes the pot for the rest of us.

Whenever you're working a gangbang, which I quickly discovered after my first ride-along months ago is always the case with Britney, you wait outside your car. There is no reason to hide—everyone, including

---

together we stage shoots. "Set-ups" are usually done at tabloid-interesting locations like the beach, a pumpkin patch, the grocery store, or even a tropical island getaway. These same celebrities will also call us on their way out to a restaurant or a shopping center if they want their picture taken, particularly if they're dressed up and looking good. Their shots are then sold to the tabloids and—this was the shocker to me—the celebrity often gets paid a percentage of the sales. As a freelancer, I didn't do a lot of these set-ups during my career (they were usually given to staffers), but it is a pretty widespread practice.

the celeb, knows you're there—and you never know if the celeb will walk down the street, pop out on the balcony, or do somersaults on the lawn. You must be prepared for anything.

It's this day, standing outside the Beverly Hills apartment complex, that I meet Adnan Ghalib, a Brit of Arab descent, whose name (not changed) you may recognize: Adnan becomes slightly famous a year from now when he dates Miss Spears herself, then decidedly infamous when she dumps him and he ends up with a forty-five day jail sentence for a hit-and-run.

Adnan gets out of a gold convertible Mercedes—a $100,000 car according to Aaron—and runs back and forth across the lawn shouting, "Fuck you, Fuck you, Fuck you," to no one in particular. (Aaron says, "That's just Adnan. Gotta love him." My thoughts are not so kind. I think he looks like an idiot.) Adnan's dressed in True Religion jeans, which for some reason are a favorite with the paps, a tight white T-shirt, and lots of rings and gold necklaces. He has a thin line of facial hair that extends from his bottom lip to his chin. Adnan's super cheesy, no doubt, but not bad-looking if you, like me (and apparently Britney), go for the Middle Eastern look. When Adnan sees Aaron, they both cry, "Mate!" and come together with a strong handshake. I stand by while they talk about which celebs are and are not giving it up these days, and eventually Aaron introduces me. Adnan nods vaguely in my direction.

We don't have to wait long. Britney leaves the building a half hour later, exiting from the underground parking lot. Britney is covering her head with a sweater, and a friend is driving her car. There is no shot. Like birds of flight, we scurry across the lawn to our vehicles to take off.

A few cops showed up at the apartment complex location to keep tabs on us, and they escort us all to Britney's next milieu. It's a questionable use of taxpayer money, but in this instance agreeable to me since it keeps the chase calm and the driving sensible. (Note: While you usually *follow* a celebrity, with Britney, it's always a *chase*.) But obviously, you can't bump lights when the cops are around, so it's easy to lose Brit. Which I do right away. Toby is first in line—he always is—so I figure he'll get me to the next destination, probably after the entry shots, but eventually.

This time, though, it's Aaron who catches me up. During the drive, we stay in constant contact over the Nextel. From Beverly Hills, we move east to West Hollywood (fifteen minutes), then without stopping anywhere, turn back west and head to Malibu (forty-five minutes). Once Britney gets to the Country Mart, a shopping center off the PCH (Pacific Coast Highway), she turns around again and heads back to Hollywood (one hour fifteen; traffic's building). She never gets out of her car.

Sound strange? It's not. Not for Britney. Lindsay Lohan and Nicole Richie do this too—drive around aimlessly as we follow. (Though to be fair, the latter two not as frequently; and soon Nicole will get married to singer Joel Madden, have babies, and quit the nonsense altogether. Lindsay, to my knowledge, is still participating today.) I *guess* if you have nothing better to do, it *could* be kind of cool to shepherd thirty cars all over town. *Maybe*. I can tell some of the paparazzi enjoy it as well—they have expressions like little boys on go-kart tracks. Personally, I find it dangerous and exhausting driving.

Finally, Britney stops. She uses the valet at a Hollywood apartment complex. There are no entry shots, but over the next few minutes thirty-something paps roll up with hopes of getting something on the exit. The stress level is high from over two hours of driving, and there's a lot of bullying and shoving. Everyone stands around waiting, hoping Britney will come out before the cops come to ticket our illegally parked cars.

But the cops have less to do than she does, and they get there first. Aaron has to go move his car. I was lucky and found a legal *park*, i.e. parking space (British), so am still in place when Britney comes out. She's wearing dreadful sunglasses with gold Chanel bling, a grey hoodie, a pearl necklace, and a short, blond old-lady wig, slightly lopsided on her head. She has a destructive expression on her face, like a smiling goblin, and I shoot from the street, fifty feet away. With few exceptions, mags love pretty, happy shots of celebrities, but Britney is currently a "train wreck" exception. With her, they'll take anything. I get some salable frames.

And just when I think I'm starting to get the hang of this paparazzi thing…

★ ★ ★

I meet Dean McDermott. Dean's ultra-famous wife, Tori Spelling, was the afternoon gangbang a few weeks ago. Everyone but Donna and I had left at dark; the other paps had their shots. I, however, was still chopping off those ever-important body parts (feet and forehead) and was short the desirable "full-length." I had only "pieces" of her.

Since there was no need to hide after the gangbang, Donna and I sat outside the offices of Tori's reality show, cameras in hand. (Donna was now equipped with a CXN video camera.) Tori and Dean were inside, and the show's van was parked in the lot. A few hours passed and a guy came out and got into the van. Twenty minutes later, he returned carrying two bags of In-N-Out burgers and struck up a conversation.

"Hi, I'm Rob," he said. Then he asked how "the whole paparazzi thing" worked, which we explained as best we knew. Before he went inside, he asked for my number, saying nebulously he could help me out. He wasn't trying to pick me up; Rob was pretty obviously another of the thousands of hot, gay guys in Hollywood. Rather, in exchange for information on Tori's whereabouts, he asked only for "some photos." At this point, I wasn't quite sure what he meant.

Since that day, two weeks ago, Rob has given me three tips. Turns out, he's a PA (production assistant) on Tori's reality show *Inn Love*. (I still haven't figured out why he's tipping me off, but I'm happy to take the tips anyway.) Today he calls with another: the show is filming next week at the "inn," a B&B near San Diego. Rob gives me the address, the layout, and everything else he can think of. I know about the back porch where Tori chats and gets makeup. I know about the dirt road where I can get a clear shot. And I know about Dean's three-foot-long monocular, used precisely to smoke out people like us.

J.R. partners me with Bradley, a good-looking Brit with a rare set of straight teeth. Bradley's only twenty-three, but he's one of the best paparazzi in the business—a spot-on shooter with "balls of steel," he proudly claims.

I arrive first, in my new (used) bright red pickup truck, which a friend gave to me because he didn't need it anymore. (Yes, really *gave* out of the goodness of his heart because he knew I needed a better vehicle and couldn't afford one. I am awed and will pay it forward as soon as I'm able to.) The truck was a definite upgrade from the '87 Mazda, but not exactly camouflage material. I park on the dirt road, per Rob's suggestion, and observe Dean through *my* long lens. He's milling around the back porch of the inn, the one where Tori gets makeup. I hope she might join him.

About five minutes into my observation, Dean picks up his monocular and promptly eye-fucks me. Then he grabs a video-camera-wielding crew-member and the pair scamper through the tree-spotted brush to my perch on the road. Confident as a drunk at a bar, Dean confronts me, "Excuse me, young lady. What are you doing?" He is a major tool, I think.

"What do you think I'm doing?" I respond with an eye roll.

Quite theatrically, Dean admonishes me and threatens to call the police if I don't "leave the private property immediately," which I can't do right then because he and his cohort are in front of my vehicle, filming me. I cover my face; having seen this done quite a few times, I've got it down.

He also suggests that I get a more discrete vehicle. *Thanks, Dean. If I make some money off your wife, I'm on it.*

I leave to reassess. I drive around but ultimately determine that the dirt road where I got busted is the only shootable angle. Somehow I need to get back there. I decide to wait for Bradley.

He finally arrives at two, and we rendezvous at the McDonald's down the street from the inn. He is not at all bothered that I've already been busted. "It's Tori. I'm not worried," he says, implying that Tori pictures are not hard to get.

In the McDonald's parking lot, Bradley opens his SUV hatchback and presents an artillery of lenses. He puts a 500mm on my camera. The "five hundred" is one of the longest lenses in use and can get shots from a quarter mile away.

Wow. The thing is huge—two feet long. And heavy—over ten pounds when attached to the camera body. "Be sure to hold the *lens* and not the camera or they'll snap apart," Bradley instructs. "And try not to use it as a weapon."

My eyes widen and my mouth turns up. This is what I needed all along: *Bring it on, Dean!*

I describe the lay of the land to Bradley, and he decides we'll go in on foot. He says we need camo (obviously)—*Sir, yes, sir! Hup!*—but since we don't have any, we put black sweatpants over our lenses, and earth-toned jackets and hats on ourselves. He pulls these from a basket full of "things paps should always keep in their car." (I make a mental note to pick up these things later for myself.) We leave my red truck in the McDonald's parking lot and drive Bradley's more subdued SUV to the street adjacent to the dirt road. Our plan is to sneak in through the dry riverbed and the sparse woods until we get a view.

Staying a few paces behind Bradley, I watch as he dances lithely from trunk to trunk and slides perfectly into position behind the largest tree. He motions for me to do the same, so on cue, I run straight across a wide-open gap in the trees, pause there with my twenty-four-inch camera lens in hand, and search for the next best trunk. When I can't locate one large enough, I dart back to my original position. Meanwhile, everyone from the film crew—and Tori and Dean—watch. If I were a deer being tracked by a hunter, I would have been shot with an arrow through the heart.

As I crouch behind a young tree, legs and arms dangling out on either side, I look over at Bradley for a signal of what to do next. He is laughing hysterically. I cover my eyes like peek-a-boo. *Maybe they didn't see me?*

Thirty seconds later, Dean, two cameramen, two boom operators, and the reality show's director are running toward me. They see me.

And they are coming at me *fast*. I panic. Then, I run. I run as fast as I can run—*Run, Forrest, run!* Still carrying the humongous lens, I run over the river and through the woods, past grandmother's house, down the road, and across the street. I haul my arse up and over a fence, and keep on going. I hear footsteps behind me. I sprint farther. For, like, ten minutes, I run.

Finally, I can't run anymore, and collapse in the leaves, my oxygen-deprived chest heaving as I look up at the clear California sky above me, praying all the while Dean won't find me. I try to quiet my breathing. *Are they anywhere near?*

After a several-minute recovery, I slide on my hands and knees back toward the crime scene. I tread softly so as not to crunch the leaves under me. It feels like I crawl for a half hour until I see the street, but just as I near it and peer through a hole in the brush, I see Dean. He is crouched behind the tire of Bradley's car, attempting to hide, and of course bust me when I make my getaway attempt.

I lie flat, trying again to breathe quietly. I am shaking with fear. *Oh, this is ludicrous*, I think. *I am not a criminal.* My phone vibrates. (Thankfully it was on vibrate.) It's a text from Rob asking if I'm OK. He's at the inn and knows Dean is hot on my trail. Apparently the entire production is "on hold" looking for me.

Still flat to the ground, I hear the director walk up and say, "Don't worry, Dean. This is great stuff. It'll make for great TV."

What happens next, I find out later: Tori and Dean re-enact the entire paparazzi chase *three times* for their reality show with Tori doing a big "Oh no!—the paparazzi!" look each take. And for thirty full minutes, Bradley sits clicking away from his perfect vantage behind the large-trunked tree. He says he doesn't believe they didn't see him. In fact, he's pretty sure that Tori spotted him but didn't say anything. "She loves it," he tells me.

It's the makeup girl who finally busts Bradley. When she points him out, he tears to his car in an effort to escape, but it's blocked by a cameraman. As the cameraman radios the crew, he apologizes to Bradley for having to do so. "Sorry, man. It's my job."

"I get it," Bradley says. "That's what I say about mine."

Dean and the rest of the crew arrive a few seconds later, and Bradley is reprimanded in a heated discussion caught—you guessed it—on tape.

Then the cops come. Somebody—we presume Dean—called them. But Dean whispers to the cops, "Be soft on him [Bradley]." And they are. (If only the LAPD treated us so well.) The San Diego cops write down Bradley's details, tell him not to trespass again, shake his hand, and leave. In exchange for the easy off, Bradley has to show Dean his pictures and Dean has "edit power." (Though, of hundreds, he only deletes two.)

Meanwhile, when I saw the cops arrive, I tore away again, making my way two miles up the road from the B&B. Now, traipsing through an avocado farm, I suddenly become acutely aware that I need to get off this private property lest I get shot. I am, after all, in *the country*, and *country people* often have guns. I dart toward the main road where I know the land is public, but where I will also be a walking target for the cops. There is no cell reception, so I can't call for help.

Think militarily, Jennifer: can't walk back because what if cops are waiting for you? Must pass B&B incognito. Best plan: hitch. (Note: I said "best" plan, not "safest.") The hitch takes a while—only two cars pass in ten minutes—and with my camera looking jarringly like an M16, I wouldn't pick me up either. Finally, another "bird photographer" stops. "Yes, the robins are beautiful, so much so that I lost my way," I concur.

My driver passes the B&B on the way to my truck at McDonald's, and when I see Dean and Bradley happily chatting it up on the side of the road, I decide it's safe to get dropped off there. As I walk toward the two, Dean spies me first and fires the same evil eye I recognize from the monocular. *She's back again.*

"Come on, Dean," I say. "Don't be ridiculous."

But Dean presses his "panic-paparazzi!" button, and the crew comes running. Then, it turns into *Good Pap Bradley/Bad Pap Jen* as they seem to have made a plot decision while I was hurdling through the avocado farm that I "lied to Dean." (Which I didn't. I never *agreed* to leave.)

Bradley smirks at me the whole time. I cover my face—*I don't want to be on TV!*—till I get bored of it, then, like Paris, give it up.

Finally, everyone shakes hands, and the crew and even Dean tell us that it is the most exciting shooting day they've ever had. Three of the cameramen personally give me kudos for my sprinting abilities.

In the end, Rob calls to say, "Sorry Dean is such a dick to paparazzi. And it's BS, because he loves it." He also tells me that he is thrilled that no one will know it was *him* who made this segment of the show a reality. That is, if he can keep his own little secret.

Chapter 7

A month goes by of continued trial and mostly error. It's now March, and today Brian is sitting on Kate Walsh, and I am sitting on Mandy Moore. Not literally, of course. Donna is in Brian's car, as she is more and more these days, and I'm riding alone. (Their relationship has been on the fast track since CXN's Christmas party.) I miss her when she's not with me; Donna's a big piece of my energy on the job day in and day out. Her confidence in me is stronger than my own, and I don't know how I would have made it this far without her. If I get abused by a nasty pap (as we've taken to calling most non-CXN paps) for getting in his shot, being a woman, or anything else I cannot help, Donna will inevitably get in his face and tell him where to go. I love watching her do that: she's five-foot-one and in her inevitable outfit of heels and a dress, she's unstoppable.

Conveniently, both Kate and Mandy live in Los Feliz, and it's a gorgeous Friday in our neighborhood. I love that about papping in L.A.: it's pretty much always a gorgeous day here. As much as I-heart-New York, I would not heart papping in the Northeast.

Around 11 a.m., Mandy leaves in her black Prius. I radio Brian, and he immediately departs his post at Walsh's and heads my way. We'll work Mandy together.

Brian and Donna catch up just as Mandy pulls into a Hollywood studio. When a celeb goes to a studio, she might be there all day working or recording so we often *leave it*. But since we're on Mandy exclusive, and since the studio is small enough that we can keep an eye on her car, Brian figures we should give it an hour.

This is only the second time I've worked with Brian (the Gwen Stefani day being the other), so I pick his brain about camera settings. Just as he starts to explain how his camera is an extension of his arm, Tori Spelling's Rob calls with a tip: "The crew's headed to the OB-GYN... if you're interested."

We're most definitely interested, primarily because Tori's OB-GYN is *not* in Beverly Hills. Most celebs see doctors on Beverly Boulevard in Beverly Hills, and because of this, paps sit near the doctors' offices waiting to spot celebs going into the parking decks. Tori's doctor is in Santa Monica; we're not likely to get jumped there.

Rob gives us the appointment time, and we head over. When we arrive, Brian makes the executive decision "not to hide" because "it's Tori and she'll give it up." But I'm a bit nervous about that decision—Dean's gonna spot my truck right away.

We park outside the doctor's building, get out of our vehicles, and stand in plain view with our short-and-flashes. Soon the beaming couple, followed by their film crew, leaves the doctor. They smile and wave at us. Dean notices my truck and points to it in recognition, but like Tori, seems pleased that I'm there. Exposing ourselves was the right call.

It's noon. One set in the bag and plenty of time for another. Brian decides we'll head to town to "trawl."

We hit Rodeo Drive first. Stores like Prada, Armani, and Cartier with front display windows worth more than most homes provide clothing, jewelry, and handbags to rich Beverly Hills's wives, wealthy tourists, and celebrities. But its worldwide fame surprises me. The shopping street runs just three city blocks, and I find it banal compared to Mulholland, the PCH, or any street in Paris.

Next, we head east on Wilshire toward West Hollywood. I'm following Brian when he radios: "Fuck me! Turn around. That was Robbie Williams!"

Brian is obviously excited. But most Americans would wonder why. *Who the heck is Robbie Williams?* Even I'd only heard of him a few months ago, and that was just because paps talked about him. But gauging from cool-headed Brian's excitement, Robbie's worth knowing.

Robbie Williams hit fame early. At age sixteen, he joined the British boy band Take That, and now, at age thirty-three, he's the bestselling solo artist in the United Kingdom and in many parts of Latin America. In most of the rest of the world, Robbie is a superstar the likes of David Beckham and Brad Pitt. But for some reason, his music hasn't caught on in America, and he is virtually unknown in the United States, where he lives in relative anonymity in Beverly Hills. Worldwide, however, his marketability is enormous—particularly now that he's just left rehab and has yet to be photographed. So if we can catch him, the international payoff could be huge.

We watch Robbie's black Range Rover enter the parking lot of Barneys. This is excellent. The inside of the famous department store is shootable with lots of light (albeit lots of security too), and Robbie has used the valet at the front door (versus underground self-parking) so we should at least be able to get him when he exits. Still though, *things could go pear-shaped*, as Simon always points out, so we better be careful.

We park underground, and Brian directs Donna and me to go into the store, pretend to be fans, and try to get a snapshot. Neither of us knows what Robbie looks like, so Brian describes him: "Good-looking, fairly tall, lots of tats. Shit, a rock star. You can't miss him."

Barneys has an open layout, and a marble walkway divides three departments on the bottom floor. The Handbag and Makeup sections never have more than five customers, so Donna and I search easily from afar. Robbie is not among the guests. We walk through Makeup to Shoes, the third department. We don't want a free makeover, and since they always ask, Donna and I keep our phones to our ears. Robbie is not in Shoes either.

In the center of the store is a wide stairwell like one you might find in a nineteenth-century estate house. It spirals upward, unhindered, toward a domed roof. We walk up the stairs to the second floor—the Women's section, another expansive floor plan flooded with light. We scan without exiting the stairwell. It's doubtful Robbie will be in Women's.

The top floor is the Men's section. Rarely are there shoppers in Men's. We don't walk around, just search with our eyes, then veer to the right toward the café in the corner. We again put our phones to our ears; we don't want to be seated. We survey the bar and the main dining room, an uncongested, dozen-tabled area where in the future I'll see Drew Barrymore sitting alone—facing me—smiling, eating, and leafing through a book. I'll be too chicken to shoot her point-blank, even though I'll have been doing this job for eighteen months by then, and even though I'll know that Barneys wouldn't do anything other than escort me out. (Drew might have given me a belting though. She's not shy with the paps.)

Donna waits at the bar, and I walk outside to the balcony and down its aisle, a dead end. "It's an amazing view. We should meet here for lunch," I tell my imaginary friend on the phone. I stroll as a tourist to take in the panoramic view of the city, the Hills, and the Hollywood sign. Robbie is at the last table, and like Brian said I would, I identify him easily. He's having tea with a friend and paying his bill.

Donna and I go back to the Men's department, get off our fake phone calls, and get ready. When Robbie and his friend exit the café and enter Men's, I know not to wait 'cause I'll wimp out.

"Oh my gosh. Oh my gosh. It's Robbie Williams." I speak loudly enough to attract attention.

Donna and I haven't rehearsed, but we connect perfectly. She giggles obnoxiously and covers her mouth. Robbie and his friend turn to look at our spectacle. Thankfully, there are no shoppers.

"Oh my gosh. Are you Robbie Williams? Can we take your picture? Oh my gosh. I can't believe it's Robbie Williams." Thick as a Fatburger-plus-egg, we lay it on.

And Robbie must like meat: he eats it up. Donna sticks her point-and-shoot in his face, and he extends a fist showing off his brand new tattoo, a letter on each finger: L – O – V – E. His wide smile and face are in the background, all perfectly in focus.

Most big celebrities will take pictures *with* fans 'cause those are rarely salable, but they often don't let fans take pictures of *just them* in case they are being tricked. Robbie's not like most big celebs—at least not on this day. He wants more photos than we do and moves from one quirky pose to another while his friend stands by laughing. To make it look real, Donna and I both get a shot *with* him (and because, truth be told, Robbie's smokin' hot, and we're both a little starstruck). But Simon's words—*Don't get greedy*—ring in my ear.

"Thanks, Robbie. We love you!" I say for a transition out.

When he's out of earshot, Donna calls Brian and proclaims, "We nailed it!" Then Brian shoots more shots of Robbie exiting the store, posing again.

We get the pictures to CXN an hour later, and the following day, our exclusive shots hit the cover of every major tabloid magazine in the United Kingdom. Over the next nine months, we each make more than five grand from that Robbie set. Oh yes, Robbie Williams is definitely worth knowing.

★ ★ ★

Perhaps, at this point, it seems that my life as a paparazzi is full of pretty good times. And it's true, I *am* having fun. But there is a dark side, one I haven't much touched on, which shadows it all.

So what's the hardest part of the job? My answer is surprisingly similar to the celebrities' response: *The Paparazzi.*

At present—four months in—the hazing I'm getting from the other snappers is out of control. It will not always be this way, but I do not know that at the moment. And right now, if it weren't for Donna, I can unquestionably say I would no longer be paparazzi.

The guys at CXN, those I've mainly written about, respect me. They can see that I'm humble and that I want to learn. Besides, if they have any inclination that I'm gonna be good, they're happy to have me on their team.

But except for CXNers (and Rodeo2's Toby), no other paparazzi will speak to me. To be clear, I mean, they will *never* speak to me. But they have no problem abusing me in other ways. To date, I have been spit on, pushed down, run off the road, and "told on" to Simon and Aaron (for things like getting in a shot or poor driving or not adhering to "rules"— rules that I was never, in fact, informed of). But, this abuse is always done silently. I am never spoken to directly.

Let me give you an example: I was outside Neil George waiting with a gangbang of men for Lindsay Lohan to get her hair done. Wayne Watermelon, a six-foot-three Mohawked American pap who drives a red car that somebody splattered with black paint (hence the nickname), decided he wanted to stand where I was standing *and had been standing for an hour*. He came over, didn't say a word, just shoved me. Hard. I toppled, caught myself, and returned to my ground. Then he shoved me harder, and I fell. Two dozen paps witnessed it, but no one moved or said a word. That was worse than being shoved. I started to tear up, but how could I leave? The other paps didn't want to get involved; it would have made their lives difficult. I understood that. If they defended me, Watermelon would have hit them much harder than he'd hit me. Plus, they wanted me gone too. Simon tells me all the time, not unkindly: "Jennifer, you have no friends in this business. Don't forget it."

In hindsight, I realize the problem. The problem—on their end—was that they did not know what to do with me. Their physical controls, the ones they used to keep people in line (like punching or shoving each other), were difficultly applied to me. (As rough as the paparazzi were, none of them really wanted to hit a girl.) But they knew that I wasn't the kind of girl who always stayed "in line," and I didn't always do what I was told, like move. Hence their conundrum, and their silent but obvious opinion that things would be much better if I were just gone.

But at this time I did not understand the problem, nor how to fix it, nor whether it would ever end. And I was starting to go down. The problem on my end was that I did not understand their rules. I did not even understand that there *were* rules. You see, paparazzi govern with "street" rules, and I had no experience on "the street." Other professions that might have similar hierarchies and rules—law-enforcement, trade jobs, restaurant jobs, and the like—I'd either never had, or if I'd had them, I generally got fired from them. When waitressing, for instance, I tried hard to be the best employee. Which was, of course, the problem. Who likes the best employee in a restaurant besides the customers? All I got was the lovely reputation as a know-it-all.

I didn't grow up on the street. I grew up in an upper-middle-class suburb of Atlanta. I went to college. Then I went to grad school. And I always made straight A's. I grew up being taught that if I tried hard and I was good at what I did, I would succeed. But all this meant to these paps was that I wasn't one of them. I didn't belong. That doesn't work on the street.

And while now I think there's plenty of bullshit in the paps' discriminatory mind-set, as well as in the idea that if you work hard enough you can get anything you want, at this point I was still onboard with wanting to be the best paparazzi I could be, regardless of whether I "belonged" or not. So when Wayne Watermelon shoved me, I bit my lip hard and glared at him. I was going to give this my best shot, come angry celebs or worthless paps in paint-spattered junk heaps. But it was not going to be easy.

$$\bigstar \ \bigstar \ \bigstar$$

This blistery, early spring Saturday, my red truck is in the shop, and Toby hesitantly offers to let me ride with him. He and his phone-sex operator girlfriend have broken up for the fifth time this month, and I can tell he needed someone to talk to.

As soon as I get in his car, Toby is paranoid. "This doesn't look good," he says.

"Why? Who cares who you ride with?"

"Just one more thing they can use against you."

As I see it, by riding with Toby, I am harming no one, eating into no one's profits; but at the moment, paparazzi rules are nonsensical with regard to me, and any change in protocol will be used as an excuse for further persecution. But I stick to my guns and go with Toby anyway.

We troll for about an hour before we run across a gangbang of paps perched on Sunset like an unkindness of ravens. "Unkindness" is the name for a group of ravens, a fact I learned from reading *The Animal Dialogues* by naturalist Craig Childs. It's become one of my favorite word usages since then.

"LMN," observes Toby.

LMN is a paparazzi agency, some of whose shooters are allegedly former members of a Panamanian drug cartel. The agency is largely made up of ethnic Americans—Asians and Latinos—and for some reason its paps seem to hate me even more than the rest do. I have occasionally feared they have a hit out on me.

We get out of Toby's car and walk toward the gangbang. It is in the center of town, and we find it on our own (versus being tipped off). We have every right to be there. To best describe my interaction with LMN on Sunset, I will quote from Childs's chapter titled "Raven":

> *I began moving toward the ravens, but very slowly. The nearest birds seemed to become agitated. A few hopped onto their toes and petulantly flexed their wings...They grumbled and cawed, their tones crass, brought up from deep in their throats. I thought I could not possibly be a threat to them...Why were they getting upset?*

Toby and I cross Sunset and walk closer to the gangbang. There are at least twenty "ravens" surrounding a building, and Toby catches wind that Victoria Beckham is inside. They "grumble and caw" as we pass by. I keep my head down. Toby tries to say hello, but no one responds. Eventually, one of them steps out in front of us, and we have to stop. He doesn't look at me or address me. He just says to Toby, "She's gotta go."

"Look man. We spotted it. We can shoot too," Toby says, trying to stick up for us.

"If you don't leave, she gets fucked up," he says soullessly.

What does THAT mean?

"Chill out. Chill out, man. We'll leave."

Toby knew the streets. And he knows, today, they aren't bluffing. He turns to me, "Let's go," he says. "They found her first."

Childs calls ravens "mobbers who gang up on invaders and attack one another if one gets out of line." By just "being there," I am out of line. And ravens, who are "skilled at delivering torment," are banding together to destroy me. It might sound melodramatic, but at this moment I do not know how far they will go. Will they expertly follow me home, sit outside my door, and wait for me to leave? Then what?

"She gets fucked up." *WTF.* At this point, I'm not so thrilled with this job anymore. I am pretty freaking scared.

★ ★ ★

Monday I collect my truck from the mechanic, stock it with "Mace Pepper Defense Spray with LED, Gun Distance" (in hot pink of course), and am back on the street.

On my way to my doorstep I decide, if I were a celebrity, I'd want to be Cameron Diaz. So slick in kicking our asses, there's no way not to like her. As pap-savvy as they come, Cameron rarely talks trash to us (she doesn't need to) and generally—effortlessly and with *style*—avoids us; *but* if she wants it, she knows how to work it. After she and Justin Timberlake broke up (not too long ago at this point), she began to oblige our shots once or twice a week, mostly after leaving her boutique West Hollywood gym dripping with svelte, sexy sweat. *Go Cameron!*

Since she's been giving it up of late, J.R.'s put Bradley and me on her Hollywood Hills doorstep. I'm not hopeful. I've never heard of anyone getting Cam from her home; rather, she just shows up when she wants to. If Cameron does come out while someone's on her doorstep, it's said she pulls up next to them, either in her Prius or her 911, smiles a giant Cameron smile as if to say, *I know you're here, and I want you to know that I know,* then drives like a fiend down the hill, past the Chateau, and onto Sunset. If she doesn't smoke the pap on the hill or on Sunset, she pulls through gated subdivisions and parking garages until she does. Or if she can't shake 'em, it's said she'll return home. Stubborn, yes, but a fair fighter: Cam never calls in the cops. I respect that. I also hear she does her own stunts in movies. I believe it.

Midday, Bradley lights a joint. Now, here's my deal with pot. I'm all for medical marijuana, but I hate smoking. Don't like the feeling at all, and only get high right before bed on occasion so I can calm my nerves and go to sleep. But this time, for some reason, I say, "Sure, I'll take a hit."

A couple puffs, I'm out. I crawl to the back of Bradley's SUV, then to the way-back and lie down. He, on the other hand, is jazzed: "Let's blow this doorstep and go get something!" We both know Cameron's not coming out, but I can't move and *no way* can I drive. Bradley has little choice but to take off for a troll with my worthless weight lying in the back.

Cam lives behind Chateau Marmont off Sunset and Crescent Heights. It doesn't take us long to hit a trolling route. We head west on Sunset, then go south down Doheny, pass the lunch spot La Conversation (patio check—no one), and swing down a little side street where Cameron's gym is. Oh what luck, her silver Prius is parked outside.

J.R. rings about this time. "Ahhhh…any action?"

"Yeah, J.R. We're on her at the gym."

"Ahhhh…Great…Ahhhh…Stick with it."

We can't expect to keep her exclusive in the middle of West Hollywood, and over the next hour, a few more paps roll in. Bradley has cajoled me out of the car, and I sit in a stupor on the sidewalk holding my camera and long lens. When Cameron comes out about an hour later, we shoot her with her head up, waving and smiling.

Bradley and I get on the follow. The other paps, apparently satisfied, let her go. Cam's driving slowly and doesn't seem bothered we're following. When she pulls into an underground parking deck in Beverly Hills, Bradley instructs me to get out of the car and shoot while he parks.

"By myself? Are we allowed to shoot here? Will you shoot with me?"

"You'll be fine. I'll shoot from the car," he says with a smile.

I'm getting screwed, I know, but follow orders, slide out with my short-and-flash which I'd switched to when we pulled into the deck, and amble toward Cameron.

"Watch the lift," Bradley instructs out his window. He means the elevator.

When I get to Cameron, I do not raise my camera. Instead I stare at her and wait for her cue.

"You're on private property. You can't shoot here," she says matter-of-factly.

I'm still a little stoned. *Hmmm, now what?* I'm standing in a dark parking deck with zero confidence (which I know she picks up on), sorely aware that if I try to bring my camera to my face, she'll just turn the other way. She's fully in control.

So, I don't try to shoot. Instead, *I've got it,* I'll follow her again. *Into the elevator.*

What the hell am I doing? I glance at Bradley who is thirty feet away snuggly in his car—he smiles and waves me on.

Cameron gets in the elevator.

I get in the elevator.

My camera's down. I'm looking at the ground.

It's just me and her.

The door closes.

Just me and her.

Silence.

No one pushes a button. The elevator doesn't move.

"You need to get off," she says.

I don't say anything and refuse to move my eyeballs from the floor. But I can feel her stare. She's looking at me like I'm a fever blister.

I'm really normal, Cameron. I bet we could be friends.

Silence.

"This is really weird," she says.

I have an MBA, Cameron. I'm smart. I'm not like them. I'm one of you. You'd like me.

She's right. This is really weird.

Cam is a *very* experienced celebrity—she knows pap protocol. And, as I can now attest, this is most definitely *not it*.

I'm super glad I smoked pot earlier.

"I'm just gonna see where you're going," I finally whisper, still staring at the floor.

Forever-long pause.

"*Humf.* Fine. I'll get off then."

She pushes the button, the door opens, and she walks out. The door closes, and I'm left alone.

Eventually I push the button, the door reopens, and Cameron, standing there, moves aside so I can pass. I never look up. When I make it to Bradley's car, he's curled up on the floor and can't talk for laughing so hard.

I whack him on the back of his head. "Get up! Let's go."

Being a Celebrity, for Dummies

Part 1

Dear Celebrities,

I feel it's about time we discussed your habits. 'Cause the way I see it, after only five months of working in this business, if you *really* don't want to be photographed, you *mostly* don't have to be. (Now, your gut probably already tells you this, but to validate: most celebrities you see in weekly tabloids are there **by choice**. You do not need to feel sorry for them. They *want* to be photographed.)

But for the celebrity who just doesn't get it, or for the up-and-coming celebrity, here are a few tips for avoiding the paparazzi:

(Note: Reverse these tactics to attract the paparazzi.)

1. Do not eat, hang, shop, go to the doctor, drive, live, or basically be

in the Beverly Hills or West Hollywood shopping areas, defined as the *City* in the Glossary of Paparazzi Terms. Ninety percent of paparazzi hang out in this two-mile radius of town. There is also a healthy smattering of us in the heart of Santa Monica and near the Country Mart in Malibu, so you may want to avoid those areas too. If you are spotted in town, you should give it up. (In my opinion.) That's the game. (Unless we followed you there. Then you may have some grounds not to.)

If you don't "want it," then move to or shop in a different part of town. There are a plethora of fantastic neighborhoods in L.A. with much cooler shopping than Rodeo Drive, Barneys, and Maxfield. (Olsen twins, are you listening?)

2. Don't be a person of habit. Don't go to the same coffee shop each day (ahem, Patrick Dempsey), the same yoga class each Monday (Reese Witherspoon), or the same Beverly Hills restaurant each weekend (hundreds of you). There's great variety in this city. Mix it up.

3. When you go out of town, use it to your advantage. You should know by now that there are paps stationed full-time at LAX— usually at the American gate. Also, some agencies have airline insiders and sort through passenger manifests so they can catch you on other carriers. Ideally, you will take a private jet. If you must go in and out of LAX, try particularly hard to keep your return a secret by arriving late at night or very early in the morning. If you alert us at the airport that you're home, expect a doorstep the next day. If you come through incognito, enjoy your L.A. freedom. (No one wants to work on someone who "might" be home.) This "out-of-town advantage" can buy you days, weeks, or more (until you're spotted, of course—so keep out of Beverly Hills. See No. 1).

4. If we manage to get a camera near your face and you know we're there, keep your eyes half-shut the entire time. You don't see this often, but it's a classic trick and friggin' funny. Mags may buy an ugly picture of you, but they will not buy one of you with your eyes shut. If that's too hard, then take a lesson from Leonardo DiCaprio: always wear a low-billed hat or sunglasses, and keep your chin curled under even if you don't know we're there. If you do know we're there, walk with your hand casually sweeping your forehead. This way, you will not look belligerent in the few places that your hand and half of face print. (Look up some pictures of Jen Aniston—she has the hand sweep down to a science.)

5. Regarding your home: where you buy a house and the layout of the neighborhood is of utmost importance.

    Ideally, your neighborhood will have at least two exits. *And even if it's less convenient, you need to use both of them.* This makes us either have to sit flagrantly on your house (in which case if you are the slightest bit aware, you will see us immediately and can simply employ other tactics, as in No. 4 above) or have to use double the manpower (i.e., we sit farther away from your home, one at each exit), which is much less lucrative for us. We still may work you but not nearly as often.

    It is also crucial that we are not able to tell if you are home. One little garage door can change your life. A variety of cars (and a mixture of real and dealer plates) is another trick.[9] If the one car that you always drive is sitting in your driveway for all to see, then we're gonna sit on you. It's like dangling a banana in front

---

9. In Cali, when you buy a new car, you leave the dealership with "paper" or "dealer" plates (or "without plates," we might also say), and your real ones are mailed to you in a few months. These dealer plates depict the dealership logo and do not have identifying numbers on them as they do in some states. Thus, if you have a new-looking car (which

of a monkey. How could we not? We don't even have to get to your house early because you are an all-day doorstep target. At any time during the day, if we drive by and see your car, we might decide to sit and wait.

Frankly, it's best we don't even see your house from the street. You could live in a private subdivision with a gate guard, or your house could lie far from the road and be shrouded in shrubbery. If we can't see your house, we can't get clues that might tell us if you're home or in town. If we are never able to tell if you're home, we are more likely to pass you up. Another option is to buy a home on a busy road or one we'll have trouble parking on (a "permit only" street, for example).

And best-case scenario, have more than one home (or stay at your boyfriend's or girlfriend's often) and switch it up. You'll be hard to keep up with or we'll have to put two paps in two locations—again, generally more effort than you're worth.

Bottom line, if it takes too much time or too much man-power to get a shot of you, *we will give up*. But, beware: you could become…*BORRRRIIING*.

Good luck!

Jennifer

---

may even be as old as two or three years), you will generally not be pulled over for driving with dealer plates. Paps use dealer plates for two reasons: one, to be less identifiable; and two, to avoid getting ticketed at red-light camera intersections.

Chapter 8

*B*ackpacking along the Mediterranean beaches in Mount Olympos on my travels before moving to L.A., I met a blond, blue-eyed Turkish girl named Elif. When she realized that I was traveling alone, she insisted I join her group on the sand. We swam in the warm sea out to a boat and to a couple of jumping rocks. A few weeks later, back in Istanbul, Elif brought me into her home where I stayed for a week and became like family. I left a chunk of my heart in Turkey that summer, and I'll keep going back for it until I die.

Like Donna, Elif is a small-statured, pretty girl you don't want to cross. Between textile jobs in Turkey, she had decided to come spend the late spring/early summer season with me in Los Angeles, but after several weeks of searching for employment—everyone wanted to see a work visa—Elif was thinking of going back home, something I really didn't want. We'd already grown very close and she was like a sister to me.

One Saturday afternoon about a month after she had arrived, Elif took a break from job searching to ride along with me. I was working Kirstie Alley.

Kirstie lives in an easy-to-watch Los Feliz home but isn't worked frequently because she never leaves. (If Kirstie weren't rich, I'm convinced she'd be a cat lady. She has a cage full of monkeys in her front yard. Seriously.) But, if you put in the time and Kirstie does come out, you can be guaranteed a sale—sadly, because the tabloids want to see how fat she is. (For the record, Kirstie isn't that fat. She may be overweight for Hollywood, but all in all, she's a very attractive woman.)

Kirstie is, however, the slowest celebrity driver I've ever encountered. She goes about 20 miles per hour on every road and turns her signal on a quarter mile in advance. This is fabulous for following. Plus, since Kirstie is rarely worked, she's not on the ball with noticing paps.

'*Appy days*! (This "Simonism" is now part of my vernacular.) Kirstie actually left her home today and met friends for lunch at the Alcove, a restaurant up the street from my apartment. She even sat on the patio where I could stay in my car on Hillhurst Ave. and get pictures of her eating, a definite score. Next, she went to Pinkberry for some yogurt. Then she queued outside Los Feliz cinemas for an afternoon movie. This was a paparazzi dream day.

I parallel parked opposite the theater on Vermont Avenue, and Elif and I sat in my truck to wait for the movie to let out. When it did, I followed Kirstie down the street, positioning my vehicle in front of her at an angle, quickly slamming it into park with my hazards on, shooting through my driver's side tint until she got out of range, and then moving in front of her again and repeating. With a card full of frames, I was no longer carefully hiding, but even so, Kirstie didn't notice me. As she neared her car, I called out "Hello" with my camera to my face. I thought she might wave and smile. And boy she did wave—she gave me a big fat bird.

When it was all over, Elif looked at me with stars in her eyes. "You didn't tell me this is what paparazzi was like!"

And voila, my little illegal alien and I figured out her job: shooting video.

★ ★ ★

Over the next month, I began to hone my video protégé. At least once a week, we would work Britney Spears, where each day outside Brit's home on Mulholland and Coldwater, dozens of paparazzi vehicles would park to wait on her. Testosterone leaked out of them like engine oil.

Britney was valuable short-and-flash gangbang practice for me, and she was Elif's favorite sit due to guaranteed action. Initially, in typical fashion no pap would acknowledge us. But when they realized we weren't going away, tolerance began to overcome disdain, and a few even seemed to enjoy our presence. For the first time, paps other than CXNers—Britney paps nonetheless, the most parochial around—were beginning to talk to me. I quickly learned the driving rules and protocol specific to Britney; and since Britney paps, like Britney herself, reward consistency, the chases became easier because someone would usually let our car in on the follow, and we had made enough "friends" to get caught back up if we lost it.

Elif turned out to be just what I needed. Donna was riding with Brian most of the time now, and I was more or less partner-less these days, which was tough for my confidence and morale. I needed a coach, or at least a cheerleader, or I would start to doubt myself. My little Turk, a gift from above, was by nature and culture fiercely protective of me, her friend. Just like Donna, Elif believed in me and that empowered me to keep at it every day, even when I failed or got knocked down.

Today, the chase begins as usual, except that Britney isn't in one of her everyday cars; rather, a large bus pulls out of her subdivision. Rodeo2 knows to follow. We get on the 101 at Laurel Canyon, and then take Interstate 5 South. The half of the procession that isn't from Rodeo2, me included, all get on our Nextels to try to figure out where we are going. About an hour south of L.A., word gets around: Britney will perform her first concert in nearly three years at the House of Blues in San Diego.

Three police cars spot our convoy, and they make it their business to escort us southbound. At one point, when the bus exits the freeway and then gets back on for no apparent reason, the cops block the reentry ramp for about five minutes. But Britney doesn't want to lose us either, and we easily catch back up to her bus just going the speed limit. (The cops ditch us after that, apparently clueing in that Brit is a star who does not want their "protection.")

San Diego's city center is full of one-way streets, and once there, paps circle every way possible trying to keep up with the prey. We need to stay close. Only a lucky few will be near enough to get a shot when the bus stops.

When it does, however, Britney is blocked by her security and ushered inside so fast that no one gets anything. Left on the steps of the House of Blues must be forty of us, half of whom I've never seen before. Frenzy ensues. The ravens, so full of adrenaline, start "grumbling and cawing" at each other, and soon potted plants and signposts near the entrance start toppling over in the chaos. Security moves in and ushers us down the street to a less noxious perch.

But despite the ruckus, there is a different tone to our group. Something about being out of town is bringing us, fierce competitors, together. There is laughter, banter, and camaraderie—like we are on vacation. It is in this melee that Wayne Watermelon turns to me and says something human, something like, "Man, that was crazy,"and the way he says it implies I am human too—even a comrade in arms to him. For a moment, I am speechless.

To put our relationship into perspective, my last encounter with Watermelon, while working on Kate Hudson, didn't go so well. He and his partner jumped her with their short-and-flashes. My partner and I, much more decently, "gave her distance" with our longs, the appropriate lens choice for the circumstance. Watermelon *savaging* her, as Simon calls it, resulted in Kate refusing to get out of her car, which resulted in me calling him a dumb %$#@*, which resulted in a barrage of insults from him, and which I returned in kind. Then, he threatened me with bodily harm, and I kicked his red and black car with the heel of my cowboy boot and ran away as fast as I could. It was a horrible day.

But for some reason, today, Wayne Watermelon wants a change. And I am game for anything that will make my life easier. San Diego marks the beginning of an alliance for us and, surprisingly, a real friendship. From here on out, Watermelon and I are buds.

J.R. attempts to get Elif and me tickets over the phone so we can get in and shoot Britney, but the concert is sold out. On a whim, I walk up to the ticket counter. Two tickets have just been returned, and I buy them on the spot.

After dinner with Toby and Mario from Rodeo2, we head to the concert. I stuff my point-and-shoot in my bra, and since security only checks our purses, Elif and I enter without a problem. The venue is small and probably holds three hundred people max. The first floor is standing room only. The upper gallery has a few rows of seats and another small standing area. We walk upstairs and greet fifteen of our "friends," mostly Rodeo-ers who knew about the concert in advance (we assume from Britney herself) and purchased tickets. It seems we've found the best position.

The concert starts at 9 p.m., and twenty seconds into the first song, "Baby One More Time," the games begin. At least twenty security guards are posted throughout the venue, and they descend on us quickly. Camera-clutching paps are booted out one after the other. I last a long five minutes, a credit to being female I suppose, and when I do get the boot, security tells me that I can come back in if I ditch the camera. They don't know I'm a pap. So out and back I go, camera again shoved in my bra.

When I return, some guy who is sitting behind a post and perfectly angled out of security's eye is chatting up Elif. The guy appears to be an obsessed Britney fan (as he thinks we are too, of course) and is happy to lend a hand. I switch my camera to video mode, hand it over, and the guy records a full two of the five songs performed by Britney. He never gets busted.

After twenty minutes, the concert is over. Britney also played "Toxic," a fantastic song in my opinion. And, man can she can dance. At $75 a ticket, I'd pay to see her again even if I weren't a pap.

The paps convene outside. Toby was kicked out early, as well as all the other Rodeo-ers, and Mario is desperate for shots. Coming back empty-handed to Channing, Rodeo2's owner, is not an option for him. In this case, there is more at stake for Rodeo2 than just picture or video sales. Rodeo2.com, the agency's website, prides itself on being the "Britney insider," and this one-off concert is big news in her world. There were no "official" press photogs at the event, so pap photos are all there is to tell the story. Since other agencies won't sell to Rodeo2—it being a competitor—the only way Channing can get material for the site is from his paps, or others, on the street.

Right off, Mario and Toby approach us to see what we've gotten. Although CXN would like to have our video, and would expect it, video is a new venture for the agency and it hasn't sold one of Donna or Elif's submissions in five months. Since I am on full commission, and Elif needs money, we are interested in talking.

At about one in the morning, Channing calls me. He offers me $9,000 for the video. I agree (of course!) and make arrangements to drop by my chip at his house when I get back to town. He'll greet me with a check.

Ten minutes later, he calls back and changes the deal to $3,000. I work him up to $3,500 but have little leverage. Evidently someone else also has video of the concert—not nearly the quality of ours, we find out later, but good enough to ruin the exclusive.

Channing's home office is situated in Brentwood, an expensive neighborhood on the Westside that's chock-full of celebrities. At 4 a.m., Elif and I knock on his door. We wait only a moment before he opens it. Channing is wearing a tailored shirt and does not appear sleepy in the slightest. He shakes our hands and sits with us on the front stoop where he apparently does all his business; no one is ever allowed in the house.

An attractive man in his early forties, Channing is polite but not charming, calculating but not conniving. In a refined French accent, he asks me to come work for him. He says he'll pay me ten grand a month. I tell him that I'm already making that. (The reality, though, is I've gotten only one paycheck so far. Which, in fact, was for over $10,000, but it was also for my first four months of work. But Bartlet told me the money would keep coming—"Your payments have kicked in now," he said, meaning that the three- to four-month lag in the initial collections from the magazines has been waited out. *Finally*, I breathed ever so slightly easier about my building debts.) Mostly though, I don't want to work for Channing because he requires bimonthly negotiations: each of his paps comes to his home every two weeks, stands on the front stoop, and makes an appeal for their salary based on what they brought forth during the period. I bargained my way through Southeast Asia always feeling like I was getting ripped off. I prefer to get paid an exact percentage of my sales, and CXN gives me 60 percent directly deposited into my bank account. That's my speed. But for one night—and $3,500—the Southeast Asia way is amenable. Channing writes me a check, and I hand over my memory chip.

★ ★ ★

We drive home down Sunset from west to east. There is no traffic and we clip through intelligently sensored lights that change quickly to green. The early morning light tints blue on the still sights of the city.

In L.A. at this time of year, the sun begins its defeat of the night at the miserable hour of 5 a.m. Though I wish it happened later, there's something satisfying in seeing the light win every day: the wakening reveals a beautiful city. It's not an in-your-face beauty, like that of Istanbul or San Francisco; rather, unlike its celebrities, L.A.'s looks sneak up on you. Think of a woman whom a man may at first dismiss as plain, even ugly— *What does everyone see in her?*—but whose splendor, like an avalanche of snow, builds and breaks and descends, suffocating him before he knows to run. In one day, he goes from feeling nothing for her to being in love with her. Suddenly, he craves this woman like his morning caffeine: he must have his fix. Her every imperfection—a gawky figure, pimples, too large of a nose—is now a beauty mark in his eyes.

This is the beauty of the City of Angels. Like the way Il Sole—where Jennifer Aniston and Courteney Cox eat—nudges into a decrepit strip mall and now flanks the priciest boutiques in town. Or the way the windows in Red Rocks cover an entire side of the bar and reveal their out-of-place hippie clientele to the surgically enhanced West Hollywood pedestrians. You can see the beauty in places like the ordinary Starbucks on the corner of La Brea and Sunset, where the extraordinary Spice Girl Mel B gets her lattes, and down the street from there at the stucco Rite Aid building where the spectacular Kate Bosworth shops for a humble tube of toothpaste.

To my left, at this moment, is the forest of the Hollywood Hills. If you
search a little, you can find buried treasures under her leaves. As I drive,
I notice the palm trees that line Sunset Boulevard. But you'll only notice
them if you look up; they've grown too tall and look like telephone poles
to the unobservant eye. As I go a bit farther and hit the Hollywood Walk
of Fame, tourist shops beckon—the Indian incense wafts out their doors
and Bangkok T-shirts hang in front windows. I love it when I reach east
Hollywood, near to my home. Here are Spanish tobacco stores, Thai
restaurants, and Armenian markets. Here, the dilapidated buildings still
reflect the mastery of early twentieth-century architecture, and outside
their doors is where the homeless sleep in cardboard boxes. One more
mile, and I'm in Los Feliz. Los Feliz is home to all colors, nations, and
ages, rich and poor alike, famous and unknown. The World is here: a
mad palette of humanity rubbing together in unexpected harmony. Life
is here. And my home is here, my beloved home.

I break the silence. "Man, what a night."

"Who is this man, Jennifer?" Elif responds sleepily. "You Americans are
always talking to Man."

I just smile.

★ ★ ★

Bartlet was right: the money did keep coming. From here on out, I never
made less than ten grand a month. Of course that wasn't all profit—I had
loads of equipment to buy, other operating expenses, and taxes to pay for—
not to mention that loan from my brother to pay back, but it was still more
money than I'd seen in years. The cash would flow on the back end too:
residuals continue, that kind of passive income that makes "dreams" possible.

But don't think I sold out for money. Papping was never my end-all,
nor was it any means to an end. It was just part of a journey, and the
money produced from it, with a light gust, would blow away as quickly
as it appeared. I knew that. Especially in L.A., a home I loved, but one
where quicksand abounds. So I paid off my debts as quickly as I could,

continued to live as I had been (with the exception of more frequently indulging in designer jeans), and saved the rest.

★ ★ ★

Summertime changes the paparazzi's typical "doorstep in the a.m./troll in the p.m." daily routine. Bathing suit shots constitute the most valuable stock in photo libraries, and it's important to rack up a few each season. Even if the shots aren't exclusive, bathing suit sets have strong residual value because they are rare: Jennifer Lopez in a bikini is shot once, maybe twice a summer. So if a mag needs a picture of her in a bathing suit (and the mags always want the most recent), then they're buying yours until she's shot again next year.

In the beginning of the season, the ocean is a welcome change. Within the Malibu city limits are several beaches, as well as the Country Mart, the outdoor shopping area and eatery which brings needed reprieve—and food—to a hot and sandy celebrity-scouting beach sit. And for every three or four hours you put in at the Country Mart, you can pretty much guarantee seeing *someone*. A- to D-list, celebrities love it.

So once May hit, Elif and I started spending every Saturday and Sunday in Malibu. Both of us had it in our heads that we could get "Jennifer Aniston on the beach" if only we were patient. My car stayed packed with paparazzi essentials: changes of clothes, extra socks and shoes, a couple of bathing suits for beach transformations, sun umbrella, beach (i.e., camera) bag, cooler to fill with camera gear, towels, water bottles, Spy Hawk GPS tracking device to attach to celebrities' cars (*Kidding!* I would never use that), and so on.

Along Malibu's beachfront, million-dollar homes run side by side, broken up only by an occasional restaurant. If the residents could pay a billion dollars to own the sand in front of their houses, no doubt they would. But God bless us, America still owns her beaches…so if you wanna plop yourself on Jennifer Aniston's sandy lawn and stay a while, ya can.

Aniston's home is perched in front of a beautiful part of the beach—not too crowded, fairly wide for Malibu, and practically speaking, accessible. If you get to the PCH by say 11 a.m., early enough to find "a park," you don't have to walk far to the beach access point near her house. Small and unpretentious compared to its neighbors, Jennifer's house has a large deck about a hundred feet from the water. This is enclosed by an unsightly waist-high plastic railing that allows her to see out but no one to see in.

We never know for sure, but since Jen's security comes out every hour, we think she's home. Even so, that doesn't mean much. Jen is a self-publicized homebody and can stay inside for days at a time. I've heard stories of paps sitting on her for a week, sure she's home—even seeing her do yoga through the windows—but never seeing her leave. Jennifer also has a home thirty minutes away in Beverly Hills. It's the one she and Brad Pitt bought together. Up a winding, narrow road past Halle Berry's, Toby McGuire's, the Olsen twins', and Keanu Reeves's, Jen's house is ten minutes from Sunset Boulevard at the tip-top of a Hollywood hill. The view kills but so would the isolation.

Elif and I have gotten familiar with Aniston's security guards because they stand out: two large men not particularly in shape, kind of like football players ten years past their prime. They are always cleanly shorn and dressed business casual in slacks, shirts, and blazers. Even off the beach, no one dresses like that in L.A. Every hour, like clockwork, they come out to patrol, standing at the corner of her deck and sweeping the beach with their eyes. They always lean down and check under her deck too—paps have been known to hide in the spaces under the beach houses.

Though they never photograph us, we've heard that Jen's men occasionally take pictures of any paps sitting on the beach. (Brad and Angie's security do this too.) I think it's just for intimidation purposes; though I wouldn't be surprised if our mugs were compiled in a monthly newsletter to all relevant parties. Honestly, that's what I would do if I ran her security. That way, if we ever followed Jen to her favorite hideaway (Cabo) and tried to stay at the same hotel (which paps have been known to do), we'd be spotted straight away. Of course, photographing paps could also have a more legitimate security implication, like differentiating us from real and potentially dangerous stalkers.

Sometimes one of Jen's guards will take her dogs for a walk. I'm always tempted to take shots when this happens—my colleague Bradley has made a lot of money off Jen Aniston's dog—but I don't because I don't want to give myself away. Not that the guards haven't figured us out. Who else would come out every weekend, even on the chillier spring days, and stay bundled up under a sun umbrella in the same spot?

Every once in a while another pap will stroll by us on a celebrity scouting beach walk. Beach paps can be spotted a hundred yards away: they don't wear a bathing suit, they wear sneakers, and they carry a bulky backpack slung over their shoulder. Although it's less practical, Elif and I take pride in making ourselves fit in. We wear bikinis or cover-ups, go barefoot, and carry "beach bags." Frankly, I don't think we look really suspect until about five o'clock when we start to shiver. We hear that Jen, like the marine life outside her beach house, becomes most active at dusk—an evening walk-the-dog shot is what we're hoping for. Besides, if we haven't left Malibu by three, we might as well wait till after seven or we'll encounter two hours of freeway standstill.

We don't just read away our time. Elif and I scan the beach for movement, and one of us will take a stroll every hour or so to scope. No sense in sitting in front of Jen's house if Courteney Cox, her neighbor by about fifteen houses, is sunbathing outside. Of course if I go stroll, there's always the chance that Jen will come out and I'll miss it. I carry my cell so Elif can call, but it's slow beach walking with the weighty camera equipment situated non-ergo-dynamically in the disguised beach bag. I usually meander to the eastern end of the beach toward Charlize Theron's. Charlize's house isn't actually on Jen's beach, but it can be seen from the end. I've heard she walks her dogs too, and who knows, I might get lucky. I used to think how uncanny it would be to stumble upon a celebrity at just the moment when she's, say, walking her dog. But the more I wander, the more I find that sooner or later—and not so infrequently—someone does walk her dog at just the moment I stumble up. *Weave your web and they'll fly in.*

Today, Elif and I see movement about one football field down the beach from Jen's. It looks like a group of people and more than the average number of beach walkers. We go check it out. Five or six paps are set up with long lenses outside a house. One of them tells me that Jessica Alba is doing a photo shoot and that the crew has made a pact with the paps: they'll send Jess out, we'll take pictures, then we'll leave them alone for the rest of the day.

Nobody's happy I've joined, but they've seen I've been paying my ocean dues, so they don't say anything. Jessica, who can't stand the paparazzi but is too gorgeous for us to ignore, comes out wearing a white bathrobe and stands statue-still and completely expressionless. We take pictures. All the same shot. Now everyone has one shot, the same one (which will sell—it is Jessica Alba in a bathrobe, after all—but not for very much). After about five minutes, she goes back inside. We wave, nod to the crew, and leave.

On the walk back to Jen's, we run into Simon, also trolling the beach.

"I don't care what *deal* you made," he says after I tell him what happened. "Jessica Alba's in a bathing suit. Go back."

"Really?"

It takes us thirty minutes to walk around the photo shoot to the other side of the beach where we must be to use the remaining sunlight. We traipse over sharp rocks and through knee-deep water. I'm carrying the "five hundred" (500mm lens), which feels like it weighs as much in pounds. It is the same lens I used to attempt shots of Tori and Dean at "Inn Love," and the office has lent it to me for my beach sits.

Simon accompanies us and is technically "jumping my job," but since I'm still learning the game and he helps me out a lot, I don't say anything. We're not the only ones with this idea either. Three of the six photogs who were there originally are now shooting from this perch.

We stand about three hundred feet away, and Jessica's really tiny even in the five hundred. I walk across someone's porch to get about fifty feet closer than Simon and the other guys. The crew has sent one poor lad with a measly piece of white poster board to block us. He's deficient in equipment and outnumbered, and I'm sure he's peeved to be missing Jessica in her bathing suit. He's also chivalrous and ignores my presence to concentrate on the men. I gratefully accept the advantage.

We shoot for about thirty minutes—a couple of wardrobe changes—until the sun is gone. I have no idea what I've gotten or if it will be salable once the images are enlarged and cropped. Jessica looks like a tiny spot in all my images.

Simon and I regroup at the Country Mart Starbucks; we'll edit together. We order coffees and sit down with our laptops and camera cards. Before he starts his edit, he pauses, "I've been thinking," he says. "This was really your job. I jumped it. I'm gonna give you my photos." What Simon means is that he won't take credit—or money—for his photos. He is going to give them to me, and I will send them in with only my name on them. This is typical Simon behavior and why he's the Most Popular Pap in the business. He's not dumb, though. The money he loses by being nice, he gets back double in information. Simon can get almost any location information or home address he needs, and he's tipped off by other paps all the time. Everyone owes Simon. Me included. But "thanks love, that means a lot" and a peck on the cheek is all I can offer for now.

We transfer the images to the computer. Simon looks at his, then mine, and then with gravity in his voice says, "I can't offer you one image, Jennifer. You out-shot me on every frame. Nice job."

I am stunned, both by my shots and, more importantly, by Simon's kind reaction. Humble, supportive, and adult: a pap anomaly. Today Simon gives me much needed money (my "full 60" percent) and, more critically, confidence.

The quality of my set is grainy due to the long distance, the low light, and the necessary pull-up in the frame, but there's no question it's Jessica Alba in a bathing suit. And that sells.

Over the next year, I'll make about $5,000 on those frames, my images superior to the competition's not because I was a better shooter, but because I had the right equipment and the gumption to crawl those few feet closer.

And finally it feels like I turn a corner. No, I didn't have the instinct to "go back," as Simon had directed, but I did have the instinct to seek out the scene in the first place, and then to shoot it. Today is a turning point for me in confidence. Now, just like Donna and Elif, I'm not worried. It's gonna roll from here.

Chapter 9

*C*onfident in the money too, Alexandra (one of "the girls") and I go jeans shopping. I buy Citizens in straight leg black, Hudsons in boot-cut washed, and Sevens in skinny blue. And just in the nick of time too.

A text from Jed, my former coworker at Tropicalia, reads:

The guy from *Entourage* with the curly black hair is at Farfalla.

"Man," I say to Elif, "I hate getting nighttime tips." I've worked all day and edited into the evening, so another set means I'll be working till ten and then editing into the night. That means nighttime tips are only worth doing if I think I can make enough on them to circumvent my following day's doorstep. 'Cause I'll sleep in. Besides, "*flashing* someone up," as night shots inevitably do, at a neighborhood restaurant—especially one in my neighborhood right next to where I used to work—is humiliating. With giant bursts of flash, everyone looks. And beyond humiliating, in this case, "the guy from *Entourage* with the curly black hair," is Adrian Grenier—my neighbor, my age, my type, and at least semi-single. Though I don't stand a chance with Adrian, I'm not going.

No, apparently I am going. Elif makes me go find Adrian. She's like a kid with a new Christmas BB gun, way too keyed up about her novel profession to let any tip go by. And, she does not think Adrian is cute in the slightest thus couldn't care less about "looking cool."

The location is only a few blocks away from my house, but we drive so we can stay in the car as long as possible. I've never shot Adrian and know nothing about his attitude toward paps. Since I don't know if I need to hide, I need to hide. Non-gangbang nighttime shots are tricky; you might be able to get one shot off before you're seen, so if the celeb is gonna cover, that first shot better be it.

Adrian is alone when he steps from the restaurant. My choice would be to wait longer (until he's gone), but Elif sees him too and is out of the car. I have no choice but to follow.

I squat in front of him, shooting him, relieved the camera is blocking my face.

Adrian stands still and stares at me. Eventually, it becomes silly. I have enough shots of Adrian standing still staring at me. I put the camera down and stare back.

"What are you doing?" he says.

"Uh. Taking your picture."

"We're paparazzi," I add. Elif is recording video, but she's not confident in her English so never says anything. Right now, I'm not confident in my English either. I pull the camera back up to my face not knowing what else to do and take more pictures of Adrian standing still staring at me. I put the camera down again.

"What are two cute girls doing being paparazzi?" he asks.

"I don't know, we just are." *Did Adrian Grenier just call me cute?*

"I'm working on a documentary about the paparazzi," he offers.

"Yeah? Maybe you should ride along with me sometime. See how it works." My voice shakes but I manage to extend this very important offer.

"Maybe I will."

Adrian's friend walks out, a girl who doesn't look like a girlfriend. "What's going on?" she asks.

"We're shooting Adrian Grenier," I respond.

She laughs. At him, not us, then corrects my mispronunciation. "It's Gren-YAY. French." I had said "Gren-YEAR."

Now I'm the one standing still staring. I am not starstruck, but beautystruck. Adrian is breathtaking. I never knew he looked like this. He did not look like this in *The Devil Wears Prada*. And honestly, there is something going on between us. I do not lie.

When his car is pulled around by the valet, Adrian hugs the girl and walks to his Prius. (In L.A., celebrity or not, there's no getting around valets. You *cannot* park your own car in this town.) I kneel in front of him again, shuffling backward as he walks toward me. His teeth blind the frames. Then he waves good-bye.

When we get back to the truck, Elif turns to me. "What went wrong with you, Jennifer? I never seen you like that."

I ignore her, but she's right. I have no idea what just happened.

★ ★ ★

Two weeks after our first encounter, I see Adrian again, this time on the set of *Entourage*. The HBO series about the movie business films at the en vogue places in Beverly Hills and West Hollywood, and no surprise, the crew is very tolerant of paps. A group of us are shooting the scenes from across the street with long lenses when Adrian sees me, points, and motions for me to come closer. I can hear my heart thud, and I immediately start to tremble. *Be cool, Jennifer. Be cool. He's just another guy.*

I walk toward the foldout chair with his name on it. When I get to him, I put out my hand. "Hi. I'm Jennifer."

"Hi. Adrian," he grins, taking it.

In front of the cast, crew, and other paps, we talk. Mostly, he talks—I'm that nervous—for what has to be five minutes. About what, I do not remember. All I care is that

Adrian pointed at me.

Adrian remembers me.

Adrian flirts with me.

Maybe Adrian will ride along with me.

Then, maybe...

"See you around," he says when he gets called back to set.

"Yea. OK," I stammer back. Then I turn and hop on cloud nine, which transports me back to my car. I do not rejoin the flock of birds still gathered outside the set. I am no longer one of them. I am one of him. At least today.

★ ★ ★

Memorial Day marks the official beginning of Malibu's summer. If you're a shy celebrity, go to Beverly Hills this weekend 'cause you won't see us: we're all at the beach.

Over the weekend, Elif and I spend the larger part of each day outside Aniston's house. Word on the street: she's home. And we're determined this time. We deserve it. Not to mention how infuriating it would be to see someone else get what we've spent so much time pursuing this spring.

By Monday at three, things are looking grim. No sign of Jennifer all weekend. I take off to the Country Mart to get some food while Elif stays on the sit.

"Jen. Copy. Jen. Copy," Aaron chirps with intent.

"Go ahead."

"You at Aniston's? Her car just pulled up."

"Copy. I'm at the Country Mart. Turning around now."

"Copy. Let me know when you're near."

On holiday weekends, paps troll up and down the PCH looking inside car windows for celebrities. A celeb in her front seat would be hard-pressed to make it through Malibu without being spotted on a holiday like Memorial Day. Besides, Jen drives a rare green Range Rover, so by being just slightly aware, and in the right place at the right time, Aaron had seen her pull out of Courteney Cox's driveway, drive a few blocks, then pull into hers. No question now: Jennifer Aniston is home.

I call Elif. She's on alert on the ocean side of the house but with only a video camera. I need to be there too. There are no shortcuts down the Pacific Coast Highway, and with holiday traffic it takes me twenty minutes to get back two miles. I see someone pulling out of a street parking space as I drive up. Score.

Aaron and I quickly make a plan. We decide to ignore the front. She could leave again in her car, but we believe a potential beach shot to be far more valuable so opt to put all our efforts there. Plus, we don't want our competitors to see us waiting outside her house and get confirmation she's home.

Aaron goes in from the north side near Courteney's house, and I go in from the south. A few other paps also spotted Jen's car and apparently have the same idea. Elif, Aaron, and I meet up and find a spot on the sand a few houses down from Aniston's. Three other paps sit nearby. Though cameras are hidden in bags, you can see that all the paps have their hands on the triggers. If shooting starts, with six of us it will be impossible to hide. We have to get an early shot before she sees us, or hope she'll give it up.

Five minutes later, like ducks, they roll off the deck: Jen, Courteney, and David Arquette holding his daughter CoCo.

"This is big," Aaron whispers.

"Both *Friends*!" says Elif.

We wait for them to descend the stairs and begin to walk before pulling out our cameras. We want them committed to the sand. David spies us first, yells and shields CoCo's face with his hand. Jen and Courteney put their heads down, and soon Courteney breaks off from the others. She knows that a picture of her and Jen, or one of her and her family, is significantly more valuable than any picture of each separately. It's a much more interesting story for the mags if "Jen and Courtney, BFFs, take a beach walk," versus if each walks alone. David and Jen soon separate too.

Jennifer is wearing cut-off jean shorts and a T-shirt. Her hair is perfectly styled, long and thick. Her face is made up naturally, and her body is expertly toned. She looks just like she has for the last fifteen years. After the first few paces off the deck, Jen pops her head back up. She's giving it up gracefully.

Alternating with Aaron, the two of us go back and forth between Courteney and Jen—mostly Jen, she's the most valuable—as we walk backward in front of them down the beach. We ignore David, who has little star power even with a child in his arms. Elif trails me, shooting video.

Adrenaline floods my body, making the surroundings blur and time freeze. The walk down the beach could have taken two minutes or ten. I'm not sure. There was no time; there was only *now*. All of us—the six paparazzi and three-and-a-half celebrities—are spread out haphazardly, like a few freckles on a hand. A couple of times I pause to catch my breath while taking it in. It strikes me that the paps look like buzzards, running in semicircles around their prey, swooping in and out, feasting and backing off, eating and retreating.

Running backward in the sand is challenging, and a couple of times I fall. Once, I sit winded looking up directly into Jennifer's eyes. She has to step around me. I feel like a twit, but not because of the way she looks at me. Jennifer seems kind and doesn't make me feel inferior. Even if she's not a fan of the paparazzi, Jen understands the media. You'll never see her with a scowl, she never looks belligerent, and rarely does she fully cover. (Only the partial hand sweep cover she's so good at.)

Before the group steps into a neighbor's party, Jen looks back at us and waves. "Happy Memorial Day," she says to the cameras.

Elif and I don't talk when it's over. Words aren't powerful enough. We had waited so many hours, so many days, wondering in our hearts if it would ever happen. We're as high as the holiday blimp above our heads.

I ring Bartlet. In a metaphor too vulgar to be repeated, he explains why my Memorial Day weekend is similar to an orgasm, then he says, "Get the pictures in *fast*," and hangs up.

Aaron takes my card, gives me a big kiss *on the lips*, and goes to Starbucks to edit and send the images. Mags usually "close" for that week's stories by Monday morning, but because it's Memorial Day a few will hold out till the afternoon. Aaron and I assume we have similar images to the other three paps since we all had plenty of time to nail it. Our sales will be determined by how quickly we get the pictures to market and how Bartlet negotiates.

Meanwhile, Elif and I go back to "protect the story." The idea is that if you already have pictures, then you need to stay on the story so you don't get scooped—a philosophy I don't really buy in to. If a shot's gonna scoop yours, then *it is*, whether you're there or not. When I get back to Jen's house, about twenty paps are gathered in front—word spreads quickly on holiday weekends. And, although not much would trump our shots, when a celebrity the size of Jen Aniston is inside *for sure*, paps will be outside *for sure*. I find out that Jen had gone to the neighbor's party for a brief appearance then walked back to her house on the PCH (a shot we'd missed, but one I never saw print).

Channing (Rodeo2) calls me an hour later. He asks if he can buy the video and some of the photos. In other words, he wants me to "split the set," a common practice among freelancers, but one that is frowned upon by most agencies because it reduces the value of individual pictures. I tell him that's impossible; I was working with a staffer on the stills, and CXN already knows about the video. This is kind of a bummer though. Channing would have given Elif at least a thousand for her video. As it stands, CXN still hasn't sold any of her videos, and this Aniston clip will be no exception. (Over the next few weeks, I cultivate a relationship with Channing. He pays us $500 cash on the spot for any decent videos we bring him. That ends up being a lot better deal than waiting for CXN to never sell them.)

We wait till dusk before we leave. Any night shot that might happen later will likely be far less valuable than our day shots and won't compete for the same story anyway.

But so much more significant than any shot I took, or will ever take of Jennifer Aniston, was the transformation that occurred today, six months into my paparazzi life. As I stood there outside Aniston's house, protecting my story, side by side with guys who still mostly hated me, something changed. I could tell it from their eyes. Subtly, and for the first time in my pap career, their looks were filled with deference. A few of them nodded at me, some quietly mumbled congratulations, and one even asked for a recap.

No pap moment thus far could compete with the pride I felt when three savages, as Simon calls all beastly and bad-mannered paparazzi, patted me on the back for *getting* Jennifer Aniston.

The tables had turned.

Side note: I barely made any money on the Jennifer Aniston shots. No one was messing with me, but there were almost no sales. A few of the competitors' photos printed, but not many, and there were no re-sales that I ever noticed. Bartlet couldn't be blamed. He was as surprised as Aaron and I were. "There's just no interest," he said. "Apparently she's *boring*."

And, it seems, that's how she likes it. So until Jen gets with her next Hollywood-man-du-jour (John Mayer it turns out), *forcing* us to take notice, one of the most famous women in the world will live virtually pap-free.

Chapter 10

*L*ike most jobs, I find the longer I work as a pap, the more predictable the job becomes. But unlike in most jobs, I welcome the routine.

At CXN, most days begin on a doorstep. We get our assignment at six the evening before, through an email or call. We have input: if we've seen someone during the day but not "nailed it," for example, that celebrity may be a good target for the next day. We will also use gossip gleaned on the street from talking to other paps about celebrities' whereabouts.

Mostly though, the paparazzi do their research on the Web. All day, office staff scans the blog sites, and in the evenings paps do this too. We check who's appearing on the talk shows so we know which celebs are at home in L.A., and who's traveling in New York. Later, when Twitter becomes a phenomenon, both "people on the street" and the stars themselves will inform us of their whereabouts. The Internet tells us both if a celebrity is in town and if he or she is selling. It is hands down most responsible for the increase in paparazzi activity over the last few years—celebs are just not that hard to find these days.

Rarely do we pick a doorstep randomly. If a celebrity hasn't been photographed or spotted in a while, we assume he or she isn't in town until he or she turns up again, often in formal pictures—red carpets or charity events—or sometimes in a candid pap shot. We also do drive-by *reccys*, i.e., reconnaissance (British), of a celebrity's home looking for signs of inhabitance: blinds going up and down, lights going on and off, cars moving in and out, etc. It strikes me as being like thieves, but the only thing we want to steal here is a good shot of the celeb. Remember, we're great anti-robber defense.

While I'm paid as a freelancer, I've latched on tight, so CXN treats me like staff. I always hope to be partnered with Aaron, who I still have a pretty significant crush on, but J.R.'s in charge of assignments and he spreads me around the staff, which is productive since I learn something different from everyone. It's been a half year since I started papping, but my learning curve is still straight up vertical.

Being prompt is key to not wasting our day. We *should* arrive at the doorstep of our chosen celebrity home by eight or eight-thirty. But not being a morning person, I'm more likely to end up there at nine. The danger of arriving much later (or even that late) is that celebrities *do* things. They often get up early to go walk or jog, get coffee, or drive to work. Most of them do not sleep in all day. Of course, a doorstep might also be out of town or spending the night out and we don't know it. Sometimes we see them come home, which really isn't that bad 'cause now, at least, we know they are there and may go out again. All in all, doorstepping is a fine way to catch a celebrity, but generally it pans out only about 25 percent of the time.

On the way to the doorstep each morning, if we're not working alone, we Nextel our partner, exchange ETAs, and discuss the layout of the house, the cars, where to park, whether to hide, and so on. When we arrive, the first thing we do is drive by the house to look for the celeb's car or signs of life. Changes may occur during the day, so we need to get the lay of the land. Next, we check for competition. Paps are easy to spot. We look in places where we might choose to sit, and for people (usually Latino males) sitting in parked cars (usually SUVs with dealer plates). Sometimes a sunshade will be covering the front windshield of a competitor's car. It is also likely the car is heavily tinted, and a window is usually cracked open. If the window isn't cracked, then the engine's on for the a.c. The occupant is often sitting in the back seat. If we know the competitor, we might acknowledge one another with a nod, but neither of us is happy to see the other.

If there are more than four competitors on a doorstep, everyone stops hiding. With that many cars, it's impossible to pull off a stealth follow, so we have to hope the celeb will give it up. If it's a doorstep of a celeb who will *never* give it up (an Olsen twin, for instance), we might cut our losses and leave.

When deciding where to sit at a doorstep, we naturally consider the best place to hide from the celebrity. But we also must consider the best place to hide from other paps. Assuming most photographers don't sit on an empty house, late-rising paps often troll doorsteps to see if another pap's already there, and if they get verification, plop down next to them. Sometimes, if we see a slow-moving vehicle coming our way, we duck under our seat in the hope that the passing pap doesn't see us and leaves. Lastly, before situating ourselves in our parked car for what could be an eight-hour day, we factor in comfort: frequency of cops and meter maids, traffic buzz, ease of watch, and direct sunlight.

When working a doorstep with a partner, we cover both street exits if it's necessary. If one person is sufficient to watch both directions (or if we know the celeb being doorstepped departs only in one direction), then we may opt to cover two doorsteps that are located close to each other, ultimately working whichever moves first. As well, a seasoned pap knows who lives in which neighborhoods and often spots celebrities whom they weren't even waiting for. For example, once I was sitting on Mandy Moore and Vince Vaughn jogged by. Dax Shepard, Kate Walsh, and Christina Ricci also live within walking distance of Mandy. And if I expand by another two miles, I can count a dozen more.

J.R. checks in between eight and nine every morning. It usually goes something like this:

"Ahhhh. Hi, Jen." (Five seconds.) "How's it going?"

"Great, J.R. She looks home. Car's in the drive."

(Eight seconds). "Ahhhh. Great." (Five seconds). "Ahhhh. Give it a go."

Then we wait, with J.R. or Bartlet checking in every few hours. The only thing worse than sitting outside a celebrity's house all day long with no action is sitting outside a celebrity's house all day long among nasty paps with no action. Nasty paps like to mill around the sidewalks smoking cigarettes, eating peanuts, and giving out menacing stares. Having a periodic call from the boss helps us keep it together.

It's polite protocol to visit with our partner for a while—morning niceties, then a review of the action plan should the doorstep move. If we're chummy, we might jump into one car to visit a bit more. When I do, I always pick my partner's brain: "What do we do if this happens?" "Let's go through the camera menu." "How does your edit workflow go?" But eventually we'll work our way back to our own vehicles, since that's the best place to be if our doorstep takes off. Nothing like busting yourself first thing running to the car in front of a celebrity.

It's amazing how much I can find to do in my car. I make phone calls to my mom, JoDeane, and Georgia; I do trade reading by browsing a tabloid or two; and I check in with a half dozen other paps. It's important to be in contact with other paps, primarily ones from your own agency so that you can share information. Unless we're on a top-secret doorstep which J.R. has forbidden us to reveal ("Loose lips sink ships," he loves to say), we call each other and report our location. It's not unlikely that another pap will have additional information about our doorstep—"Beckham flew out yesterday," for instance—and this saves many wasted hours. On the other hand, if we check in with our competitor "friends," we don't tell them who we're on at the moment. They may not know he or she is in town, and we don't want our story scooped the next day.

Once our doorstep moves, we radio our partner (if we have one) and follow. Unless there's a reason to be seen, e.g., the celeb gives us better pictures when he or she knows we're there, we attempt to hide. We may be on our target all day, or he or she could go immediately to an unshootable location, a studio for instance, in which case we may "leave it" right away.

If our doorstep goes to pot, i.e., we lose the celebrity or he or she goes somewhere and we don't think it's worth waiting, or if the doorstep doesn't move by 1 or 2 p.m., then we generally head to the city. I prefer to get to town by 1 p.m. for lunch-hour spottings. I troll cafés on

Melrose and Beverly, the Fred Segal department store, celebrity gyms, and Robertson Boulevard. All paps have similar paths, so we're constantly passing one another on the road.

When trolling, paps look for celebrities' cars—both on the road and in parking lots. As well, we look *in* cars, on sidewalks, and on restaurant patios for the celebrities themselves. We also look for other paps, or their cars, engaged in a follow or lurking outside an establishment. Memorizing other pap vehicles—and their drivers' reputations for productivity—is as important as knowing celebrities' cars.

Most paps are too lazy to get out of their cars and instead rely on outside clues (other paps, the celebs' cars) to tell them if famous clientele are inside. I've found, however, that actually walking in stores and restaurants significantly improves my hit rate. Interestingly, when scanning a restaurant or store, it is not necessary to look at each person individually. By simply breezing one's eyes over an area, the subconscious will, without fail, register "recognition." I'm not exactly sure why this works, but Malcolm Gladwell covers it in *Blink: The Power of Thinking without Thinking.* Soon I will come to see celebrities out of the far peripheries of my eyes, when I'm out with my girlfriends, not even looking for them. As well, more and more I am beginning to spot celebrities by their builds or gaits, so I can easily recognize them even if their backs are to me. If I've seen someone once, I find I see them frequently. If I do make a spot, I *post up* strategically on the sidewalk or in my car, try not to get jumped (by actively watching for and ducking when I see another pap), and shoot the celebrity exiting. Depending on the location, I occasionally attempt to shoot inside, but mostly I reserve that for the paps more experienced than me.

Late in the day, I may ditch the car altogether and go for a stroll around the Grove or traipse through Barneys in Beverly Hills where celebs enjoy shopping for items over a thousand dollars apiece. Or sometimes I just park on Sunset or Doheney and wait for them to drive by—and get stuck in my web.

★ ★ ★

It's been months since he first tipped me off, and Rob, *Inn Love*'s deep throat, shows no signs of stopping. He tells me that he doesn't feel guilty giving me inside information about the boss because she and Dean do the same thing. As I mentioned, in exchange for tips on Tori's whereabouts, Rob asks not for money but "for photos." I wasn't sure what he meant by this at first—*pictures of Tori? Of celebrities?* Eventually, however, it became clear: Rob wanted pictures of…himself. Rob wanted to be papped!

We did this a couple of times on Robertson. He shopped there, and I was always passing. He loved it. Before long, it turned into a full-on fetish with Rob texting at least twice a week:

> **Rob:** Shopping at the Grove if you're nearby; taking Tori's dog to acupuncture at 2; with my cousin on Robertson…dressed alike—it would make a great photo.

After I take his picture, I edit the best few images and email them to him. I do not ask what he does with them.

Today Rob texts:

> Going to the Standard with a few friends at 6. Dressed up. Will make a great photo.

He always adds that it will make a great photo, like that determines if I'll come or not.

> **Me:** Let's stay in touch

Turns out, the hotel, which is also a bar and restaurant, is going to be on my way home, and at six I'm nearby. Little effort for the next Tori tip. Here's how it goes down, in texts:

Rob: I'm 2 minutes away.
Me: Don't go in yet. I'm not ready.
Rob: Circling. Give you another min.

I find a lucky meter on Sunset and get out with my short-and-flash, the camera Rob prefers. The titillation apparently comes when others think he's famous, so a long lens from inside my truck is not the point. There are a slew of valets in front of the Standard, and I'm not sure what the hotel's attitude is toward paps. Some locales embrace us as healthy publicity, while others pride themselves on being celebrity hideaways. Of course Rob isn't a celebrity, but the valets won't know that, and I don't want to cause a scene on Sunset *over Rob*. Feeling like a tool, I crouch behind a potted plant with my camera in my bag.

Rob: In a black Prius. I'm driving. Three other guys.
Me: OK. Almost set.
Rob: I'm here. Do you see the car? I'll get out on the street side.
Me: I'm in the bush. I see you. Wait a sec. [I fiddle with a few settings.]
Me: OK, go.

Chuh-chuh-chuh, flash-flash-flash.

I'm not sure what he wants exactly—*Pictures of him alone? All the guys? Is everybody in on the ruse?*—but I think it's better not to ask now. I say, "Hey, Rob. How you doing tonight? Don't mind if I get a few frames, do you?" I concentrate on trying to be professional and not doubling over in laughter.

He doesn't respond. He acts coy, like he can't much be bothered by the camera but will "tolerate" it. He doesn't smile, but doesn't cover (of course!). He gives me the peace sign (the money shot?) just before he goes into the hotel. Once they're gone, I hurry back to my car hoping no one's seen me.

A couple minutes later:

Rob: How was it? How did I do?

Me: Perfect Rob. You're gorgeous, so my pictures are gorgeous.

Rob: There weren't that many people there to see it?

Me: [I think I know where he's going with this.] Oh, there were plenty. A car stopped on Sunset to ask who you were.

Rob: Really, what do you tell people when they ask?

Me: [Uhhhhh…"whatever you want me to tell them," or "nobody."] Oh, I say you're from a reality show.

Rob: :)

Me: Just wondering…What do you tell your friends? Do they know what's up?

Rob: Oh they just think it comes with the territory, working for Tori.

★ ★ ★

It might be easy to laugh at Rob's vanity, but he is not alone or even uncommon, especially in L.A. The intensity with which people crave fame here is unbelievable. I sometimes wonder if I could make more money as a hired pap who gives nobodies the thrill of feeling famous than I do by going after real celebs. But at least the Rob mystery is solved.

I am also discovering that it is not unusual to have insiders among the stars, or insiders who *are* the stars. Many celebrities make themselves famous or more famous through active participation with paps and tabloids—i.e., they give it up all the time or they set up their own jobs. For example, it is well known that Rodeo2 has some sort of arrangement with Britney, and I know several of "Lindsay's paps" who have her personal cell phone number, and I've seen what appear to be her texts. Besides the two of them, Nicole Richie, Denise Richards, Jenny McCarthy, Hilary Duff, Tori Spelling, many of the Bachelors and Bachelorettes, Hayden Panettiere, and even Katie Holmes and Angelina Jolie, at different times in their careers, have purportedly coordinated with us or the tabloids (or had their agents do it for them). These are just a few I have heard of; I am sure there are many more. Everyone has a different deal. Some do it just for the publicity, but many also make money off their photos.

"Speidi" (Heidi Montag and Spencer Pratt) is a classic example of working it for the money. I know about the couple because their deal was with CXN, and it was no secret. It started in 2007 when CXN set up bathing suit shots with Heidi. "Spectacular" shots were put out each subsequent week, and before the year was over, the girl that only a few of the *Hills*'s viewers recognized was on the cover of *Us Weekly* talking about her nose job. The kicker: Speidi made 40 percent of all the sales, and CXN and the photog divided the rest.[10]

Once *Keeping up with the Kardashians* blew up, Kim reportedly entered into a similar situation with another photo agency. Other celebrities like Tori and Dean use a company called StarTraks Photo for their setups. I don't know whether they get paid or not, but at the very least, notice that an image with a StarTraks, WireImage, AP, or Getty photo credit usually looks posed[11]—almost a guarantee that the celeb was complicit. Just leaf through mags with a conscious eye; you'll find it easy to spot the setups.

---

10. Specifically, what happens is this: Spencer calls Bartlet and they brainstorm. "What would make a salable picture? What haven't we done already?" Sometimes Bartlet will ring the mags. "What do you want to see Speidi doing this week?" Remember, the mags like pictures *and stories*. Over the next several years, Spencer (the business mind of Speidi) and CXN create comic-genius, salable sets one after the other: *Heidi at the grocery store strategically holding two melons; Spencer and Heidi in rabbit ears at Easter; the couple on July 4th waving American flags outside the U.S. Capitol;* and *a perfectly coiffed Speidi caught kissing in a row boat.* Not only do these self-made millionaires make money off their photos, but the mags also pay them for exclusive stories, clubs pay them appearance fees, and companies pursue them for product endorsement deals. Spencer bragged on David Letterman that in two years he and Heidi made over $3 million in "self-promotion." Gotta give him some credit; that's not easy.

11. These four photo agency names have not been changed. They sell celebrity images, but they are not paparazzi agencies.

Chapter 11

Two weeks before she goes to jail for violating probation by driving with a suspended license, a small gangbang of men—and I—meet up with Paris Hilton as she departs a building into underground parking. Three savages form a semi-circle around her to get the front-facing shots and to prevent others from doing the same. This isn't "allowed," but no one else is big enough—in stature or status—to prevent it. Their blocking pushes me to the left, so I come out with only side shots of Paris.

I am furious. Profanity spews from my mouth like crud from a clogged sewer. Elif has to drag me back to my car. "You can't win every time," she says, trying to calm me down.

It isn't until we get home and I look at my photos that I notice something interesting: Paris Hilton is holding the Bible. And it isn't until a few days later that I realize the value of one photo: I had gotten a shot with the full "Holy Bible" words exposed. And no one else had.

That shot made nearly every tabloid and major newspaper in the United States. It claimed the entire front cover of the *New York Post* and was printed in papers around the world. It was the punch line of the late night talk shows. Even CNN bought the picture. Had I been shooting Paris from the front that day, as the three guys were, I would have shot only the rim of the book. From my angle, I got the whole Holy Bible.

I may not have realized what I was getting when I shot Paris from the side. *But she did.* When Paris walked out that day toward her car, she had neatly tucked the Bible under her arm, along with *The Power of Now,* and she had feathered them in a way *no one* carries books. She had it all planned out.

The best thing about that shot, though, was the Bible itself. It was a hardcover, golden-colored Gideon's Bible, the kind you find at hotel chains. I betcha all the money I made on that shot—five grand at least—that it came right out of one of Daddy Hilton's hotel rooms!

★ ★ ★

But saved or not, Paris still went to jail. After her release, the media genius (and I'm not being flip) selected Larry King to conduct her first interview. So after Paris's midnight walk from the jailhouse, CNN's studios became paps' first opportunity for a photo-op with Paris as a free woman.

I arrive early at CNN wearing the "Free Paris" T-shirt I bought at a tourist shop on Vermont Avenue. My plan was to get a space on the second floor of the parking garage, enabling me to get a head-on shot of Paris when she exited the building. I knew everyone else would be on the street fighting for a ground-level shot, and I wouldn't have much of a chance in the throng of aggressive men. Regardless, I didn't come today to make money; I came to witness history.

I get into position as planned and over the next few hours watch the media converge. In one location, I've never seen more—we are well over a thousand. By 1 p.m., every U.S. news agency and many photographers on location from around the world are at the Cahuenga and Sunset studios, hoping to get a glimpse of Paris.

Her limo—a large blacked-out Escalade—arrives at three, but she is blocked by officious security and there are no entry shots. During her hour-long taped interview, we wait, hoping the exit will be different.

It didn't seem possible that Paris's celebrity could get bigger. But it did. I'm not convinced that she wanted to go to jail, but I am sure she used her internment to her advantage. To be clear, Paris is no dumb blond. Quite the contrary, this bombshell knows *exactly* what she is doing. All

Of The Time. She controls her media, not vice versa, and hers is a beautiful performance to watch. Even when you think that it's an accident that she's wearing something, holding something, doing something (even perhaps going to jail), you come to realize later that it was no accident (or if it was, she's turned it to her favor). Paris thinks ahead. Of all of us.

While she is inside, I soak in the scene. From my vantage on the second floor, Cahuenga buzzes electric and excitement swirls around the entire city block. Like steam rising off the street's asphalt, the paparazzi and the news media rise, erect and ready. Most people are smiling and I don't see any ravens today. We are beautiful blue and yellow hummingbirds, sparrows, and starlings. To witness something so newsworthy is electrifying. I haven't felt this kind of human media energy since I worked in CNN's Control Room. Thankfully, this is a happy news day. We all missed Paris while she was away. Twenty-three days is a long time.

★ ★ ★

The only person who has the idea to shoot from the garage is me, so the space is mine to maneuver, and I position myself facing CNN's exit door, one level up. We know the time the interview is supposed to end, and I have a former colleague from CNN who will text me confirmation. About an hour after Paris entered the building, I am out of my car, camera up to my face. I expect her to come into my view for a split second when she walks out the door before she descends the stairs to her limo.

"Paris!" I scream her name over the street noise when I see her. I am hoping she will look up and I will get the shot.

And she does—she looks directly at me and smiles.

And I get it.

And we have a moment. (Or at least I do.) I may only see her through my lens, but when I do, the media silences and like an old black-and-white slow-mo turns a half-second into about five. Paris and me. Just us. And for the first time—*in real life*—I see emotion in those stoic doe eyes of hers. There's true joy in them, no doubt. She is happy to be a free woman. Yes, twenty-three days is a long time. And I'm not embarrassed to say it, I choke up!

After my shot, Paris walks down the stairs and gets into her limo.

UPROAR! The media and the paps are standing behind a blockade on Cahuenga and cannot get a shot. They are being blocked, unintentionally, by Larry King's car which has been pulled up behind the Escalade.

Par-is! Par-is! Par-is! Everyone begins chanting.

From inside the car, she sees the media's dilemma and she reacts. Arising like Sleeping Beauty from her castle bed, Paris pulls herself up and out the door. Then, standing on the seat of the car, her head and torso well above the massive vehicle (a slightly unladylike move that normally she would not do), Paris waves wildly to the salivating photographers (also a very non-Paris-like gesture). Even though my shot is no longer exclusive (though it is the one they pick for People.com the next day), her action pleases me more than my loss disappoints. I pat a moist eye dry. Paris missed us too.

★ ★ ★

Cardinal Rule of the Paparazzi (per Aaron): Do not need or desire to be liked by these people.

But I can't help myself. I am completely schoolgirl giddy. Adrian Grenier checked me out—subtly but *definitely*—not once, not twice, but *thrice* tonight. Yep, three times. Up and down. Maybe it was his girlfriend he was with, but they honestly didn't look like they were having much fun at dinner.

I had gone to the movies alone, one of my favorite indulgences. Ocean-moist air was floating around the city, and the evening energy felt hot and exotic. On my way home—I walked—I passed Figaro, the French café. I was wearing a long, fitted summer dress cut down the front and my thin-strapped silver Havaianas. Casual but sexy. I had slept ten hours the night before and knew I looked my best.

He was sitting outside along the Paris-style sidewalk, and I passed his table. We saw each other at the same time, and I stopped. We both smiled and he scanned my body, but not in an obnoxious way, more in an automatic way. I was not looking like I do at work. "Jennifer," I said awkwardly, to be polite and to remind him of my name.

"I know," he said. He introduced me to the girl he was with, and whoever-she-was, we ignored her for the rest of the conversation. I stood next to their table and close to him. He reflexively touched my arm and my hand familiarly as we spoke. Again, he looked at me, all over.

"What are you up to tonight?" he asked. And we chatted about the movie I'd seen and movies in general. He didn't mention to the girl that I was a pap, and we didn't talk about the paparazzi. He never acted like he wanted me to leave, and he kept a slight smile on those amazing kiss-me lips, unquestionably his best feature. When I thought I couldn't stay anymore—maybe five minutes—I leaned down and kissed him lightly on the cheek. It was an automatic gesture, like it was what should have happened. As I left, he looked me over once more, a bit less subtly.

So, the next morning, my celebrity crush in full force, I digress a la Bridget Jones: Must find way to get phone number to Adrian Grenier. Think pushing ride-along card is best way to go. That way don't come across like a groupie—can't have him thinking I want him too much. He must want me. But ride-along will make it seem like I only want to make money off him (versus make love to him). The Cardinal Rule is stupid.

Boy, I was in trouble.

★ ★ ★

Bitch—that's another derogatory and sexist term the paps use. A bitch is a celebrity who makes getting his or her photograph difficult.

Drew Barrymore qualifies. I put her in that category with reverence, however. Drew's smart, just like her friend Cam. Both girls are a guaranteed sale but not easy to get—and Drew's often not worth the time put in. Besides her dreadful outfits, she's just not that interesting and goes to her office, an unshootable location, all too frequently. A shot of Cameron

Diaz will sell over and over for reasons of fashion. One of Drew will sell only once, for a fashion faux pas.

Still, Elif and I like working her. She lives on an untrafficked street in Hollywood—less than a ten-minute drive from my house—and Hollywood neighborhoods are pleasantly more low-key to doorstep than their counterparts in West Hollywood or Beverly Hills. As well, there are lots of other celebrities who live nearby if hers goes to pot.

Drew's main pap-avoidance strategy is based on her assortment of vehicles: she's got more cars than a CarMax lot. Sometimes when I arrive, I peek under her iron gate and into her wide driveway and note which vehicles are nearest to the exit.

Drew's house is situated atop a steep dead-end street, and when you doorstep her you can't sit right outside the house. (If she saw you there, which she most definitely would, she would never give you a shot.) Instead, you must sit down the hill and look inside every car that passes. She may still see you, but by giving her "space," you won't immediately piss her off, and she might give it up.

At around noon, one of Drew's many cars comes out—a Prius. A young guy is in the driver's seat, and through the car's untinted windows, I see no one else inside. I grab his eyes intentionally. He averts my stare, which is odd. Though I delay, I follow. I am able to catch up to the car after about a minute. Still, I see only his figure inside. If a celeb were "hiding by ducking," she normally would have popped up by now, especially because I hadn't followed at first. But this is Drew. I don't trust her.

A few blocks later at a light, I pull into the adjacent lane and from the high cab of my truck am able to see inside the car. And there she is, scrunched up on the passenger seat floor like a Nordstrom's shopping bag. *Nice one, Drew.* I pull in behind the car, but the driver U-turns and goes directly back home. Drew continues to stay down—stubborn, won't even admit she's caught.

Probably we're now wasting our time—Drew knows we're here and is obviously not in the mood for it—but neither Elif nor I feel like trolling.

We "park up" and wait for her next move. There will be a move; that we know. She wants to leave.

We get out of the truck and sit on the curb. In the middle of a Los Angeles summer, it's too hot to stay in your vehicle unless the a.c. is on or the windows are down. Since Drew now knows we're here, we might not get anything, but at least we don't need to hide in the truck anymore.

Aaron beeps. "Any action? Any action?"

I tell him what's happening at Drew's. He tells me he's just shot Naomi Watts, exclusive, and is now *trawling*.

"You got Adrian out of your head yet?" he asks. After the Figaro encounter, I fessed up to Aaron about my Adrian crush. It made him angry. I don't think he was jealous, just more protective, which was pretty sweet too.

"You know, Aaron, it's not out of the question that I could date a famous person."

"Ahhhh. Yes. It is. Your crush is juvenile and ridiculous, and more than that, dangerous."

Whatever.

Over the next hour, three cars pass us in the direction of Drew's house. We follow them up the hill and watch as they enter her gate. She's surely devising a plan.

We're back in position when we hear a loud motor coming down her street. It's her old pickup driven by the same guy, this time disguised in a low-brimmed hat and a different T-shirt. I am standing outside my car, and again he doesn't look at me. It's suspicious.

The pickup rolls by *too* nonchalantly, and it's moving so slowly that I am able to tiptoe up and peer inside. There's a dog curled up on the passenger seat floor, but that's all I see. The truck carries on.

It takes a minute to register: no normal dog would lie on the floor curled up in a ball when he's just gotten into the car.

"Elif, get in the car! Drew's under her dog!"

We race. But it's too late, and they're gone.

It's that simple, celebs. You don't want us around, then make our job hard. If you checkmate us too often, we'll find a weaker opponent.

★ ★ ★

When you enter a hotel or any private commercial property in America, unless "No Trespass" signs are posted, you cannot be cited for trespassing. And those look unsightly: no fancy hotel or venue is gonna tack them up. Besides, hotels and restaurants want to *encourage* patrons—they want *most* people to enter. It is not until you are at some point asked to leave the private property *and you refuse to do so* that you become an official trespasser and could be cited.

You might wonder, since it's not illegal to go "inside," why don't paps do it more often? A few reasons: One, depending on whose interior is in the shot, the magazines are sometimes scared of lawsuits. Perhaps the pap they bought the photograph from was asked to leave but didn't. The mag is usually the one slammed with the lawsuit (in addition to the snapper who took the picture). Two, interior light is usually too dim to get a magazine-worthy image without a flash, and while we could use a flash, that would mean getting right up in the celeb's face, spraying white light all over him or her, then facing the consequences of the inevitable bust, which brings us to number three. Hands-down-no-question, the BIGGEST obstacle to interior shooting—and papping in general— comes down to one measly human factor: the Fear of Embarrassment. Yep, even paps have the desire to fit in, to be "cool" and "normal," and like you, we dread public humiliation, *especially* in front of our "clients," the celebrities.

It's worth mentioning one exception to this code: crashers. A crasher is a person (not usually a paparazzi) who lives for that intestine-knotting rush that makes most of us vomit. Crashers (think *The Wedding Crasher* but at celebrity events versus weddings) don't do it for the money (or to meet girls) but for the thrill. And for the recognition from other crashers, a small tight-knit group who lurk within Hollywood.

I am aware of only one crasher-pap—a guy who was recently recruited by the iPIX agency and who would probably love for me to mention his real name, but I'm just gonna call him "Crasher Joe." Over the last twenty years, Crasher Joe has gone ticket-less to hundreds of events including at least a dozen Super Bowls and most Oscars and Golden Globes (the events themselves and the post-parties). Per Crasher Joe, the sole objective of the crasher (at least before he started carrying a camera) is to get as close to as many celebrities as possible. The bigger the celebrity, the bigger the crash (obviously). At the Oscars, for instance, a coup would be to sit near enough to an award-winning celebrity so that when he or she gets up to accept the Oscar, the crasher would stand along his or her side and shake the celebrity's hand. Not only would the crasher have "touched" the celebrity, but he would have done it on television in front of the world. Even though it's his little secret, *everyone* has seen it. Later, the crasher may run into another crasher at a post-Oscar party and get a subtle nod, a sign of envy and approval.

Now that Crasher Joe carries a camera and is his own special kind of paparazzi, he does things like walking into fancy restaurants, going up to tables where celebrities are eating, and flashing his giant SLR in their face. He doesn't use a long lens or hide. He doesn't break any laws or trespass. He leaves when he is escorted out. And he keeps the picture.

The reason I bring up Crasher Joe is to illustrate who the paparazzi are by showing you who they *are not*. It feels to me like "crasher-style" paparazzi is how the media often portrays us. Take Courteney Cox's bomb of a TV show *Dirt,* for example, whose main character was a schizophrenic paparazzi who would do things like sneak into hospital rooms with his spy camera and take million-dollar photos. That is ludicrous. What is also unbelievable is that Courteney, who's been a Hollywood star for twenty-five years, doesn't get it. But I'm finding that's the norm. Except for the paparazzi themselves, no one gets our world.

To be clear, paparazzi *are not* Crasher Joe. There is Crasher Joe, then there is everybody else. And everybody else may have more kahunas than Average Joe, but other than that, the paparazzi are… Just like *You!*

The Battle of Bosworth, Round 1
Kate: 0; Simon and Jen: 1

Eventually, it came time for my dear Elif to return home. She had only planned to stay for a couple months, and her family and country were calling her back. I understood. Teary-eyed, I put her on a plane to Turkey. More than a sidekick, more than good company, for three critical months—those in the infancy of my pap career—Elif was my inspiration. Like Donna, she believed in me when no one else did. She knew what pained me and what thrilled me, and she picked me up each time I fell down, which was often. Elif was my biggest fan and often my only one. So when I wave good-bye to her at LAX, I know I will miss her a lot.

After eight months, I am becoming somewhat self-sufficient. Still, I know I need a partner. Combatting heroes, nosy neighbors, nasty paps, and moody celebrities is not possible with a single person's energy, no matter how positive. Simon says yes to my pleas.

"If you're my new partner, luv, it's time you met Kate," he informs me.

Kate Bosworth is a two-man job: if Kate has any inkling you're on her, you will never get a shot. It's my first time on her doorstep, so Simon fills me in with the logistics. Pap No. 1 (this time, Simon) will post up on the popular Runyon Canyon jogging path nearby her house, walking in about fifty yards from the street. From there, he can see Kate's whole property in a bird's-eye view. Ideally he will be equipped with binoculars useful in making out license plates parked in her drive and looking for signs of life.

Pap No. 2 (me, by default) will post up in my car (making it look empty by ducking when passed or by sitting in the back) near enough to Kate's drive to go whichever direction her car departs but far enough away to not alert her that someone's on her doorstep. Kate lives in the

Hollywood Hills on a remote road where it's a challenge to hide. She also has more than one car and can go *down* the canyon or *up* the canyon, and on the way can take at least twenty different routes in the maze of streets.

At around 11 a.m., Simon beeps. "She's out."

"Copy." I start my car.

"Going down hill. Repeat, she's going down hill."

"Copy," I repeat.

I lose reception just as I start the follow. We're prepared for this. There's limited cell service in the adjacent Nicholas Canyon which Kate follows toward town. I don't pick up the car right out of her drive, but when I do pick it up a few streets down, there are too many detours to follow loosely. It takes about five minutes to get down the switch-backed streets, and I have to hope they don't suspect me.

Not until we get to Hollywood and hit Franklin am I able to get a clear look into the car. Turns out, it's only Kate's current boyfriend, British model James Rousseau, inside. Simon's tipster is Kate's best (and *only* from what Simon says) friend's tennis coach. We knew from her that James was in town, which was why we decided to work Kate.

I can't imagine that James has ever been papped, so I'm a bit surprised when he clocks me. Simon figures that Kate briefed him on how loved she is in the States, so he was on the lookout. James makes his way to the Grove, and then gives me a nasty look as I pull in behind him in the valet line. *Oh park your own car, lazy teenager*, I think.

About that time, Simon makes it down the hill to cell reception. "Let's leave it, Jen. He's worthless without her."

Though we've been gone only fifteen minutes, we decide not to go back and wait on Kate. Our gut tells us she's either not going out without him, or she's gone straight out after him (and her garage was shut so we wouldn't be able to tell). Instead, we'll spend the afternoon trolling.

When you start the day with a partner and Plan A, your doorstep, either finishes or goes to pot, you have the option of doing the day's remainder together or splitting. Simon and I, fond of camaraderie and each other (and now official "partners"!) tend to stick it out. I take one troll route to check certain restaurants. Simon scouts the opposite side of town. If I see something I may shoot it myself, but I'll put his name on it, or if there's time or it's complicated, I might call him in. And vice versa. Doing the day together cuts our *cut* in half, but it also doubles the chances that we'll get something. So if your partner has an equal skill and reliability level to your own, partnering up makes sense. As well, you may spend an hour or so in the same car: this means less of a sun-headache from not having to drive *and* spot, and with all the parking difficulties around town, it's much speedier to jump out if you see a gangbang or a lone celeb walking down the street.

After four unproductive city hours—Simon and I seem to turn up to every star sighting just as paps are dispersing—he suggests finishing the day at Kate's. "Maybe the car's back? Maybe they'll go out for an early dinner?"

About fifteen minutes ahead of Simon, I'm not in a rush and meander through the curves toward her street. Halfway up the canyon, a car catches up to me and a quick glance in my side-view mirror reveals James's eye-fuck. Uncanny.

I divert my stare. *Maybe he's not certain*, Simon's advice reminds me. James leans his torso out the window to make sure I see him. He seems certain. I ignore her street and continue to climb the canyon. For intimidation purposes, James follows for a few curves before turning back.

I wait only five minutes before heading to her doorstep. Then I plop my car fifty feet from her drive so I can see both directions. James has already busted me, it's late in the day, and I've got nowhere else to go. I radio Simon to tell him to stay in Hollywood, that this sit isn't promising enough for two of us to pursue.

I notice a security camera outside Kate's gate and assume I'm being watched. I take out a tabloid. Soon enough, James walks up the driveway and strolls by my car. I stare at the underwear model. He looks so young and unintimidating. His features are classically handsome, but his unblemished skin is too feminine for my taste.

"Hi," he says and keeps walking. He's on his headset with Kate instructing his moves, I presume.

I smile, nod, and continue reading.

A couple minutes later, he wanders back and engages me. I listen half-*arsed* to his theoretical discussion on the evils of the paparazzi business. I'm not rude but don't make much effort to converse.

"You do it for the money," James accuses in a pretty Prince William accent.

"What money? You see my truck?" I respond pertly. The red pickup's probably worth about $1,500.

"Why don't you use your photography for creative purposes?" he says.

"Why don't we get some shots of you guys together? Could be good for your career."

His face turns scarlet.

Soon James runs out of things to say, shuffles his feet, and leaves, no doubt frustrated about not having converted me.

"Not happenin' today," I beep Simon, then head for home.

Bartlet calls. "Why do you two waste time on Bitchworth? [That's what Simon and Bartlet call her.] She's not worth that much anyway."

"She's a challenge. We'll get her tomorrow," I reply.

Then, he makes some off-color comment about her uptightness, says, "I'll put you down for Kate. Gotta go," and hangs up.

It's his "thing." Bartlet always has to be the first person to sign off. I care little for this kind of power so let him have it.

★ ★ ★

When I get in my car at around 9 a.m. the next morning, I beep Simon. We know Kate's a late riser so don't bother to get there early.

He doesn't answer. A few minutes later, he texts:

Getting me arms waxed—please hold.

I roll my eyes.

He beeps a few minutes after that: "Ya know, Jen, if they had a pill that would get rid of all me hair, I'd take it." I roll my eyes again.

We come up with a plan over the Nextel. Both of us will post up on the Runyon Canyon trail. That's half because we don't want our cars to be seen and half because it's more fun to hang out together even if it cuts the follow dangerously close. Based on yesterday, we think we'll have about sixty seconds from the time we see her exit the front door to when she pulls out of her drive. If we run, we can make it back to our cars in that time, and if she goes *down* the hill, although we'll be two minutes behind, we can catch up before she hits Franklin Avenue and Hollywood, a mass of traffic. If we catch her too early, she'll bust us anyway. We don't think that's gonna happen, though. Simon is sure Kate will assume we are on her again today, so she'll take a convoluted route to wherever she's going. He thinks that even if she goes to Hollywood, she'll go left out of her drive, up to Mulholland, then back down to Hollywood on another canyon. Going that way, she'll have to pass by the joggers' parking lot where we park for Runyon, so we'll pick her up there. Kate doesn't know Simon's car, and for this tough job, I've cunningly resurrected the stealth blue station wagon, which I've yet to get rid of.

We get to the trail at the same time, hike in, and plop down on some rocks. It's a gorgeous Los Angeles morning and a haze-free view from the hills. We can see the entire city and all the way to the sailboat-dotted ocean. I love these views. Simon grabs his powerful binoculars, which he spent $500 on.

"I don't think these have ever helped me get a shot, but they sure are entertaining. You know, the other day, I saw through Eva Longoria's white shirt with these lookers. That right there was my money's worth." Once more, I roll my eyes. But Simon makes me laugh, and I'm happy he's my new partner.

Our Peeping-Tom binocs scope out Kate's house, check the cars in the drive, and look for movement through the windows and on the back deck. We relish knowing how infuriated Kate would be, if she only knew.

"She'd have the cops all over us," Simon says.

He's worked Kate enough times to "know" her, and he can't stand her. He spends a lot of time dissecting her motives. "Her life's purpose is to be Audrey Hepburn," he notes. "That's gotta be a lot of pressure." He also thinks she wears her hair pulled back from her face so that it's fully visible to all, at all times. "I hate having to look at that *whole* face every time I shoot her," he says with disgust.

Kate's not Simon's type. Simon likes double-D fake boobs and bleached-blond Playboy bunnies.

In my opinion, Simon's taste is off. Truly, Kate is exquisite. Her skin was churned for eons until God poured her, and He no doubt had a goddess in mind when He sculpted her perfectly symmetrical features. Kate's body is waif-like but still sexy with long, feminine limbs. The only physical flaw I can find is her unfortunately thin hair. ("Which is why," I tell Simon, "she wears her hair pulled back.")

But there are lots of ethereal stars in Hollywood. Why Kate? Why does she sell? What makes her so *interesting*?

Though she'd like it to be, her acting is not why we photograph her. Kate's breakout role in the surfer movie *Blue Crush* established her in Hollywood, but since then she's never commanded leading-lady roles. And it's not her beauty alone; we know that's nothing special in Hollywood. Her boyfriend was once Orlando Bloom, but that's not it either. Kate sells for something else, something quite specific, and something that she is *fully* in control of: clothes. That's right, Kate's a fashion diva, a first-row guest at every "Fashion Week" around the world. And the mags pay to see what she's wearing. The way they hang on her petite body and frame her baby-doll face is just what the designers intended. If Kate didn't dress so well, we wouldn't be nearly as interested. In fact, we might not be interested at all.

"Smug Bitchworth," Simon continues. "All she'd have to do to put James on the map is be photographed with him a few times. But nooooo."

"Just wait till she dumps him."

"He's gonna be bangin' his head."

At about 10:30 the back door opens, and James comes out for a fag and tea. "Good British boy," says Simon. I smile.

James is in his boxers, a great confirmation they've just arisen and are still at home.

"They've had their lie-in and shag. Probably head out in about an hour." Simon, like Bartlet, always presumes morning sex is the norm with women who sleep in.

Throughout the morning, we watch the FedEx man deliver a package, the flower man deliver a several-hundred-dollar bouquet, and Kate's one friend stop by. Simon says she's too paranoid to have more friends. (She should be more paranoid about her best friend. That's where the leak is.)

By noon, the sun is scorching and we send me on a Gatorade/food run. It will take at least thirty minutes, leaving Simon alone for the two-man job.

Right when I get to the bottom of the hill, he beeps. "She's on the move."

His Nextel goes blank, and I know he's running for his car. I can't do anything to help, so I post up on Franklin at the bottom of Nicholas Canyon Road to see if her car comes down, and wait for Simon's call.

He beeps about five minutes later. "Go to Laurel."

"Copy."

Laurel is the street one over from Nicholas.

"She's in her black Ford Escape. She's alone," Simon says.

"Copy."

"We're halfway down Laurel. I'm two cars behind."

"Copy."

My adrenaline rushes my senses. I'm on.

Turns out, as expected, Kate tried to avoid us. She took a left out of her drive, up the winding road leading to nowhere. Simon lost her almost immediately—she took an even more circuitous path than he anticipated—but his pap instincts told him that she'd cross over to Laurel Canyon and head back down to Hollywood that way. Simon navigates L.A. streets as well as he does porn sites, and he cut her off midway down the canyon. The constant flood of cars on Laurel kept him obscure; meanwhile, I was shrouded in the crowd of cars in Hollywood so could take over the follow when they got to the bottom. *Well played, Simon.*

I spot them easily and roll in a few cars behind. It will be a tough follow—lots of cars to hide behind but lots of lights to get stuck at. We are discreet and stealth for a few blocks; then suddenly Kate pulls a slick right-hand turn from the left-hand lane, forcing Simon to blow his cover. He has no choice and screeches across three lanes of traffic.

"Oh, that little bitch!" he says over the Nextel. "Did you see that move?"

"Did. I'm three cars behind. Drop back."

"Look at her now," he snarls. "Panicking. Weaving all in and out. Checking in her mirrors. Poor little girl probably peed her pants."

Kate speeds up erratically. Simon drops back like he's lost it, and I move in to pick up the follow. She's got no idea about the station wagon and doesn't realize I'm on her as she pulls into the Chevron at the corner of La Cienega and Holloway. She stays in her car, so I post up where I can see her but far enough away she won't notice me. I wait for her next move.

A motorcycle cop drives up to her window. I beep Simon. "She's called the cops. Lay low."

From a crack in the top of my window, I take shots of Kate talking to the cop. After a few minutes, we leave the gas station. It's Kate, me, and our police escort, and thanks to the latter, we have no problem hopping through traffic. They have no idea I'm attached to the train.

Kate waves as the cop drops her at Planet Nails. I salute too: *Thank you, LAPD.* Then, *chuh-chuh-chuh, chuh-chuh-chuh,* several lovely shots of Kate feeding the meter and sauntering up the sidewalk in a picture-perfect green and blue horizontal-striped dress. She never knows to look for me.

"Done. Nailed," I beep Simon.

"Excellent, luv. Nice work."

Our adrenaline's our crack. We've beaten Bosworth and made a thousand each, we reckon. Simon picks up the food that I never did and meets me at the manicurist.

If Kate sees us when she exits, it's not a big deal since it's already nailed. But, for story purposes (e.g., Kate's "Just like *Us*"—she gets her nails done by the Vietnamese), we want the salon in the background. Simon posts up out of the car where he knows she'll bust him but hopes to get off one shot first.

After an hour, Kate exits. One frame, head down. Already in my car, I pick up the follow. She smokes me out with a few darts in and out of side streets, but I stay on her snug. We've got plenty of salable frames; we're just making a point now.

Simon chimes in on the Nextel. "You know why we are still follow-ing you, little one," he says in a laughable stalker voice. "You know you need to give it up. Your head down, that was no good, luv."

Eventually, Kate pulls into a tight alley in Beverly Hills and parks. I stay in my car and lean out my driver's side window with my long lens. She makes a fifty-foot runway walk toward my car, not smiling but not looking belligerent either. Her head's held up the whole time. When she gets to my car, she leans down and with unconcealed disdain says, "Will you leave me alone now?"

Simon said it: *Kate's smart. She knows what we need.*

"Of course," I say. "Thank you very much. Oh, and *hasta la vista.* Have fun in Mexico."

Kidding, I don't really say the last bit. We know from the tipster that she and James are going to Mexico tomorrow. Kate would surely change her plans if I had said that. We wouldn't want her to have to do that; we're not *mean,* after all. (We're just really f—king annoying.) And she did give it up in the end and didn't *have* to. She could have played it like Demi Moore and never, *ever* give it up.

Chapter 12

*A*t this point, I publish a lot. Each week, I have at least one and often three or four pictures in *People*, *Us Weekly*, or other U.S. mags. In addition, many more print online on sites like PerezHilton, E! Online, and the Daily Mail (in Britain). I've stopped saving hard copies unless I'm particularly fond of the photo, or it's a cover, but I still crack a smile when I'm queued up (another British term I've adopted) in the checkout at Safeway or Rite Aid and see my name, and handiwork, staring back at me.

As long as the paychecks keep coming, I personally don't care if the average Joe knows what I've shot; however "getting known" is a critical part of earning respect from my fellow paps. CXN—and not all agencies do this—credits the photographer as well as the agent when a photo is published. On blog sites, you find the credit directly under the image. It might say *Jennifer Buhl/Celebrity X News*, or if I shot it with Simon for instance, it will say *Buhl/Landingham/Celebrity X News*. Most rags credit at the bottom or side of the page in itsy-bitsy font you'd never notice if you weren't looking. Because of these credits (and the fact that a female name stands out), other paps are constantly reminded that I am getting published. My online credits are especially important since blogs are the paparazzi's main source of daily information. Paps are now seeing *Jennifer Buhl* at least twice a week. They figure if I am getting pictures then I probably know what I am doing, and they respect that. Since the Jennifer Aniston shot, no pap has trash-talked me, and I've even started to notice that some guys look to see what I'm doing—where *I'm* standing, what lens *I* have on. It seems, now that everyone realizes I'm not going away, we're finding a way to live together.

★ ★ ★

The first thing most people want to know when they find out that I am a paparazzi is how I get paid, and how much. I've already told you "how much"—I never gross less than ten thousand a month, and sometimes I make closer to fifteen. Based on what I know about other CXN salaries, and what Bartlet tells me, that's in the top 10 to 20 percent of pap paychecks. In terms of "how" I get paid: generally a freelancer makes 60 percent of his or her photo sales and a staffer makes roughly 20. (Staffers also get paid a base salary and have their equipment and vehicle provided.) If you shoot with a partner, your percentage is cut in half. The agents—who do the obvious, selling—get the rest. For that giant percentage, which has made many of them very, very rich, they also line-itemize each photographer's paycheck by sale: picture, price, media outlet, and country. Sales outside the United States, United Kingdom, and Australia are often outsourced to international agents so a pap is getting a percentage of a percentage, but those little bits add up. I probably make half my money in U.S. sales, the other half internationally; and although the pictures somewhat sell themselves, relationships are important, especially with exclusives, which Bartlet individually negotiates with each publication. Non-exclusives are usually priced using standard page, half-page, and quarter-page rates, which change all the time but at the time of this writing are around $500 per quarter page but can go up if the non-exclusive is *the shot*—a truly exceptional one, for example, Paris's Holy Bible shot.

Making a larger percentage as well as having the final say in my daily destiny keeps me freelance. But there is another huge advantage: residuals. As a freelancer, I own all my photos, which means that I get residuals forever. Today, "forever" is really only important for a year; regardless, when a staffer leaves his or her agency, he or she is lucky to get paid out for three months. To a person like me—who has historically taken long sabbaticals to pursue her "dreams"—residuals are a big perk. As well, owning my own photos means that I can use them wherever and whenever I want without giving my agency a cut and, more importantly, without getting its permission.

Because I am prolific and one of a half dozen girl shooters, I know if I desire, I could work with anyone in town. Female shooters are always needed as we blend in better on "CIA-type" stories, for example if we must follow a celebrity into an interior location, or if "a couple" looks more natural doing a job and checking into a hotel in Maui. (Sometimes female tabloid reporters will be used for these kinds of stories.) And sometimes it's tempting to jump ship. I do get bored of the office staff's Tall Poppy issues, and whenever Bartlet calls, he always manages to insert the P-word (the same one Dylan used in reference to Britney's) in the conversation. *I don't remember Charlie ever talking to his Angels like that.* But it's the snappers who keep me from leaving. One thing I love about our staff (and our staff-like freelancers, like me) is around three or four in the afternoon, when all the paps are "scouring the tank for final bits and bobs," as Simon says, we'll meet up for coffee and cupcakes. And, as it happens when you're doing life in Beverly Hills, you might just roll across a late-day jackpot sippin' his or her joe alongside you.

I know Simon says I have no friends in this business, but I think he might be wrong. I'm starting to really care about these guys.

★ ★ ★

Subconsciously I've been nurturing my crushes. When boys occupy my mind, it takes the focus off the black hole in my gut: the dark, empty space that only a baby can fill. I just can't imagine ever being happy without one.

Claudia is CXN's new female pap. She came over from the United Kingdom for a "trial run" last year before I started working, then moved here with a proper work visa last month. She told me, "Jen, everything in my nature goes against this job." Claudia wears dresses to work. If someone takes her spot, she finds another. When a celeb asks her to leave, she does. Claudia is a lady. Bartlet says she makes half the money I do. But then, the boys like her. Particularly, Aaron seems to. I think that's why she took the job.

Claudia knows I have a crush on Adrian. I think she wonders about Aaron too. Thankfully, she doesn't ask. Honestly, I'm finding it impossible not to like her. Claudia's a gentle, empathetic person, and how can I blame her for being ladylike at work, or if Aaron *fancies* her? She must long for the same things I do.

"Why don't you just work on him?" she suggests (about Adrian, not Aaron, of course).

"He doesn't sell. Least not well enough to warrant a doorstep."

"Hmmm, right. Well, maybe you could work on him, then not shoot him. Just make it an accidental bump-into."

I give the idea brief consideration, but what if Adrian actually sees me on the follow, I don't realize it, then I feign happenstance. I mean, it's not like I'm trying to have Adrian's baby, I just want to date him. But still...

I explain this to Claudia.

"You're right! That could be seen as bunny boiler behavior![12] Can't do that."

It's kind of odd for me to hear that even I have limits. So much seems doable now that I'm paparazzi.

Nonetheless, I opt for a note instead of a follow. I have confirmation from the tabloids: Adrian is, in fact, doing a documentary on the paparazzi, so I decide to work on that angle instead.

Dear Adrian,

If you just wanted to hang out with me, you didn't have to go so far as doing a documentary on the paparazzi...

---

12. Bunny boiler is a reference to Glenn Close's character in *Fatal Attraction*. The British guys use it a lot to describe "psycho girls" who won't leave them alone.

That ride-along offer is still open. See you around, neighbor.

xx *Jennifer*

My roommate checked it over and OK'd it. I also included my card (making it professional and at the same time giving him my email and phone number)! Then I got up all my nerve, ran up Adrian's driveway, taped the note to the front door (which creaked open!), ran back to my car, and drove away.

It's three days later and I haven't heard from him. *Nice one, Jen. Now he just thinks you're crazy.*

"What did you expect? A celebrity's not gonna call you," scolds Aaron when I tell him what I did. "Forget about him. And don't do it again. You'll get arrested."

"I won't get arrested."

"You might."

"I wrote 'neighbor.' That makes it a friendly thing, not a psycho thing." I try to sound self-assured but don't feel that way.

"Are you listening to me? A celeb does not think *you* are normal. To them, a pap is not normal. Full stop."

"Maybe I shouldn't have put the x's?"

"Maybe you shouldn't have."

I wish I could chalk it up to jealousy, but I don't think that's it. Aaron's clearly thinking about Claudia these days, not me. The two work together frequently, and when she's around he pays more attention to her than me. All signs of a new romance are there.

"Well, we're just two hippie artists living in Los Feliz. Why shouldn't we hang out?"

"To be clear, Miss Buhl: Adrian. Will. Never. Be. Your. Friend. And more importantly, he will never, *ever* be your boyfriend."

"I bet he doesn't think I'm an artist. With my photography."

"Probably not."

Adrian's a catch, I know. And, of course he could have any artsy, gorgeous girl he wants. Admittedly it's a stretch, but *why not me?*

"It is art, you know," I say.

"I know it is. Leave it now. Don't make him call the police, Jen. Because he will."

★ ★ ★

I call Claudia. She'll be more understanding; she's a girl.

"I know he's a celebrity, but that's no excuse for being impolite and not calling when a girl has put herself on the line and given out her number," I complain.

"You left a note on his door?"

"Yes. Now I'm humiliated. But I'm pissed too. He looked me up and down *three times* if you remember. How could he not call?"

"*You left a note on his door?*"

"I'd wager that I'm at least part of the reason he decided to do his documentary. Maybe he was thinking about it before, but I bet I was the impetus to get it rolling. He's probably too self-absorbed to realize it came from me…" I can hear my ego-protecting bumptiousness as I speak the words.

"Stop," Claudia says in a rare forceful tone.

"What?"

"Paparazzi don't leave notes."

"But it was a *friendly* note. There wasn't…"

"Jen, no."

"But…"

"Promise me. No more notes."

One week, two crushes crushed. I am beginning to lose hope.

★ ★ ★

You could say "Anxiety" is a proper noun in my life, a female demon inside of me that is deserving of capitalization, and she is psyched for the battle with Dejection. Her strategy: an adrenaline drip. If my body starts to relax at any point day or night, she just opens the drip and lets more adrenaline in. Awesome, right? *The more hours you're awake, Jen, the more you can be looking for love,* she encourages.

So between the drip and my *actual* bruises, the latter being visible externally, I was up most of the night. Yesterday was "team building" paintball, organized by Donna and Brian: CXN versus West Coast Wing, the paparazzi agency full of Tall Poppies. This morning, I had seventeen round, bloody spots covering my body. Paintball is a game for men. Just like paparazzi.

I can feel my mood, foul like black tar, creating something nasty in my stomach. This life is starting to get to me, and the ugliness of the paps is beginning to reach my insides. If only I had someone to love, then I could balance the hatefulness that surrounds me every day. But I'm beginning to think I might be asking too much. I mean, a girl in her mid-thirties has to lower her expectations—there just aren't that many "soul mates" left. My age, thirty-six now, constantly haunts me. In most women, the biological clock starts ticking at around age thirty; in me, the alarm is BLARING. I can't shut it off; frankly, I don't want to shut it off. But it's the only thing that I can hear, and it's making me crazy.

A few hours into the start of my miserable morning, Claudia and I are "dug in" outside La Conversation. (Simon loves to say he's "dug in like an Alabama tick," which is particularly funny because he has no idea where Alabama is.) We're waiting on Shakira.

"Who the hell is that?" I beep Claudia.

Neither of us recognizes the car, and we can't see the driver through his limo-tint. We know it's a jump because it's a blacked-out SUV that pulled up in shooting position and no one got out.

"I'm gonna find out who it is."

I get out, walk to the car, and when no window rolls down, I make a scope with my hands and attempt to look inside. I can't see anything so I stand there a few seconds more looking at my reflection. Whoever it is knows I want them to roll down the window, but they don't. It's confirmation: a pap.

I'm unreasonably furious as I walk back to my car. The combination of sleep issues, paintball bruises, and male rejection has left me unequipped *to deal.* All my anger re-channels toward the Jumper.

I beep Claudia again. After several expletives, I take a breath and admit, "I'm really stressed out."

"Yes, I can tell. What's wrong?"

Right, like I can tell her.

The jumper's outnumbered so I decide, "There are two of us. You pick up Shakira. I'm blocking."

Claudia pauses for a few seconds before she responds. She would never intentionally block someone, particularly with her car, and she knows I've never actually tried. We both recognize it's not a safe choice, but it's my story and my decision, so she uncomfortably agrees.

The Shakira tip had come two hours prior from a waiter at La Conversation, the charming French café in West Hollywood. La Conversation is the kind of place where you can sit for hours, sipping coffee, and no one hassles you for the table. The waiters are refreshingly pleasant, non-Hollywood guys sans the "I should be *acting*, not serving you" attitude typical of the rest of Los Angeles. La Conversation is over-priced but an oasis. Not to mention, it has the best coffee in all of L.A.

It is also—and this is chiefly why I go—one of the finest locations in town to spot celebrities. Seventy-five percent of the time, I see someone. Ryan Phillippe was once sitting next to me. (I didn't even recognize him until another pap drove by and snapped him.) My favorite celebrity diner here was Scott Wolf. Remember him from *Party of Five* as Jennifer Love Hewitt's boyfriend? He didn't sell. One time Queen Latifah jogged past me. She sold.

But from the restaurant, I mostly spot celebrities in cars. Hundreds live within a few square miles, and La Conversation is located on Doheney, a major artery into town. I like to go in the mornings and watch for stars heading south to their errands and lunch dates. The restaurant is also near the little street where Cameron Diaz's gym is, and every once in a while Demi Moore and Penélope Cruz work out there too.

The waiters at La Conversation know what I do. They know if I suddenly disappear, they should save my food and I'll come back. I pay in advance. My car is always parked by the closest available meter next to the restaurant, and I leave my keys inside, ready to roll.

Today, the best shot of Shakira will be one of her exiting, but having no idea which car is hers, I don't know if she'll go to the left or the right out of the restaurant. Since it was necessary to stay hidden in my car due to La Conversation being a trendy jumping location, I needed another shooter—and that's why I had called Claudia.

My tipster, Mauricio, a server at the restaurant, has been keeping me abreast of the situation via text:

There are four in Shakira's party. They are eating slowly.

Claudia and I have managed to stave off paps for the entire two hours, Claudia in the back of her SUV and me slumped down in the driver's seat of my red truck. Now, just as Shakira is paying the bill, we get jumped by the thug who refuses to identify himself.

From her position, Claudia can see Shakira's table through the front window of the restaurant. When the party gets up to leave, she radios me. We pull our cameras to our noses and keep our hands on our door handles ready to rush out when we see her.

We wait. But no one exits the restaurant.

"They should be out by now," Claudia beeps. "Where did she go?"

From my position, I can see the rear of the restaurant. Suddenly, the back door, where the cooks and waiters exit, opens and I see legs. I don't wait. I jump out of my car and race to the back, arriving just as Shakira steps into a mammoth blacked-out Escalade which pulled up as she walked out. She must have gone through the kitchen, though we don't know why. She couldn't have known we were there.

I have no shot and run back to the truck. Claudia, the jumper, and I pull out behind Shakira's chauffeured ride, and almost immediately it turns down a side street and stops in the middle of the road. We stop too, and other cars have to swerve around us.

"What's he doing?" beeps Claudia.

"I think he's trying to figure out what to do."

Shakira's chauffeur is definitely a rookie—there is no reason to stop in the middle of the road. We are stopped for quite some time, five minutes maybe.

"I'll be right back. If they move, she's yours," I beep to Claudia and get out of my car.

I go over to the jumper's SUV. This time he rolls down his window. An inch. "What the hell are you doing?" I say.

"It's Shakira. I pay my tipsters well. If you ever touch my car again, I'll punch you," he says through the crack then rolls his window back up.

I return to my car.

The critical point here is that he knew it was Shakira. Since he didn't walk into the restaurant, and from his position couldn't have seen her on the way out, he had to have had an inside tip. So, technically, he didn't jump me. He has as much right to the story as I do.

Regardless, he could have told me this politely when I walked over the first time. I know I shouldn't expect civility from paps, but my anger won't recoil. I walk back over and knock on his window. He cracks it again.

"What's your name? Who do you work for?"

"Barclay. West Coast Wing."

"Barclay, if you ever fucking threaten me again, I will call the fucking police."

Obviously, I'd lost it. I was making no sense. I can't call the police on another pap—*I'm a pap!* Even if he did punch me, they wouldn't care. I walk back to my car.

After another five minutes, the driver of the Escalade accepts that we aren't going away. He screeches off, down Doheney and across Santa Monica Boulevard where he begins circling in the middle of the road. We have no choice but to circle too. Now all four of our vehicles are blocking both directions of heavily trafficked lanes.

Next, the Escalade tears down a side street and heads toward residential neighborhoods. From one narrow road to another, hopping over curbs and jumping red lights at 40 to 60 miles per hour, we weave our way into Beverly Hills. With adrenaline spiking through my system, I am able to stay with it. Claudia loses it, and soon Barclay does too.

Shakira's vehicle continues through parking lots, out the other side, down alleys and around office buildings. My concentration is on driving, and I can't get to the Nextel to catch up Claudia on where we are. Not that she'd want to re-join.

There's no hiding now, and to even have a chance at a shot of Shakira, I know I'll have to get in her face when we stop. I manage to change my lens from my long to my short, a hazardous task while driving in this manner, and a great example of why a fully kitted pap has two camera bodies. I do not.

As the hideous drive continues, I ignore the sense in me telling me to stop. *I won't let them win* is all I can hear. *At least I can control this.* Stupidly, I put my life in danger. I know it. But Shakira's driver puts hers right up there too, and I doubt she does. Suddenly, it reminds me of what happened to a beautiful princess many years ago.

Finally, the Escalade pulls into the Peninsula Hotel where no fewer than ten bellmen are standing outside doing nothing. I screech in behind it and jump out of my truck, camera in hand.

Shakira's door opens, but she stays put casually talking to someone inside. Meanwhile, her driver comes around with an umbrella. *Oh, please!* The horde of bellmen begins to catch on and they yell at me to move my car.

"We'll call the police," they tell me.

I know the police can't get here that fast.

As the bellmen move in, the petite Columbian singer hops down out of her beast of a vehicle and into the crowd.

Fifteen feet mark the path between her and the hotel entrance. I position a yard in front of her, walk backward with my short-and-flash pressed to my face, and hope the tomfoolery will clear for a split second.

"Hi, Shakira. Could I get a quick shot?" I ask.

Through a crack, I can see her. She's smiling and trying to dart beneath the chauffeur's umbrella, around a girl holding up a blanket, and through the bellmen's hands. "It's OK. It's OK," she's saying to them.

They don't hear this.

I still haven't taken a shot and step out of her way so she can enter the hotel. With a quick maneuver, she turns, ducks down under the block-ades, smiles, and waves at me. I get one shot. Of her head.

In case you are wondering, there is no shortage of Shakira headshots in the world today. The mags need a full-length. They've got to show what she's wearing and that she's visiting L.A.

I am not lucid as I walk back to my truck. "You are all fucking idiots!" I scream several times at the dozen men.

It's the only thing my rage can form. After that incredibly stressful chase, I got *this*—a worthless picture!

When I get to my car, the head bellman is waiting. I try to get in, but he holds my door closed. We play tug-of-war, and he's stronger.

"Just wait. Just wait," he says over and over.

He can see that I'm out of control. Finally, I realize that his goal is not to prevent me from leaving but to talk to me. My energy drains, and I stop pulling on the handle. We stand quiet for a beat.

"Did you see what happened?" I say weakly.

"I know."

"She wanted it."

"I know," he confirms gently. "We were just doing our job as security."

"I know you were, but you see what you did, right?"

"I know. I saw what happened. I'm sorry."

He's sincere, and I take it in. They really were just doing their job, and hotel bellmen should be on the side of hotel guests. They just didn't know which side she was on.

"I'm sorry for yelling at your guys." I extend a quivering hand with my apology. He takes it, then opens the door for me.

"Thanks," I say. At least he understands. That's all I can really ask for now.

I pull out of the hotel driveway with the Shakira-less Escalade in front of me, when it stops—*again!*—in the middle of the road. The driver motions for me to pull over down the block.

Oh, why the hell not.

I pull over and he pulls up in front of me. A small-statured black man who looks to be about forty gets out of the SUV, lights a cigarette, and leisurely works his way to my car. I stay put but roll down the window.

"What's your name?" he asks, putting out his hand.

"Jennifer." I take it and we shake.

There is a long pause as he inhales and exhales a drag.

"You're a pretty good driver, Jennifer."

"Yeah, not bad for a girl."

"Not bad for anybody."

Another long beat. I don't try to make conversation.

"So, uh, sorry about that back there. The driving. The blocking," the man explains.

"Yeah, kinda sucks."

"I didn't know she wanted it."

"They often do."

★ ★ ★

The one shot I did manage to get of Shakira under the umbrella is used on People.com the next day. It's the only publication that picks it up. After paying Mauricio and splitting my cut with Claudia, I make twenty bucks.

Twenty bucks. It could have been at the cost of my life. Or someone else's.

That evening, my body feels like it's been through La Conversation's dishwasher. I blubber to my roommate about my life's loveless void, and we down half a batch of Nestle Toll House chocolate chip cookies. In the end, I was somewhat vindicated, but my behavior was not. It remained deplorable.

And my mind returns to *its* comfort food: Aaron. Now that Adrian has overtly rejected me, the slightly less far-fetched fantasy of this handsome Scotsman revives. Who knows, maybe I'm wrong about him and Claudia...

Being a Celebrity, for Dummies

Part 2: Driving, Following, and Covering

Dear Celebrities,

Following the Shakira incident, for everyone's safety, I feel it necessary to offer more advice. Many of you stars *do not* have this down.

To avoid paps around the city, take note of these points:

Chauffeuring. Take cabs. We never notice cabs *'cause you never take them.* They'll get you to your destination as expeditiously as a limo and much less pretentiously.

Your personal vehicle. To anti-pap your ride:

1. *Heavily tint your windows.* Often we don't know your car but see your face through the windows.
2. *Keep your dealer plates on, or no plates, or better yet change them up all the time like we do.* If you haven't figured it out by now, we memorize your plate numbers.
3. *Own and use several vehicles.* Draw some lessons from Ms. Barrymore. My favorite in her fleet is the Crown Victoria, the ancient cop-car variety.
4. *Ensure your car is black, white, or silver.* No strange colors. Have no bumper stickers, colored rims, or other distinguishable features on your car. Christina Applegate has an old "WTF Bush" sticker on hers, particularly unnecessary since we know her politics already. One of the Olsen twins (I can't tell them apart) has a black Mercedes G-wagon with red brakes, which show through the rims. She might as well spray-paint "Olsen Twins" on the side of the car.

5. *Buy something other than a $100,000 sports car, a Range Rover, or a Toyota Prius.* As of this writing, most celebs drive these cars, and every time I pass one, I look inside. It's a habit. If you don't want to be seen on the road, buy a silver or black Accord or Camry like the rest of America. Jake Gyllenhaal drives a Camry. We never see him.

The follow. If you are followed from your house, do not drive like a maniac trying to lose us. (Or allow your limo driver to, as per previous section.) So often you do this. *Why?* You endanger your life just to show us how fast you can drive? We usually catch you anyway. Besides being stupid, it's absolutely unnecessary. As I will now describe below, there are more sophisticated ways to hinder our shots.

When you are followed, allow the follow. Repeat, *allow the follow.* Do not get fussy about "power" on the follow. When you arrive somewhere, power shifts—always and automatically—into your hands. (Female celebs take note: Though you may *feel* powerless, *if you own it,* you actually *retain* power. A pap will never physically touch you; thus if you can overcome the feeling of being the weaker sex, you can still win.) If you'd like to prevent a photograph, do it *not* while in the car but *at your destination.* You can utilize one of the following in-control, yet safe options:

1. *Be thoroughly infuriated.* This might not work the first time, but with repetition you will triumph. Cuss us out, hammer us to the ground, perform a good ole American shock-and-awe campaign—*How COULD we?* We're people too. We hurt too. And sometimes paps need a butt-red belting and this course may be in order. I must admit, however, it isn't my favorite option. I think it's...mean. People shouldn't talk to other people

this way in general, pap or no pap. (Peninsula bellmen, I apologize again.) And besides coming across as a complete a-hole (not to mention ruining *your* day with all that bad energy), you must be extremely careful of *video*. You don't want your rant ending up on TMZ that night.

2. *Go somewhere we can't follow.* For instance: a studio, a private residence or hotel, or the Scientology building. I realize this isn't always possible, but it'll make us think twice the next time we're trailing you in the same direction.

3. *Don't give it up.* Cover! Or just look down. (Way down. Chin to neck.) This is the simplest, kindest, and most effective option. You can use a hat, jacket, hand, or book; in fact, most any object will work. Gwyneth Paltrow used a pillowcase once. (Though I don't recommend that. She looked so ridiculous the shot published.) Plenty of big-time celebrities use this tactic: Jennifer Lopez, Natalie Portman, Orlando Bloom, Jessica Simpson, Mila Kunis, Halle Berry, Jessica Biel, and on and on.

   Critcally, by covering you control the situation. For it to be permanently successful, though, consistency is necessary. *Cover each and every time.* If you only cover sometimes, we'll keep working you. (Which may be your goal. You may only want to cover when you don't look good.) But to effectively rid yourselves of paps—if that's your objective—you need to not give it up *at least 90 percent of the time.* People like Drew and Cameron give it up 20, maybe 25, percent of the time. What this does is make them "sometimes getable," and since they're "rare," worth a decent mint. So, even though Drew and Cam are toilsome targets, if we're in the mood for a challenge, we'll work them. On the other hand, unless Demi Moore and Ashton Kutcher are embroiled in a lusty story (as in their later divorce, for instance), a pap will never be waiting on them because they'll *never* give it up.

Bottom line: celebrities, if you make it too arduous for us, if we waste days tracking you and never get a shot, *we will give up.* Time is money. You're either *money* or *not money.*

Note: Reverse tactics if you *want* to be photographed.

Good luck!

Jennifer

P.S. How to Lose a Pap from Your Vehicle

Though I never recommend endangering your life by trying to lose a pap from your vehicle, if you insist, don't drive fast; try these tactics instead:

- "Force" the red-light ticket for the pap by driving through a yellow-turning-red light at a camera intersection. Most of the time, you aren't worth a ticket. (In L.A., the punishment does not fit the crime and we're looking at about $400 and a point on our license. Though we may have the *skill* to run the light and possibly get your photograph, rarely will the sale of your photo make up for the cost of the ticket and the increase in our car insurance.) The Mercedes-G-wagoned Olsen twin did this to me, and I got a picture in the mail from the DMV with the back of her vehicle flippin' me off.

- Drive in and out of manned parking decks. Cameron Diaz's trick. The technique: Once she knows you're in, she heads out. While you wait to pay the attendant, she's blown you. Or a studio. George Clooney and Teri Hatcher do this. No one can get into a studio lot without a pass, and once you are in, there are too many exits for a single pap to cover, so you're free. Or as aforementioned, head to the Scientology building. Katie Holmes, Kirstie Alley, and Penélope Cruz use it. I don't know one pap in L.A. who will follow their prey into that abyss.

- Become a world-class driver. This can't be emphasized enough. If you aren't an exceptional driver (Hilary Duff), you will never lose us, you will frustrate yourself, and you may kill someone. We who are following you are exceptional drivers (from lots of practice). Stars like Dempsey, Diaz, Nick Lachey, and Bosworth, who fall into the "outstanding driver" category and drive like badasses even when they don't know they're being followed, are the only ones who should ever attempt to lose us.

- Lastly, if you're trying to lose a pap, man up and do it yourself. Don't call the cops; that's just plain sissy.

Chapter 13

I stop work at four to meet Aaron at his house. I've dropped by under the ruse of returning his camera chip, but we both know that's not the reason I'm here.

Sexual tension, he keeps saying, is why we bicker so much. Unclear diction is what I think. But when he says, "We need a good romp to sort us out," I actually listen and wonder if it's possible.

I know he's not the way to go—it's obvious Aaron *fancies* Claudia—but considering I haven't slept with anyone in a long, long time, I need to take advantage of opportunity when it presents itself—even if it means being second choice. And of course there's always that possibility that he'll kiss me and suddenly realize I'm the one he really wants. Right? I know it sounds desperate, but somehow I can't help myself.

So here I am. I ring the buzzer outside his Hollywood high-rise.

"Hello, Jennifer." His voice is deep and flat, serious through the intercom. "Be right down."

Aaron is never serious with me.

He holds the door open, doesn't say anything, and doesn't touch me. Only stares. For a long time, he holds my eyes.

We ride the elevator up in silence. *Is this really gonna happen?* In truth, I've lusted after Aaron for months, but nothing's ever happened. I'm doubtful.

Once inside his apartment, he strides away and paces the living room. I babble nervously about the pictures on the wall and the heat.

"Here's your camera ch—."

He cuts me off. "I feel like I'm at the prom."

"Is there prom in Scotland?"

"No."

"It's not *the* prom, by the way. It's just *prom*."

I walk to him, face him, and gently place my fingers in his hands. He squeezes them tight. His eyes become fervent and he pulls me to the sofa. I sit on his legs and cup his chest with my hands. Aaron always tells me how women hit on him, and how much he loves that. I never hit on guys. Can't handle the rejection. But I badly want him now.

"Let's forget it. Wait till we're drunk," he says, his eyes darting everywhere but not meeting mine.

Seriously?

My upraised brows relay my disbelief and more emotion than I'd prefer he see. I need to save face. I get up and move toward the door.

"I'll walk myself out."

As I reach for the doorknob, I feel his hands grab my shoulders. He turns me around. Again, intention is in his eyes, and there are no words. He picks me up off the ground, sets me on the sofa, straddles me, and, finally, kisses me.

It's a tender, passionate, exceptional kiss. His lips fit perfectly over mine and his tongue makes love to my mouth. Nerve endings spread the sensation throughout my core. His hand hangs loosely around my neck and with the palm resting on my breastbone drives me back against the couch, pinning me. Our breathing is choppy and heavy. My body becomes limp. I am unable to move anything but my mouth.

When we break the kiss, I look into his eyes. They are no longer serious. They tease and flirt like they normally do.

Awkwardness replaces titillation on my part.

"I gotta go," I say, wanting to be the first to initiate departure. I can tell we're not going "to romp." At least, not now.

"I'll walk you out."

On the way down, he pushes me to the back of the *lift* and kisses me again, rougher this time. The elevator stops, and I pull away and turn to leave.

When I look back one last time, it's at his eyes. Lust and desire.

The Battle of Bosworth, Round 2
Cumulative score: Kate: 1; Simon and Jen: 1

Nine days later, Aaron invites me to meet him and the Commonwealth paps at happy hour. They do this a couple times a week at their local, and though I never go (I see enough of them during the day—I prefer my girlfriends and Figaro for my evenings), I can't stop myself this time. I haven't seen him since The Kiss. I want to see him.

Meanwhile, with only one set in two weeks (the celebs have been winning *a lot* recently), I'm demoralized. Kate Bosworth came back from Mexico, her boyfriend James is still here, and Simon and I spend a third day trying to get a shot of them. We're giving it a third day because we're stubborn, not because it's smart. Our only hope is that we'll wear them down.

Bartlet, always pragmatic, won't speak to us today. He says we're making it personal with Kate and James and that's gonna get us into trouble.

After eight hours outside her house, we admit defeat. She never leaves. I rip out a page from a tabloid that's in my car—a page with her picture on it—and write a note.

Dear Kate,
(Copy James)

What do you think about stopping this nonsense and working together?
    Lots of advantages:
- We will not sit outside your house all the time and agitate you.
- We will not give your address to the five hundred other paparazzi who work in L.A.
- If you let James be photographed with you from time to time, you may actually help your boyfriend with his career.

- *You will get publicity shots once a month, which as we all know are an important part of a healthy, long-term Hollywood career.*

  Here is what we suggest:

  We take some unobtrusive, controlled photos approx 1x a month. You have our word that only the two of us will "work on you" from our agency. We will not tell anyone else where you live and do our best to have no one find out. We will discourage other paparazzi from "working on you."

  If this sounds reasonable, next time we are "on you," let us follow you (safely). Give us a few shots at the first place you go. We will leave and you will be on your way.

  No crazy dangerous driving (which we hate). No nuisance photographers. Only pretty shots of you. Think about it. We are reasonable. Hope this works for you.

  P.S. We won't bother you the rest of the week. Enjoy!

We don't sign it but leave the note in her mailbox. She'll know it's from Red Truck and Silver 4Runner.

When I get to happy hour, Aaron pulls me into his arms with one of his six-second hugs. After an hour and lots of rounds for the Brits, he wraps his arms around Claudia, and in front of everyone, kisses her. Just like he kissed me.

In that instant, I realize Claudia is dating a quack, a quack who kissed me nine days ago. And yet...I still envy her. Nothing short of imbeciles we women are.

★ ★ ★

People have always told me that I look like Kirsten Dunst, so how could I not like her? Plus, she just seems *cool*. Somebody I'd want to be friends with.

But I don't think she likes me.

I'm waiting for her at the bottom of Nicholas Canyon Road, same place Kate Bosworth (if she's not being paranoid) comes out. Kirsten lives a bit higher up the canyon from Kate. Simon and I can't figure out why so many twenty-something actors choose to live there. It's stunning real estate, no question, but it's not hip in any way. The neighbors are sixty-something, and you can't walk to anything. I'd hate it.

Kirsten's an easy spot in a black Prius with a dented fender and TOY on her plates. It's actually TQY but it looks like TOY, so that's what we all say. Every pap knows the car. She comes down around twelve-thirty and smokes me out immediately. Kirsten's tactic is to weave in and out of side streets, then abruptly stop in the middle of the road and wait to see if anyone's following. She sticks her hand out the window and motions for me to pull up. I've heard she does this—always wants "to talk."

"Hey, Kirsten," I say, window to window.

She blurts out the automatic question all celebrities ask, though of course they know the answer. "Why are you following me?"

"Don't you think we look alike?"

Just kidding, I don't say that. Her skin is *so* much better. It's like creamy mayonnaise. Mine's more like tartar sauce.

I actually say, "You must be so over us right now—I get it—but you've been gone all summer and now that you're home, people wanna see you. It'll only last a week or two, then we'll be gone."

Kirsten has been in the United Kingdom following around a new boyfriend and being photographed mostly in little villages outside quintessential British pubs with five-hundred-year-old brick facades.

She doesn't have to give me *anything*—she can cover—but I honestly don't think she cares enough to bother. She never covered in England.

"Well, I'm not gonna pose for you."

"Of course. Don't pose. Just go wherever you're going. I'll take some shots, then leave."

"I feel sorry for you guys," she says and seems to mean it.

We continue. She drives slowly now, not trying to lose me.

Had the stars been aligned, I do think Kirsten would have given me a few shots today, but as it happens, around the next corner sits a cop. Kirsten pulls up beside his car, chats for a second, and then drives on. The cop falls in behind her Prius and then stops in the middle of the road, blocking it both ways. Trapped, I watch Kirsten escape.

After a minute, the cop moves out of my way and lets me pass.

I yell out my window, "What's your problem? How'd you like it if we messed with your job?"

Lucky for me, he doesn't respond.

Regardless, I hope the cops aren't stupid enough to think the celebrities like them. Nobody in L.A. likes the cops. They're as reviled as the paparazzi. They gotta know that.

★ ★ ★

After Kirsten goes bust, trolling is my option. I circle the city and then stop by a boutique gym, a small house in Hollywood where celebs like Jessica Simpson and Eva Mendez get personally trained. John Mayer's distinct New York-plated Porsche Cayenne is parked outside.

Three hours later, J.R. calls. "Mayer's in New York," he says. "Musta left his car there while he's traveling."

Awesome. My frustration as a pap no longer comes mainly from nasty paps, tainted cops, and nosy neighbors. It now lies in the repetitiveness of my daily routine and the boredom of waiting for, but not necessarily getting, the frame. Today, as on many others, I've spent hours squeezed in a hot front seat watching the California sun move from one side of the sky to the other.

The only thing that seems to stimulate me these days is the thought of having a baby. It's honestly like there is an unborn child inside of me who's been there since I was a child. I crave its life as much as I crave the preservation of my own. He, or she, or both is not just something *I want*; it's a true *need* of mine. In Maslow's hierarchy, it comes at the bottom as the biggest priority: there is *baby*, then there is *food, shelter,* and *clothing*. And I know celebrities have babies well into their forties, but I can't guarantee my eggs are golden, and I definitely don't have thousands to spend on IVF. I gotta get going. Now, I'm starting to not even care so much about the guy; with my biological clock clamoring, I just want the kid.

★ ★ ★

Late in the day, I follow Ellen Pompeo to Griffith Park. I catch "Meredith Grey" by doorstepping the *Grey's Anatomy* set, which I've found highly profitable: there's never competition, everyone from *Grey's* sells, and the actors don't always go home after work. Besides, it's convenient, only two blocks from my house.

The light is extremely low—it's cloudy and almost 6 p.m.—and I'd like Ellen to *not* know I'm here. I'm unsure what her reaction would be should she see me, and I want her looking natural. Right now she is: she's playing fetch with her dog. And I know that animal shots *always* sell.

A flash is ideal, but impossible. Short-and-flash requires getting in my subject's face, not practical in a game of fetch. Without a flash, I will take a hit on the number of usable frames (many will have action blur) and the quality of frames (they will be "softer" and "noisier" than they would with a flash or in strong light).

I select my six hundred, a fixed 600mm lens, a beast of a thing that Aaron has loaned me. He doesn't like it because it's too heavy. I would like to shoot through the tint on my car window—this would allow stealth—but that's impossible in the existing light. I crack my window and at times hop out and hide behind my car, which besides Ellen's is the only one in the vicinity.

After fetch, Ellen gets in her car and pulls up beside me. I hang my head low—I've been a bad dog. I knew she'd seen me halfway through the shoot when she put her sunglasses on.

"I understand you have a job to do," she says. "I don't like it, but I know you're gonna do it anyway. Next time, I just want to know you're here."

This is the first time a celebrity has said this to me, and it makes perfect sense. It's how I would feel. Of course, what Ellen doesn't factor in is that when a celebrity knows we are there, she doesn't always cooperate or she becomes self-conscious and does something like put her *sunnys* on, as Ellen did, making herself less identifiable and thus less valuable. There are good reasons why we hide.

But I'll respect Ellen's request. "Sure. OK. I won't try to hide next time."

She adds, "I'm not the kind of girl who's gonna get all dressed up for you. I just like to know when someone's taking my picture."

"I understand."

Then I can't help myself. Ellen, this itsy-bitsy woman, has a *giant* Northeastern accent, something you never hear on *Grey's*.

"Your accent," I say. "I never knew."

She smiles, blushes, and says, "See you around."

"Make 'em smile" was Aaron's advice to me in the beginning; and from here on out, I will always announce myself to Ellen and she will always smile for me.

★ ★ ★

It's been three months since I followed Katherine Heigl home from the same *Grey's Anatomy* studios. I barely knew who she was then. Now she's won an Emmy and the tabloids pick up every set of her I take.

When someone starts to get hot, they get hot *fast*. There's a window, and by catering to the public's interest during that window, a celeb can make a significant impact on her future star power.

With Katherine's convenient Los Feliz home, close to my apartment, I am working her at least once a week. Other paps haven't caught on yet, so I usually have her to myself. My secret won't last long, though, and I know it's wise to take immediate, unrelenting advantage when it exists.

After getting seen by her a few times—as you inevitably do when you overwork a celebrity—I realize that when my friend Katherine Heigl knows I'm there, she looks down the barrel, smiles, and waves. She actually gives me *better* shots when she sees me. (Aaron constantly reminds me: "She's not your friend.")

Whether she is my friend or work acquaintance, Katherine Heigl is my new favorite celebrity. One day as she orders a soda at an outdoor kiosk in the Grove, I put down my camera and approach her. I want to say thanks. Plus I see her all the time, and it's starting to feel awkward that I haven't introduced myself yet. Often it's just the two of us, walking around, running her errands.

"Hey, Katherine."

"Katie," she corrects.

"Right, Katie." I suddenly have shaky-voice-syndrome; talking to a celebrity still makes me nervous. "I just wanted to introduce myself—I'm Jennifer—and also say how nice it is that you're always so agreeable and generous with pictures. It's really pleasant to work on you."

I say "work on you" and know that sounds strange. I don't know how else to put it.

"No problem," she says. "Some people just take it so seriously."

"Well, thank you, Kath—I mean Katie."

"Sure," she says smiling. Then she says, "And, thank...*you*."

"Huh?"

"I would have killed to have my picture taken by you guys for the last fifteen years. So yeah, thanks."

Sssssnap! It sure is nice when someone finally admits it: *I need you, darling paparazzi, as much as you need me.* 'Cause even us paps like to be appreciated!

★ ★ ★

"Katie" lives about a half mile up Griffith Park from Adrian. When I work her, instead of sitting right on the house (which in pap/celeb etiquette isn't very polite), I usually hang near Adrian's house in a shaded area where I can keep tabs on his doings as well. There's one problem with Adrian's doorstep: the bathroom.

By now, it's probably obvious that if I were to leave my doorstep to go pee at Starbucks, the celeb could come out during that time, and I'd return to an empty house and never know it. Depending on the doorstep, there are a few peeing options. At this particular location, besides peeing in a cup, which the guys do and which, as I've mentioned, I've tried and *hate*, the only option is the front lawn across from Adrian's house.

Horrible! Believe me, I know. Claudia refuses to use it. But this morning after a Starbucks Venti Misto, I'm desperate.

His neighbor's lawn is sort of a small field, about thirty-by-thirty feet, and full of tall, willowy grass. I make my move and race to the field. A cursory scan of the area reveals no one and I quickly kneel. I am squatted when—you know it—Adrian pulls up. Shit, I will never get a date with Adrian if he catches me publicly urinating in his neighbor's yard. Half done, I pull up my drawers, fall flat to the ground, and do not move a muscle until I hear his front door open, then close, then count to twenty. Then I scramble back to the blacked-out safety of my truck. *Phew.*

Twenty minutes later, Adrian leaves and I make a quick decision to ditch Heigl and file behind. On the way to wherever we're going, I pin my hair back in a decent ponytail and apply some makeup. Adrian hasn't seen me since "the note," and although my crush has waned, I still feel gauche. I even consider hiding—he'd never notice me—but then, I want to discuss his documentary project and push, again, the ride-along idea. I opt for being seen.

At this point in his career, Adrian is rarely followed so he has no idea I'm on him. I trail his steady-paced Prius until we end up downtown, where he pulls into an exterior parking space, gets out, and feeds the meter. I hop out next to him and take pictures. He looks at me. To eschew awkwardness, I attempt conversation. "Is it true? Are you dating Paris?"

We both know the latest tabloid rumors are absurd. Paris and Adrian have nothing in common. Besides, paps are on her 24/7 these post-jail days. There's no way he could sneak in or out unnoticed.

He doesn't answer. When his friend walks up, Adrian turns to me. "What's your name again?"

"Jennifer," I say incredulously. He must know it.

He introduces me to his friend, they chat for a while, then he turns back to me. I'm standing ill at ease, camera down, having already *nailed* what little there was *to nail*. By now, I should be back in my truck moving on.

"Was that you who left the note on my door?"

I feel my face flush. "Yeah."

"Well, you know that was trespassing."

"You're my neighbor. I jog by your house every day," I manage to stammer out this non-response but am *mortified*. The note was supposed to be "cute."

At this moment, I dream of crawling down a manhole, slogging under the streets of the city, and re-emerging in the grassy field facing Adrian's house.

"Do you want to do an interview?" he asks.

"Huh," I say, a little confused. "Of course." I may not be able to sell his photos, but I bet I can sell a video. And I'm very excited to change the subject.

After more discussion, however, it becomes clear that Adrian is not offering himself for an interview. Rather, he wants to interview *me*. For his documentary.

Now, here's the thing about paps: with few exceptions, we do *not* want to be famous and we do *not* like to get photographed. That's not why we're in the business. I back off a little.

"Maybe. I'll think about it."

"Think here. Give me your number. I'll call you in five."

I jot it on a scrap of paper. He leaves and goes into a building with his friend.

In that five, my nerves react, my throat constricts, and I can barely breathe. I know I should consider his offer—it could help me in the future—but I suffer from severe stage fright. I consciously hurl all my Adrian fantasies under the red truck. (It wasn't that hard. He killed me at "What's your name again?" and stomped on me at "That was trespassing.") I try to pull myself back into paparazzi mode: *Get what you can out of them. Don't care if they like you. Don't need them to think you're normal.*

My phone rings. "Hey, it's Adrian."

I smile. I can't help it. I've never been called by a celebrity.

"So you'll do it?"

"I don't know, Adrian. I really don't wanna be in a film."

"Ah come on. It'll be good for you."

"Why? What's in it for me?"

"Well, what do you want?"

I want a lot of things, but I don't think that's what you mean. So I say, "I suppose if you interview me, then I should be able to interview you. You know, perhaps I could make some money…"

"Deal."

"A ride-along interview," I add.

"Deal," he says again. "Wait there."

Thirty minutes later, he comes out, says, "Can't do your ride-along today, but we'll do it soon. Promise," and before I can respond begins instructing his four-man crew with setting up cameras, lights, and mics. The crew obviously thinks I *want* to do the interview. I suppose since they are making such an effort, I should give it up.

★ ★ ★

Two exhausting hours later, we wrap. I guided the majority of the interview, and the crew couldn't get enough of me. Adrian's questions made no sense—he's obviously better at acting—so the co-director took over. He sparred with me, equating papping to pornography (but worse, because according to him, porn has merit while the paparazzi don't).

Everyone was, in general, clueless about the way paparazzi work, and nobody wanted to hear that many pap/celebrity relationships are symbiotic. (None of them had ever heard of doorstepping either. *Did any research go into this?*)

When it was over, the crew was extremely impressed (of course, I'd redirected their whole documentary project with my one interview)[13] and told me that they thought there was hope for me of one day escaping the dark and evil world of paparazzi.

"Very nice," said Adrian as I was leaving. "I'll call you."

As much as I told myself, *Stop it!* I was giddy again.

The "Loo"

Home renovation crews abound in L.A.'s rich neighborhoods, so much of the time paps can take advantage of the Port-O-Lets that crop up conveniently. But since we can't always count on one being nearby, male paps pee easily in a cup or bottle they keep in their cars expressly for this purpose. Simon has had the same plastic Baja Fresh cup since I first met him, and he empties it strategically: "Always pour me piss out on Montana. Love it, dirty Brits soiling the Westside." I witnessed Aaron swigging out of his once (his own that is, not Simon's), which was quite funny.

I did experiment briefly with "the cup" technique, but as a girl I've come to discover a much more agreeable modus operandi—*en plain aire*, a hassle-free and sanitary system so enjoyable that, lately, I've taken to using it even on my days off. It works as follows: First, I find a tall fence, a row of thick bushes, or a steep slope of land next to the road. These block the view of my "bathroom" from homes

---

13. A few years after this, Adrian invited me to the screening of the documentary, titled *Teenage Paparazzo*. I chatted with the film's editor for a half hour and he confirmed: "Your interview changed the whole film. We all owe you." That was nice to hear!

(which in L.A. are generally near to the curb). Next, I employ my truck as a blockade, angling it such that the front of my truck is jutted out about three feet while the tail is snug to the curb. I put the vehicle in park and walk to the curbside, opening the passenger door to serve as a shield for the "jutted out" angle. Then I eye-sweep the view, giving special attention to strolling pedestrians, and do my business. It's much cleaner than a public restroom, and it feels like I'm out camping.

Like a man's best friend, I do have my favorite spots at different celebrity doorsteps that do not necessitate concealment-by-truck. Britney's street, Mulholland, is steep enough to pee off the cliff, providing a scenic and breezy loo. Kirstie Alley's neighbor has a giant oak with low-hanging branches that is situated on a hill by the curb. And at Adrian's, well, you know about the small field at the neighbor's house.

Chapter 14

*H*eigl is a chain-smoker. When I arrive at her doorstep the following Saturday morning and do my requisite drive-by, she is sitting on her front stoop, five feet from the street, having her morning fag. I roll down the window and wave. "Don't worry, I won't photograph you," I call out. (Mags don't like smoking shots anyway. Remember, celebs are beautiful people doing beautiful things.)

"Thanks. I don't expect you guys here this early," Heigl says cheerfully. It's nine forty-five. Not early. That she thinks it's early makes me love her more.

To take advantage of my window, I've been working Katie to death. Only she's not dying, but blowing up. My sets publish in several mags every week. I've been trying to get her alone so I can ask her a question. The opportunity presents itself now—no paps and no people, other than Heigl.

"Would you mind if I talked to you for a sec?" I ask.

"Sure. Of course."

I pull to the curb and park, walk to her steps, extend my hand, and remind her of my name. Unlike Adrian, she acts like she remembers.

"So, this is kind of a strange question." My breath retracts and she looks at me expectantly. I begin to ramble. "The thing is, you and Josh are getting married over Christmas, and I was thinking about coming to shoot your wedding, but that would mean missing Christmas with my family and, well, I was just wondering if you could reschedule it." Heehee. Of course I don't say that last part. I mostly just want to know if she wants her wedding featured in magazines or totally private.

You probably can imagine that this is not something a pap typically asks a star. But Bartlet has offered to fly me to Utah over the holidays where it's well publicized that Heigl's wedding to musician Josh Kelley will take place.

Katie smiles kindly. "I'm so sorry. I would have you there in a second. But I can't. We've signed an exclusive."

What she means is that one mag has bought the wedding story and photo rights from her in exchange for lots-o-cash. With most celebrities (not Heigl), I find the signing of exclusives quite hypocritical. You'll often see celebs who claim to dislike us (Drew Barrymore, Halle Berry, even Brangelina) making deals with the tabloids—which are, effectively, our employers—for photos of their weddings or new babies.

She continues, "If we give any shots to other photographers, the magazine will pull the deal."

I get it. I also know that when mags spend that kind of money on exclusives, they spare no expense on SWAT teams to quarantine the area. Unless CXN wants to hire a helicopter, getting a shot of Katie's wedding without her permission will likely be impossible. Plus, I couldn't do that to her. It's like…we're friends. (Aaron's Cardinal Rule buzzes in my ear: "Do not need or desire to be liked by these people." *Shut up, Aaron.*)

As Katie and I talk, others come by—her brother finishes his run, her dad walks out of the house, and Martin the neighbor stops by. She introduces me as "Jennifer, a photographer." I love that she calls me that. It humanizes me.

I don't seem to be bothering anyone but don't want to push it. One more question, then I'll go. "So, the honeymoon," I say. "Is that part of it too?"

"No. We don't have a deal for the honeymoon. But you probably don't want to come to Cabo."

"Well…actually…I probably wouldn't *mind* coming to Cabo." I try to sound like what she's told me is No Big Deal. But it is. It's a HUGE deal. Her honeymoon plans are unpublished.

I continue, "I could pap-scout for you. Make sure there are no other paparazzi that get photographs. You'd, of course, have full edit power on my photos."

"That might be nice. Make sure no bad bathing suit shots get out."

"We'd only use perfect shots."

She laughs. "I'm not sure how many of those you'd get with my bikini-body!"

She plugs my number into her phone and promises her publicist will call me next week. Then, later that morning, she leaves with a girlfriend and gives me an exclusive mani-pedi set inside a Los Feliz nail salon. *'Appy days!*

★ ★ ★

While I've been chasing down my new friend Katie, I've also been chasing Aaron. I can't help it. I'm desperate and he knows it fully well. We've still only had the one kiss, but the sexual tension is mounting again and the flirting is out of control. He called last night to tell me that he and Claudia were over. Then he said he wanted to give me a massage.

"I don't like it when you do that, Aaron."

"Do what?"

"You know what I mean. You can't play with me."

"Ah, come on. Don't be mad."

Amy, my roommate, tells me moving to a different city is the best way to handle a guy you can't say no to. But it's too cold to pap in New York. Anyway, the truth is, I'm into him. I want Aaron. He wants me. Though not enough for a husband or babies, which is still what I want more. Why can't it be, when you find a guy you actually like, reciprocal? 'Cause I do *like* Aaron. I fancy him. There, I said it. And while I know he jerks me around (and can't speak properly), he does have many redeeming qualities. For example, he's hot. And he has a great body. And he's clever, intelligent, and very, very funny. Mostly though, I like Aaron because, Claudia or no Claudia, we have chemistry. That's what always gets me. I never end relationships—or stop them before they should begin—if there's chemistry. I'm addicted to pheromones. No matter what the guy looks like or how he treats me, if I feel *him* in the pit of my stomach, my senses go out the window and I turn into a "sixteen-year-old boy." So, while my head knows this will probably never go anywhere with Aaron, my heart—or maybe just my libido—will not listen.

★ ★ ★

In the morning, however, my head is in control. Before heading to my doorstep, I stop by Rachel Bilson's, Aaron's sit in Los Feliz, to have the talk.

He walks over as I pull up.

"I know we're not going out, but this has got to end."

He has a goofy smirk on his face.

I continue: "You disappoint me…I drive you crazy…you infuriate me…we fight. Worst of all, you hit on me—and never finish."

He's attentive as I speak, half amused, half sheepish. When I'm done, he smiles, says "you're right," leans in my car, grabs the back of my neck, and pulls me to him. I can feel his breath mix with mine and we almost kiss. And even though I don't want to, I melt. Then he says, "I'll come over and say good-bye after work."

"Fine."

I drive off. *Weak, weak woman,* I chastise myself.

At four-thirty, he calls. "Gotta check out the Will Ferrell set. I'm not sure if I can make it."

He's just not that into—

"Of course you do."

"Stop having a go—"

"Never mind, Aaron. We're done. Good-bye."

But then, as it happens when you're a pap in Hollywood, another celebrity intervenes. I'm driving toward home an hour later when Katherine Heigl's bright red Range Rover passes me. I U-turn and follow her to the Grove, next door to Aaron's apartment.

After the shoot, I call him. "I'm at the Grove. Should I come over?"

"Yes," he answers immediately. "I'll call you when I get home."

I wait at Starbucks. Thirty minutes later, he calls.

Ten minutes later, I'm outside his door.

Aaron comes down when I buzz, grabs my wrist, and yanks me inside. He pins me to the lobby wall and we kiss. His hands grope my body and I pull at his hair. After a minute, he leads me to the stairwell. We run upstairs and stop at the top and kiss more. Still attached, we move toward his door. He fiddles with the knob till it opens, then pushes me inside. My back to him for the first time, he scoops me up, takes me into his bedroom, and lays me on the bed. He pulls his shirt over his head and lies on me. My nails dig into his back, I wrap my legs around his waist, and pull my body into his. He lifts my shirt and his lips move to where his hands have been.

Then, the buzzer rings. Aaron looks up, petrified. "Who the hell...?"

He gets up and goes to the living room. "Hello?" he says through the intercom.

"Hey, it's me."

Claudia.

Then there is a blood-curdling "FUUUUUUUUUCK!" He presses the intercom again and says, "Be right down."

And, that is *truly* the end of that.

The Battle of Bosworth, Round 3
Cumulative score: Kate: 2; Simon and Jen: 1

In retrospect, perhaps the note we left in Bosworth's mailbox was a bit psycho. Maybe it would have been better if we didn't effectively write, "If you cooperate with us, we will not tell anyone else where you live." *I guess* that could be construed as "burglar talk" or "stalking." But we still like to think that's a stretch.

Clearly, Kate is not scared of us. And she's not scared of the camera either. She poses at every red-carpet event and every "Fashion Week" around the world. Honestly, Kate doesn't know what being bothered by paps means. I wish I could tell her how bad it could be.

Today, Simon clocks the porcelain goddess (as he calls both Kate and his toilet) pulling out of Nicholas Canyon onto Hollywood. He wasn't even actively working her. He just happened to spot the car. He gets on the follow and beeps me immediately. "Got Bitchworth."

She runs her first light at Hollywood and Fairfax, pops two more, then speeds down a quiet side street and pulls into a random driveway.

"Well, no question here. She's onto me," he says.

"Stay with her. I'll be there in five."

"Jen, if she drives like this, it's gonna end bad, and they're gonna blame me."

He manages to stay on her, and I catch up at the same time they arrive safely to a photo-free office building off Doheney and Sunset. We know there isn't a shot possible in the garage—too dark, too ugly, and too short of a walk to the elevator—and we know security will be stationed on the first floor and up. There is a possible shot in the outdoor lunch garden, if she chooses to lunch there, but we aren't going inside to see. Today, "the paranoid girl will be checking for us in every crack, including her rank arse," says Simon. "You may be beautiful, Kate, but your arse still smells like the rest of ours." Oh, he can't stand her.

Simon and I park on the street next to the garage and discuss waiting or not waiting. She could be here all day. We decide to give it an hour.

A few minutes later, a car pulls up and parallel parks next to us. A man gets out and approaches Simon's car. I immediately drive off. I don't know who he is, but I know I don't want to talk to him.

I beep Simon—"Don't talk!"—but it's too late. He doesn't respond.

Ten minutes later, Simon calls. "What happened?" I ask anxiously.

"It's over, Jen. It's over." Simon's always-chipper voice is fully deflated.

"Oh no. Tell me."

Simon begins the play-by-play. "Well, he saunters up in super-snug, tapered jeans. Not Pete Wentz–tapered, mind you. More like The Gap 1988–tapered. Larry—the Tool—circles my car. He taps on my windshield, asks for ID. What was I thinking, Jen? I handed it over."

"You weren't thinking. You're a great pap, but sometimes I wonder about your brains."

"He was wearing a gold police badge on his belt. He looked serious," Simon says defensively.

"Right, the kind the sheriff wore in *The Dukes of Hazzard*."

"Yeah, the kind the kids wear in cops and robbers. But I'm an ex-pat. You know I can't mess with the law."

"Larry wasn't the law."

"But I didn't know that. You got the smarts, luv. Not me."

"What happened next?"

"Well, Larry's copyin' me license…"

"Ugh."

"…and I ask him what this is all about. He says, real official and all, 'I will respond to your questions after I write down all your information.' That shut me up."

In the end, Simon acceded to all of Larry's demands, including staying five hundred feet away from Kate and not photographing her "ever again." He eventually figured out that Larry was Kate's hired security guard and not any sort of law enforcement official, but he didn't care. Larry's scare tactic had worked. Simon was done.

★ ★ ★

But I hadn't agreed to any of that. And I was mad. *How dare he threaten my Simon! Imposter!*

I drive back to the office building and the Tool is standing outside. Good, that means Kate's still inside. Larry immediately approaches my car. I refuse eye contact. He bangs on my window and tries to open the door, which I locked—I had a feeling he was going to do that.

"Give me your details right now. I'm gonna call the cops."

"I thought you were a cop," I mouth and point to his badge.

He makes a lot of noise, a lot of demands, while furtively trying to block my view. But I know what he's doing. I see her. The doe is exiting the parking garage. I try to pull away, but Larry pushes his tapered-jeaned legs to my car and won't let me pass.

Somehow I manage to maneuver my car around him. This is quite unfortunate. It would have been better had the day ended here.

I cut off Kate at a side street and end up in front of her. I pull to the shoulder and wait for her to pass. But, like me, Kate's a fighter. She pulls up behind me and lays on the horn. She honks—continually—for at least a minute. Like a baby's incessant crying, it starts to get to me. Rage circles my head like ravens their prey, and I exit my car and walk toward her knowing I can't hit anything but wondering if I can stop myself.

"*What the fuck!*" I respond like any normal adult would.

She and her (one) friend call me names: "loser, bitch, whore," etc. Then I have a thought. I go back to my car and grab my camera. Bitchworth (I've started calling her this now) moves quick. She pulls her car out in front of mine, and then I follow her to where I know she is going: the Beverly Hills Police Station.

Like blood from a freshly cut wrist, indignation is gushing out of my being. I should stop—I know—but I cannot. I am out of control. Kate pulls into the emergency parking space at the station, and I pull up next to her. Then Larry swoops in behind me, blocking me in.

"*Move, asshole!*" I yell. At this point, I've gained enough sense to know I don't want to be here.

But it's too late. Larry gets out of his car and is not going to move. He removes his *Dukes of Hazzard* badge.

Then come the cops. One after the other, like clowns out of a Volkswagen, at least a half dozen Los Angeles police officers exit the station.

"This guy's blocking me in. Is that legal?" I say to one.

"Lots of things are legal in my book *little girl*," the cop spits out.

Oh, great, so that's how this is gonna go.

The cops get busy and take statements from Larry, Kate, and Kate's friend. No one talks to me, the criminal.

After about five minutes of doing nothing, I take out my short lens (the flash seems a bit over-the-top, so I turn it off), walk up to Kate who is tattling to an officer, and start taking pictures. It's *so* obnoxious, but I'm past any measure of dignity.

Kate shields her face, but neither she nor the cop say anything.

When the "little girl" cop who is now talking to Larry sees me, he belts out, "I will not allow you to make a spectacle out of me! Go sit there," and he points to the curb like I'm in time-out. "My time is being wasted on nonsense," he continues.

Yeah, mine too.

When I look around, I see clearly excessive coppage—at least ten now. More have come out to see what's going on. I recall a recent ballot measure to add more police to the L.A. streets. Just what we need, more police who have nothing to do.

While sitting on the curb, I pop out my memory card (I'd like to keep those shots of Kate talking to the cop—never mind that they probably won't sell due to my "involvement") and then detach my Canon lens and replace it with my less expensive Tamron one. The "little girl" cop told me that he was going to take my camera as "evidence," though of what crime, I am not sure.

I sit for ten minutes. Everyone is hard at work. Slowly some of the cops begin to leave. I stay seated on the curb watching the violation of my rights by the lead "little girl" cop. He is transcribing my driver's license into his notebook, and Larry is looking over his shoulder like a parrot, transcribing the same.

Eventually, Kate drives off. She looks smug but wrecked. At least I ruined her day too.

"Where's your gold badge?" I say to Larry as he walks toward his car. He ignores me.

Now it is just me and "little girl" cop. He hands me back my ID and asks for my phone number.

"Why'd you need that?" I say, too late. I should know by now: *Always question cops.*

"Oh, it's for my little black book," he smiles. "You can go."

I get back in my car—no ticket, no citation, and all "evidence" still in my possession. As I pull out of the emergency space, another cop falls in behind me.

You've got to be kidding! They're gonna get me on a traffic violation, I realize, sick to my stomach.

But he doesn't turn on his lights. Instead, he pulls up beside me and rolls down his window.

"Are you OK?" he asks.

His face is kind, and that breaks me. Tears pour out. "I was just doing my job."

"I know. Hang in there. It'll be OK."

I'm grateful for this gesture. I keep crying, but some measure of respect returns. Maybe I just haven't met the good guys yet.

On my drive home, the words merry-go-round in my head— "extortion," "letter in the mailbox," "we have her on security tape"—all words I heard Larry whispering to the cop. At home, I look up "extortion" on Wikipedia. It mentions a maximum of twenty years in prison.

I can't afford to fight Bitchworth, and money always wins. Will Gloria Allred, the high-profile attorney, take my case? What if I go to jail for five years? All for *what*? This job that makes me money but is slowly taking my life?

Chapter 15

The next Saturday, still queasy over the Bitchworth incident, I am back at Heigl's. Her publicist hasn't called about Cabo, which makes me feel foolish more than anything. (As much as Aaron has warned me against it, I'll admit I was starting to feel like one of them.)

To add insult to injury, when I rock up this morning to Heigl's, there are ten other paps. Last weekend, I was alone. I guess everyone had the same idea when they saw my mani-pedi set, and StarNP got pictures of her sister's wedding, which apparently happened later that same day.

"You got scooped," Bartlet barks when he phones for his morning check-in. "You should have stayed on."

"She gave me enough at the salon," I respond defensively. "Besides, I wouldn't have crashed her sister's wedding."

"Well, you lost money because of it. StarNP's pictures went all over. And now Heigl's gangbang material, so deal with it." Bartlet goes on to say that he read Katherine prefers to stay in on the weekends and "make love" (he doesn't use this term) with her fiancé, so she's probably not coming out.

Ulysses Bartlet is an interesting guy. Over the phone, he's a commander. His directives are precise and stalwart, and he's usually right. He could lead an army or a ship with his voice or, like Charlie, a kick-ass trio of girl detectives. His deep, punctuated British accent never wavers or bends, and though he's thirty-three and technically younger than me, he sounds like a middle-aged man. Bartlet doesn't have misconceptions about the business being slimy or feel the need to stroke his "journalistic integrity" like other agency owners do. He cares only that the money is good. His expectations are high, and though he suffers from a severe case of Tall Poppy Syndrome, he's empowering as long as he has the upper hand. For these reasons I like him, as does most of the staff. Which is why we all deal with his crass remarks.

Bartlet was wrong. Heigl comes out around one. Her gangbang is ready. Ten cars fall into line behind the red Range. I am first. Normally, on a gangbang follow, female paps almost always get pushed to the back; however, the paparazzi are moving into my territory cautiously. They know Katherine is *mine*.

The reason men don't like women in the lead is because they think we aren't gonna keep up. Aggressive protocol goes along with multi-car follows such as this one, and it's important that the cars at the lead are staying close to the celebrity's car by popping all possible lights and blocking out "foreign" cars, i.e. cars not related to the follow. Otherwise, the cars at the back of the follow will never keep up.

As the first car behind Heigl, I need to get my camera ready. Today's lens choice is unclear. It's Katie, whom we "respect," so we want to "go long"—she will give everyone time to shoot—but with so many paps, can we stay out of each other's frames?

Katherine stops at the Rite Aid in Los Feliz. She has a baseball cap pulled low on her head, which I've never seen her do, and she pauses before entering the store to tell us she's sick. We all have on long lenses and shoot her entering and exiting, but the shots are mostly worthless—you can't see her eyes.

Back to our cars, we follow her to a magazine stand on Vermont and Melbourne. Heigl takes her time browsing and soon lifts her head and smiles. She must be thinking about the prospect of so many of us leaving with nothing. She'd feel guilty if she wasted our day.

There are ten of us crowded on the small sidewalk. It's an obvious short-and-flash photo-op, but everyone has long-lensed it so they are getting extreme close-ups, less than desirable as they tell less of a story. I've "shorted it" but without a flash to make it "look long." (It's the "flash" of the short-and-flash that is considered rude. By putting the short lens on my camera, I can get wide-angle frames showing Katie is magazine shopping but still give her "respect.") While we huddle around the newsstand, I call out instructions—"Give her space," "Watch out, guys," "Back up—she's sick." I hate it when paps do this—act like they own the celebrity—but I can't help myself. Amazingly, they listen to me. Everyone is on their best behavior.

Nearer to her than the others since I'm on a short, I whisper, "If you ever want to avoid us, exit right, the long way out your subdivision. No one will see you."

She doesn't respond or seem to process my comment in the moment. And, I would miss her too if she did that, but the tables are turning and it's time Katie learned the game.

My frames outsell the competition's. I'm learning the game too.

★ ★ ★

Aaron and I have been distant for a month now, and it's been good. We talk only when work necessitates. We have barely seen each other, and my self-esteem has risen.

Word on the street is that he and Claudia despise each other. I don't want to know the details, so I don't ask.

Today, Aaron calls to see if I want to get a couple's massage, his treat.

I am obviously not going to pass up a free massage. And since for the coming weekend I've already purchased two tickets to Josh Kelley's concert, I invite Aaron to go along. I don't know many of the songs sung by Heigl's fiancé, but since she does so much for me, the least I can do is be a Josh Kelley fan.

Date night arrives, and we meet at Aaron's apartment. The moment I lay eyes on him, I realize I've missed him. I can tell he feels the same.

We start with a Thai massage on Abbot Kinney, the fashionable street in Venice Beach; then stroll to a perfectly lit restaurant where we have dinner. "This feels like a date," I say.

He responds by wrapping his fingers around mine.

When we get to the Troubadour, a historic concert venue in West Hollywood, Aaron holds me from behind as we listen to Josh and sway to the music. It's so natural, so comfortable being in his arms. When the show is over, we make a point to find Katherine. We didn't bring our cameras inside and need her to see that. Aaron says it's important in celeb/pap relationships to *not* photograph them sometimes. He says it gives them some power back and humanizes us.

Katie greets me with a giant bear hug and thanks me for coming. I gush over Josh, who *was* truly fantastic, and her neighbor Martin says hello to me, reminding me that we met once outside Katie's house. The girlfriend who was with her on the mani-pedi day smiles at me too. Seems I know all of Katie's friends who are here.

This is the first time I've been in a level social setting with a celebrity and her entourage. Honestly, it feels no different than if I were talking to any other interesting new acquaintances.

Drink in hand, Heigl is in a fabulous mood and doesn't seem to care whether I've brought in my camera or not. The others are a bit more perplexed at how this paparazzi thing works and appear to be peering into my purse expecting me to bring out the guns. I hang with Katie's crowd for about five minutes until I feel like one of the gang. Sensing that, Aaron gently escorts me back to the car where he reminds me, "You're not one of them. She's not your friend." (He makes me repeat it back. I am begrudgingly thankful for the reminder.)

The night ends as picture-perfectly as it began. We snuggle on the sofa. Aaron caresses my face with his hands, then moves down my body.

"Let's not rush things," he says. "We'll have plenty of time."

Jennifer, I say silently to myself, Aaron will never love you. Remember what it is you really want in this world.

I repeat it.

And again.

★ ★ ★

I don't sleep with Aaron that night, nor do I sleep over. I know those are unwise choices for "attachment" reasons. A few days later, my prudence pays off.

The incident occurs at a kids' swing set store in Calabasas and doesn't seem like that big of a deal at the time. It is a Britney gangbang, but with only a dozen of us, very manageable.

There is plenty of parking in the dirt lot across from the store, and along with a few others I walk across the lot toward Britney's slow-circling vehicle when I happen in front of John, a British guy from West Coast Wing who is visibly upset that he is last in line on the follow and is not yet out of his car.

"Get out of the road, bitch," he yells, leaning his skinny frame out his giant SUV. John has a soft, young face so he has to bark extra loud to be taken seriously.

Obviously, I should ignore him, but "Fuck you!" spews from my mouth, and for extra spite, I slap his window as I pass his car.

John's passenger, Adnan (the pap who would soon have his first date with Britney), reciprocates with a "Fuck you!" back at me.

Now, normally, I'd ignore this exchange—worse happens—but Adnan and I have become friendly acquaintances, and although John never talks to me, he is friends with my CXN coworkers. During a lull a few minutes later as we were waiting on Britney, I ask non-confrontationally, "What was going on there, guys?"

"Go fuck yourself, bitch" is their general response, and suddenly sensing that Tall Poppy Syndrome has them in its grip, I don't say anything further.

We shoot Britney, then follow her back home.

Two hours later, she comes out again. This time she has a larger entourage in tow, but she never gets out of the car—she just goes for a drive down Robertson to pick up more paps, around Beverly Hills three times, and back home. Now parked beside thirty cars on the shoulder of Mulholland, I am in my car when the phone rings.

J.R. is speaking as fast as I've ever heard him speak: "I've fielded several phone calls about you today, and I'm tired of it."

"What are you talking about?"

He goes on to say that if I don't leave Britney's right then, the threat on the street is that any and every CXN shooter will be blocked when working on her in the future.

"I can't have you fucking it up for my staff," he slurs.

Many of his words are unintelligible, but what I am able to piece together is that John and Adnan have corralled their friends into calling CXN and "telling on me." I don't know what they said—truth or lies—and I realize this sounds like grammar school, but tears well up anyway. I am really upset that they would stoop to such low tactics for such little payoff. But more importantly, I am stung deeply by J.R.'s reaction. What boss doesn't stick up for his worker to some snitch paps with little to go on, especially a worker who gets to the job on time, who's responsible and responsive, and who frankly nails it more often than most of the salaried staff?

When we hang up, Bartlet calls a minute later. In a tough-love attempt at sympathy, he tells me to ignore J.R., quit crying, and "more than any-thing…don't let *them* see you cry."

Which, I realize, is just what they need to see. I hang up, and with a red, tear-stained face, walk over to a large unkindness of ravens. John and Adnan aren't there, but enough witnesses from the swing set store are. They fall silent, immediately giving me full attention.

"I need a break." No one moves when the tears reemerge and I am unable to speak for ten seconds. I continue. "I shoot well. I drive well. I know what I'm doing. You don't have to like me, but you all need to lighten up."

Heads stay low and voices quiet as I walk back to my car. The group quickly disperses, and a couple of guys murmur "sorry" under their breath as they pass my car window. One even leans in to pat my shoulder. I know this group, made up of mostly Rodeo2 Brazilians, are not the culprits, but I know word will make it back to those who are.

Nextels spread gossip as fast as chirps through a cicada field, and my phone starts ringing. I ignore most calls but answer Aaron's.

"Are you OK, babe? What happened?"

I start to cry again.

"No tears. I'll be right up to sort it out."

It takes him fifteen minutes to get to Brit's estate on the edge of the Valley, and he greets me with his usual I'll-take-care-of-everything hug (and even a little kiss). He listens patiently as I tell him exactly what happened.

"I'll go talk to them," he says like a man.

He will punch them, I think. At the very least, berate them in my defense.

From the car, I watch as he walks up to John and Adnan, gives them high-fives, and offers them a handful of sunflower seeds. Ten minutes later, he returns with a big grin and word from the enemy, "So, here's the deal: John just doesn't like you. You're gonna have to live with it."

My heart stiffens. Ice shoots through my veins. I am furious and it shows.

"What! And that's an acceptable reason for you?"

Aaron's brush-off response is, "What do you want me to do about it? It's not my fault. Stop having a go at me."

What did I really expect from him? Beginning to cry again, I ask him to leave. And he does.

On my way home, I Nextel Simon and tell him the story. "What've I told you, Jen? *No one* is your friend in this business."

"But *you're* my friend. You would have stuck up for me, wouldn't you have?"

Simon stews on that for a while. Then he comes out with, "I do like ya luv, but really, I barely know ya. It's been less than a year."

And that's when I truly realize how alone I am in this business—and how this business probably isn't all that different from any other industry. Few people in our world today stick their necks out to right a wrong, regardless of whether it's for a friend or a stranger. The paparazzi are no exception.

The Battle of Bosworth, Round 4
Cumulative score: Kate: 3; Simon and Jen: 1
GAME OVER

"Neighbors are complaining. You're gonna have to move on, ma'am," a female member of L.A.'s blue coats says to me as I sit unobtrusively on the side of the road at the bottom of Christina Aguilera's street.

Most likely, Christina's Beverly Hills neighbors have never met one another, never left their house on foot, never even smiled at someone on their street. But I betcha all of them could tell you if a foot slipped off the sidewalk onto their lawn. They keep tabs. And they should: many have worked eighty hours a week for the last thirty years to obtain their million-dollar properties. If something happened to them, what would have been the point?

"I'm parked legally," I say, energy-less. I already know I won't win this argument.

I'm a fine-looking female in a fine-looking car (I got a new Prius recently!) and not at all threatening. The cop knows perfectly well what I'm doing, and she knows I'm no threat to anyone but Christina (who likes it anyway) or possibly Penélope Cruz, who also lives on the street (who hates it, but on a side note is the most beautiful woman I've ever seen). The cop also knows she can't *make* me move.

But I move anyway. With the Bosworth incident still fresh in my mind, I don't feel like getting my name in any more little black books.

And speaking of...

In my mailbox that evening: legal papers from Ms. Bosworth and her attorneys at Lavely & Singer, who Bartlet says are *the* celebrity attorneys so I should be proud. Eight pages of legal documents on heavy stock paper stating that Simon and I "placed Ms. Bosworth in fear for her personal safety and well-being." Saying that we "laid-in-wait..." (I like this term; it sounds like we're tigers) "...for approximately two months…" (This simply isn't true; we doorstepped her just five days over the course of two months) "…and threatened to publicly disclose private and confidential information regarding Ms. Bosworth, absent her agreement to succumb to [our] demands." (Oops. That was what she got from our friendly note?) It also says that we "chased Ms. Bosworth's vehicle at a high rate of speed, recklessly swerving in front of Ms. Bosworth's vehicle and then abruptly stopping in front of her preventing her from driving forward." (Quite by accident I ended up in front of her. She could have gone around, as I motioned for her to do. She chose not to. Besides, we don't "chase," we "follow.")

The letter talks about our attempt at "extortion." (Which, according to my friend Georgia, who is a lawyer, Ms. Bosworth's attorney needs to read up on since my note is not an example of extortion. "Maybe blackmail," says Georgia, "but definitely not extortion.")

The letter warns us not to come within one hundred yards of Kate or further legal action will ensue. It neglects to mention how Larry, Kate's *Dukes of Hazzard* bodyguard, obtained my name and address, or why he was running around L.A. with a badge from a Cracker Jack box.

I must admit, I am relieved. At least now I know the card she's playing, and it's only a warning. I won't have to drain my account to hire a lawyer to explain to a judge that the note I left in Kate Bosworth's mailbox, like the one I left at Adrian's, was "cute," and she needs a better sense of humor. And, most importantly, I won't have to spend time in jail while my eggs rot. (I kid you not, that thought has kept me up many nights.) Simon and CXN get the same letter—another relief as misery loves company, especially company with more money. Plus, they don't seem all that worried.

Kate's stubborn, but a solid game player. She fights as well as she drives, and at least for now has won. Simon and I will not go anywhere near her house or the Runyon Canyon lookout point. Though she may do well to change her nail salon—if I see that Black Ford Escape at Planet Nails again, I just might be tempted to arrange a little gangbang upon her exit. Then she can meet the real savages of this world when they follow her to her secret home in the Hollywood Hills.

And considering half of the paps are illegal, I imagine it would be "hella" challenging for Larry to get all their addresses.

Chapter 16

These days, it takes about as much time to get famous as it does to fill up a bathtub. Over the last few months, I've watched Katherine Heigl and Hayden Panettiere become household names. No pap knew them last season. Now they're worked like 800-count cotton and worth as much.

At the moment, Zac Efron and Vanessa Hudgens, newly hatched pretty-young-things and currently coupled, are at their dawn of fame. Except for tweens, no paps knew Zac-essa six weeks ago.

I wasn't particularly anxious to work Zac. I'd heard he was a bitch, a term usually reserved for female celebrities, but one bestowed on Zac because of the way he drives. I actually think paps are just jealous his car's so fast.

Zac lives in a nondescript apartment complex in Studio City. Vanessa lives around the corner at her parents' equally modest house. Though Vanessa is the easier *get*, I have less desire to work her—she just doesn't excite me. In my opinion, Vanessa's star power is all on the coattails of Zac, her *High School Musical* co-star, and these days, as the money is rolling in consistently, I'm getting pickier about who I work.

But all signs point toward Zac becoming *big*, and it's important that paparazzi know how to work all big stars. You never know when your paths will cross. So, one late afternoon when I'm in the area, I troll by his place. After keeping it to themselves for two weeks, my coworkers were glad to hand over his address, tired of the near-death follows and lack of shots. Along with the address, they told me how to check for his car through the iron-gated parking garage to see if he is home.

I peer in and see his sparkly black Audi jutting out from the last space. Finishing the day here is as good as anywhere, so I pull to the side of the street and park where I'll easily notice if his car exits. There's one other pap waiting, a young Armenian guy who waves at me. I wave back. It's nice to be cordial for a change.

About twenty minutes later, Zac's supercharged Audi pulls out so quickly that the other pap, who by then was standing outside his car talking to me, never even gets on the follow. I feel a pang of guilt for contributing to his loss, but not enough to answer my phone when he calls four times hoping I'll catch him up. Following Zac at 60 miles per hour through small subdivisions requires my full concentration—and now I have him "exclusive."

Zac spends about five minutes darting down random streets trying to lose me (the Prius has a feistier engine than you might expect) before getting on the bottlenecked 101 South at Laurel Canyon. For an instant, Zac is trapped. I take the opportunity being presented and pull up beside him.

It is the first time I've seen Zac in person. *Aww, look at him. So young and harmless* are my thoughts.

"Window," I mouth and motion for him to roll his down, a move I'm sure he's never seen before. He's curious and complies.

"Hey, Zac." I try to sound flirty and powerless. "I'm the only one on you. Is there any way I could have a couple of shots?"

"Are you sure no one else is on me?" he says copying my lingo. He swings his head around, scanning the freeway.

"I'm sure. The other guy lost you at your house."

"Well, I'm just going to a friend's, but if you want, you can. And, by the way, anytime you ask, I'll give you shots. I just wanna be asked."

I wonder if he'll kiss me if I ask. He may only be twenty, but *whoa!* he does not look harmless with the window down. Oh no. Zac is one smokin' hot boy.

We drive the remaining distance slowly. When we arrive at the friend's house, I wait while he primps in the reflection of his car window. With skinny jeans and a backpack slung over his shoulder, he turns to me, winks, and flashes the peace sign. I fire five or ten times. *Chuh-chuh-chuh, chuh-chuh-chuh.*

"Sorry for driving so fast," he says. "There's another guy who drives your same car. I can't stand him. Thought you were him."

"No worries. Have a good night. And thanks," I say sincerely.

Wonder what Zac thinks of Mrs. Robinson? Or, if he even knows who she is.

★ ★ ★

The next week, taking advantage of my window, I work Zac again. This time, when he pulls out of his garage I immediately roll down my window and wave so he can see that it's me and not "the pap he can't stand." He pulls to the shoulder, leans out his Audi window, tells me where he is going, then drives there slowly. When we arrive, he blocks the other paps from getting shots and smiles just for me. I'm appreciative. I'll take all the bones he throws. No doubt, it occasionally helps to be a woman in this biz.

But, woman or man, the pattern's always the same: like a prime steak over a hot flame, Zac'll be "done" in a few months. So I have to strike while the iron is hot.

Pap My Ride

The Ideal Pap-Mobile

When I replaced my reliable yet hard-to-miss red truck with the shiny, spanking-new, fully loaded silver Prius, it still wasn't fully outfitted for the job. Vehicles are as critical to paparazzi as their 70–200mm lenses, and serious considerations go into pappin' one's ride.

1. Tint

For the obvious reason, tinting car windows is favored by paparazzi: it provides you with cover.

Every car window can be individually tinted, and no surprise, there are pros and cons to each shade. Thus, how dark to go? On first thought, as dark as possible—"limo tint" it's called—'cause if you're completely blacked-out, then no one can see in. The celeb won't see you. If you're hiding as an "empty, parked car," security won't see you. If you're on a movie set where you aren't supposed to be, all-round limo tint is fabulous.

But stealth isn't the only factor when deciding the degree of tint. Equally important is the shot. Since you often shoot through your windows, you must consider whether you can "nail it" through a heavy tint. Every camera has a different ability to shoot in low light, so those of us with better quality cameras can go with more tint. Even with the best of cameras, though, a perfect frame is often elusive with limo tint—it's just too dark. Limo tint requires sunshine, so on a dreary day or in shadows, you won't get a clean frame.

Finally, while limo tint might make you completely invisible, everybody knows that what you *can't* see is often suspicious. I've watched plenty of stare-downs into heavily tinted windows by distrustful security guards and paranoid celebrities.

2. Windows

An ideal pap-mobile has a completely vertical back window that can be rolled down via front controls. Sadly, the 4Runner is the only vehicle that I am aware of with this feature. The second best option is just a vertical back window (that doesn't roll down)—my red pickup, vans, and the Mini Cooper, for example. At least this way, you can press your camera directly onto the glass and shoot a clean photo.

The reason this is so critical is that *any* slant in a window produces distortion in the frame, so if you're going to shoot through a window, it needs to be vertical, or almost so.

3. SUV (or Not)

SUVs have advantages and disadvantages. They are more expensive, but they have extra space. But the car's size also makes them more conspicuous and harder to park. And a "blacked-out SUV," especially one without plates, is the stereotypical pap car so a dead giveaway.

4. Hybrid (or Not)

Hybrid vehicles are also more expensive vehicles, so like any driver, a pap must weigh the gas savings with the higher price tag. And in city traffic, which constitutes most pap driving, a hybrid can be very cost-effective. With a Prius, a pap might spend $150/month on fuel. In comparison, a non-hybrid sedan might guzzle up $500/month at the same pump, and a large SUV could cost $1,000/month.

Hybrids also have direct physical benefits to the driver. Sitting in your car all day long waiting, day in and day out, is worlds more comfortable in a hybrid. The car can stay "on"—including the air conditioner—without the motor running. This is a BIG deal. There is no gasoline smell or that headache-inducing car vibration you get with a non-hybrid car.

The Prius is a popular pap car, and bonus: with its immense popularity in L.A., we almost always blend in.

5. To Plate (or Not to Plate)

Another way to be stealth is through your license plate, or lack thereof. As I've mentioned, in L.A., plates aren't completely "necessary" on new-looking cars; temporary dealer plates are just fine. (You are legally allowed to drive "plate-less" for about two months after purchasing a new vehicle; after that, if pulled over, you could be fined.) But to a cop and to a celebrity, a "no-plate" car—just like a heavily tinted car—is a major red flag for "paparazzi." So even though the cop or celeb or a competing pap can identify you through your license plate number, it may still be better to drive with your plates on, so that your vehicle is not immediately suspect.

Should a pap decide to go plate-less, he or she must decide *which* dealer plates to use. The in-town dealership where Simon bought his 4Runner has colorful, memorable rainbow plates. Simon is a believer that everything pap must be subtle, so he drove to Glendale, thirty miles from his home in Venice, to pick up less flashy plates from a dealer there. The problem: when you're driving around Beverly Hills with Glendale plates, you also look suspect. *Why are you in Beverly Hills if you are from Glendale? Are you a pap?*

Some paps keep multiple plates on hand—a couple of dealer plates plus a real one. Then, after a questionable follow, they might switch around their plates and become a "new car." (Not that I would ever do anything like that, mind you!) Adding a hat or a change of sunnys may be in order too.

★ ★ ★

I spent the evening, November 21, at Aaron's thirtieth birthday party. Out of obligation. I haven't gotten over that day at Britney's and how he essentially fed me to the wolves all over again, but I have gotten over Aaron (at least 90 percent). It's *much* better this way.

I knew John would be there since Aaron had told me last time we spoke, "You and John are *equally* my friends." I almost gagged when he said that.

And sure enough, he was. And Adnan came as well. He was on crutches since John had run over his foot. Now, if a female paparazzi had run over someone's foot, she'd be forced out of the business, hazed mercilessly for incompetence. But since it was John who did it, and Adnan who had jumped out of a moving vehicle, everyone thought it was funny.

What I thought was funny was that Adnan would be out of work for weeks, and there's no workers' comp in the paparazzi world.

The night crawled by and the Brits drank like Brits.

John approached me after midnight. "No hard feelings. Work is work, right?" he said, giving me a slap on the back.

"Sure," I responded curtly.

Later, Adnan slipped on his own vomit.

And I was reminded that sometimes paybacks are best left to karma.

★ ★ ★

"Hey, sexy. How have you been?" I ask my new favorite celebrity. I haven't worked Zac in a week. I'm trying to make sure he doesn't get sick of me.

He pulls over to say hello, then tells me, "I'm just going to play basketball."

The other paps tell me that when I'm not there he drives like a maniac and tries to lose them.

"Basketball again," I Nextel Simon as we fall into line behind the Audi—me at the helm, next Simon, then two Rodeo2 shooters who we're friendly with.

"Copy."

Simon and I are partnering today in case Zac and Vanessa need separate follows. Lately, I've been shooting alone; I make more money. But I'm coming to realize that if I don't partner up at least twice a week, my morale plummets. There are just too many negative forces that bombard me in this industry. I gotta have somebody to pick me up and make me laugh.

Vanessa often shacks up at Zac's overnight, then is either dropped home by him or picked up by her parents in the morning. This morning there was no sign of her, so when Zac left, we all followed. We don't expect to make much money (the basketball ritual has been photographed several times and is unlikely to sell again), but guaranteed shots are hard to pass up. It's like Dule, an Armenian pap who works for iPIX, always tells me: "They could come out with balloons, Jen. Balloons. Ya never know." His point: don't ever leave a boring story 'cause they could come out with balloons. And by golly, *that* would be *interesting*!

Everyone chats up the cheery, fit movie star as we shoot him long-lensed walking to the indoor courts. We wait behind the gates lest we trespass (or make him mad), but each time he makes a trip to the water fountain, he kindly lets us know how much longer is left in the game.

The Rodeo2 duo is Margot, a reputable French pap and one of the few other women in the business, and Moss, a native Caribbean guy. I don't trust Margot for *une seconde*—she's sneaky and driven by money—but I respect her. True to her French roots, Margot always dresses well. Whenever she sees me in sweats, she says, "You need to look nicer. What if you have to follow someone into the Beverly Hills Hotel in *that*?" She has a point, but when I'm mostly crumpled up in a hot car all day, I opt for the more comfortable look.

Moss is a quiet, big-hearted guy who struggles with his English. He's owed Simon money for two years—money Simon will probably never see again. I made a similar mistake loaning $500 to Toby, whom I call each week only to get his voicemail. I had never thought twice about lending money to friends before, but this too reminds me: we paps aren't friends.

"I have an idea," I offer. "There's no way Zac's gonna sell another basketball set. Let's mix it up."

The boys can't be bothered, but Margot, all about the money, is game. We spot a giant rose bush in the parking lot and make a plan to hand Zac flowers on his way out. Flowers in one hand, basketball in the other—sure sales.

It goes as splendidly as planned: Zac accepts the flowers, and laughs. Simon and Moss take stills. And after we give him the roses, Margot and I shoot video.

Back to our cars, everyone is upbeat, and we lazily follow Zac home.

As I resituate myself into an available parking spot outside Zac's apartment, I hear, "Hey. Hey."

I look up and the smokin' hot movie star is beckoning me to his door. I hurry over without my camera, but titillation passes immediately—his face is full of angst. Zac is not calling to invite Mrs. Robinson up.

"Were you trying to set me up back there?" he says.

"What do you mean?"

"Everyone in Hollywood is calling me gay at the moment. And you go and give me flowers."

"Oh no, Zac. That was really, *really* not the intention. You're obviously not gay. You're so straight. And so hot," I add.

He nods. Waits for me to go on.

"You shouldn't read PerezHilton. He's an ass."

About every other day on Perez's blog, Zac gets called gay because he's so pretty. That's gotta be hard on any twenty-year-old, famous or not, gay or not.

"Well, Perez is gonna have his story of the month," Zac says.

I tell him, at least five more times, that everyone knows he's not gay, and equally as many times, he's hot.

He eventually goes back inside, believing that we meant no malice, but not looking happy. Margot and I feel especially awful: Perez can be spiteful; Zac is as virile and hetero as they come. With ten years of weathering, he's the next Brad Pitt.

The next day, Perez doesn't use the photos, although they do run most everywhere else (sans gay comments). It's the Zac set of the week.

Simon says celebrities have short memories—"Zac'll be over it in a week, Jen"—although a few days later I hear that he ran out of basketball practice with the ball in front of his face.

And, I'm betting The End is near.

★ ★ ★

The end of the year is near too, which means Katherine Heigl is about to get married and go on her honeymoon. In all likelihood, *Cabo a la*

Jennifer is not gonna happen. Katherine's publicist hasn't called, but my old days of corporate due-diligence compel me to follow up.

For weeks, I've been working Heigl every Saturday or Sunday or both. Her honeymoon is only one month away now; *did she forget she told me I could come?* Every time I see her hasn't been the right time to bring it up—either there are other paps or the mood's just dark. To me, it feels like a giant white elephant is always with us, but I'm not sure celebs think enough about their promises to paparazzi to notice the beast.

It's past four and I've wasted an entire sunny Saturday sitting in my car waiting on Katherine. I'm at the bottom of her hill where we always sit when we wait on her, near Adrian's house, but I think she might be taking my advice about sneaking out the back of her subdivision. Next time I'll have to sit right on her house—intrusive, but no other choice.

At dusk, I'm about to leave when Adrian comes out. He wasn't my target, but I figure I'll follow him anyway. Besides, this may be the last time I'm on his doorstep: Heigl is moving after she gets married.

He goes to Silver Lake, not far, and parks on Sunset outside my favorite vegan restaurant, Flore. This happens to be where my friends and I are meeting in an hour, which is very inconvenient because I'll have to delay our dinner plans or he'll think I'm stalking him. I lean out my car window to shoot, not even bothering to get out. I hope he notices how little effort I'm putting forth. Maybe if he thinks I'm not impressed he'll be more likely to want me—*even celebs* gotta want what they can't have, right?

Adrian stops before he enters and stares at me for a long time, like he did the first time we met outside Tropicalia. Finally, I put my camera down. "Too much of the same pose doesn't sell," I say. *Damn, can't we just forget about this movie star business and spend the rest of the evening together?*

He keeps staring at me.

"What?" I say.

He's still staring at me. His eyes flirt and his expression teases. They say he wants me. (Seriously!)

Leaving my camera inside, I slowly get out of my car and walk over. "I have a bone to pick with you."

He raises his brows. He's enjoying the attention. "You haven't called," I say.

He's confused. Yes, how quickly promises to paps are forgotten.

"The ride-along? I have no desire to be in your documentary. I did it for *your* interview."

It finally registers. "Oh, yes. Yes. I'm gonna call you. I will."

I keep his eyes for several more seconds, neither of us speaking, then turn and leave while he watches me go.

I smile at my nice touch: I left first. That's not how paparazzi do it.

★ ★ ★

The next Saturday, I get Aaron to work Heigl with me. I need the power transfer that comes when we outnumber the celeb.

At around noon, she comes out, and we're on her exclusive. She parks on Hillhurst and walks toward the Mustard Seed, another fabulous restaurant I frequent. The time is now.

I am shooting video—it gives me an excuse to talk—and Aaron is on stills. Just before Katherine turns into the restaurant, I put down the video and say, "Just wondering, Katie, is it still possible for me to photograph your honeymoon?"

"Oh," she responds cheerily, "you should just call my publicist." It's like she just plumb forgot.

The next day, I call her publicist.

"Hi. I'm a celebrity photographer friend of Katherine's," I begin. "*Katie* wanted me to call you about her honeymoon. She was thinking it might be nice to have someone she knows photograph it."

"Oh, right. Of course," says the publicist. "Hang on a second."

I am on hold for no more than a minute. Then the publicist returns and tells me that the agency has decided that Josh and Katie deserve some privacy on their honeymoon. "She's just been so bombarded of late. So many photographers."

"Well, Katherine Heigl's the hottest new star. I'm not surprised."

"You know, one paparazzi even had the nerve to follow her into a salon while she was having her nails done."

"Oh, really? That's awful."

Ouch. I feel the punch to my stomach. I thought Katie had enjoyed my company at the nail salon. I thought we were, at least, "work friends." Aaron's words…

With that, I hang up the phone, go immediately to the Internet, and book a flight to Bangkok for five days later. My bank account has spare cash for the first time in years, and instead of going home for Christmas, I've decided to fly to Thailand with my backpack. It's the end of year-one as a pap—a year of fifty- to seventy-hour work weeks; a year of mental exhaustion but overall true professional accomplishment (*I'm a damn good pap*); a divine year, but all in all, a year I'm happy as heck is over!

Happy Holidays, Hollywood!

Year 2

Chapter 17

I still aspire to meet someone, and fall in love, and get married, but that is a very high risk scenario, and I want a baby now. I'm thirty-seven.

—Tina Fey in Baby Mama

Coconut, pineapple, and mango helped re-juice my half-empty self as I took reprieve in Southeast Asia. Throughout the beauty of it all, however, there was but one thought that repeatedly consumed my mind's every idle moment and burned like a red-hot branding iron in my gut: *ROTTING EGGS.*

OK that might be a little vulgar, but it's not preposterous. At thirty-six, I still hoped for a husband, I still hoped to fall in love, I still hoped for a child one day. But it was far from a sure thing, and that constant ticking of my biological clock was reminding me: time was running out. How was it that despite my relentless pursuit of happiness, I was left with no one? I was wanting to love so badly, my heart hurt physically.

But instead of facing the music, I extended my trip twice. I found it took six weeks before I could again face life—and celebrities. Upon returning to the States, I discovered what was new this year:

- There is a recession. Bartlet says mags have slashed rates and lower paychecks are on the way. My thought is, that's a plus: any guys grossing less than thirty grand will be forced out of the business, and even if my paycheck is cut in half, I'll still make more this year than I have in the last ten. I won't like it, but I can survive a drop.

- Adnan is officially dating Britney. Despite most paps being foreigners, the beat on the street about the new couple is very American: Adnan's a prick but an opportunist, and "good on him" for playing to his advantage.

- There is a pap-festation. I didn't think we could be more, but the sky's grown darker. I'm told that Heigl has moved to daily gangbang status, and we've savaged Zac and Hayden to the limit.

- I am rusty. Simon says this happens with even two weeks off. I was lucky to get a set of Hayden on my first day back—spotted her outside of Whole Foods (since she doesn't tolerate doorstepping anymore). It sold, but my pictures were less than professional. I blanked on my settings and was shaking like an old lady. The worst part was my lack of *style*. The only thing I could think to say was, "Hi Hayden, I've been on vacation for two months," to which she did not respond, "Oh, I've missed you. Tell me about your trip."

- And, the biggest news of all: Forget about the Year of the Rat. I declare that this will be the Year of the Baby.

★ ★ ★

A few weeks after getting back into the swing of things, I run into Adrian. Instead of the humorless stare I've gotten the last few times, he greets me with a giant *Hey, how are you!* smile that sets off his four thousand sparkly-white teeth and *those lips*. He even initiates conversation: "You're changing it up," he says. Today, I have my video camera versus my still.

I walk backward, video rolling, feeling like a proper celebrity reporter. We are in the parking lot of a strip mall.

"Your pictures aren't selling, so I thought I'd try video," I say cheekily. Then my voice turns serious. "Adrian, I have an important question for you."

"Sure."

He appears in a fabulous mood. I suppose this could look good to a first date, which he seems to be on. Before arriving at our present location, the strip mall, Claudia and I first followed Adrian to an apartment complex where he picked up a girl and greeted her with a "new acquaintance" hug. She looked petrified. He didn't look nervous enough to be remotely interested in her, but you never know.

I continue, "You're doing a documentary on the paparazzi. Based on what you've learned, do you believe we are to blame for Britney and her situation?" (Britney is currently being hospitalized for something or other.)

Adrian responds ineloquently, a pattern I notice when he hasn't memorized lines. His bottom line is that the paparazzi are "partially to blame."

I follow up with a question I've been planning ever since I heard the Adnan story: "And what do you think of Adnan, the paparazzo who's dating Britney?"

Adrian continues to poorly express himself—"It's strange. Postmodern. Weird," he says—but gives me the perfect segue into my follow-up question.

First, I peer over the video screen and grab his eyes. After a dramatic pause, I ask, "Would *you* ever date a paparazzi?"

In perfect movie-star style and brilliantly on cue, Adrian stabs my eyes right back and says, "*You're* kinda cute."

We flirtatiously continue the piercing stares for a few seconds longer while the forsaken date, who has way overdone her hair, makeup, and clothes for a one o'clock lunch, refuses to look anywhere but the ground.

Before he steps into the restaurant at the corner of the mall, he says to me, "I owe you that ride-along. I always keep my promises. I don't know if I have your number anymore. Give it to me again."

"You're gonna call me?" (The video is still rolling.)

"I'm gonna call you," he assures me.

So I give him my number for the *third* time, and he plugs it into his phone. I shrug to myself. He probably won't call, but it doesn't hurt to dream.

★ ★ ★

Bartlet and Simon have stopped calling me Jennifer. They now refer to me only as "Jen-Full-Sixty" (as in my 60 percent cut of my photo sales), like I am greedy. But if you don't need a partner, or if a partner actually impairs you and gets you busted by the celebrity—which many of them do—why not take the full cut and be successful at the same time? Hey, they wouldn't question a man doing that.

But, as I've said, working solo too frequently destroys the soul. The negative energy that circles me each day *does* penetrate, and I need support. Thus, I am thrilled to have made a new friend. Abbey is my age, petite, and has a pixie hairstyle that accentuates a delicate and beautiful face. Her looks don't match her character, though: she is tough, with a manly voice and a heavy step. Abbey is a lesbian but tells me not to call her that—"I'm a dyke," she explains. Her partner, an equally adorable and minuscule Asian girl, holds the female role in their relationship.

Abbey works on staff for TMZ and shoots video. Since I shoot mostly stills and TMZ isn't a pap agency—although it does *buy* our material, it doesn't *sell* its own video to anyone else, and it only hires "video paps"— the two of us can easily share information. We met a couple of weeks ago outside the Beverly Wilshire Hotel waiting on Rihanna and hit it off so quickly we speak several times a day already.

This afternoon, after a nasty, multi-car Lindsay Lohan follow from the Valley into Beverly Hills, Sid, a hulk of a guy from West Coast Wing who doesn't like me for who knows what reason, comes over to bully me. He spouts fallacies about how I drove poorly and blocked his car on the follow, hollering out these inaccuracies for others to hear. He wants people to think I was out of line, that I didn't obey "the rules," and hopes they'll use it against me.

But I'm not worried. Sid and I both know I can outshoot him. My reputation strengthens every day, and it's clear to everyone.

That doesn't mean his cruelties don't hurt. The negative energy he hurls my way has an impact like lead balls slamming against my stomach. They bruise and will eventually lead to permanent scars. That's my fault, though.

When I'm asked by an outsider to explain the paparazzi world, I describe it as an ungoverned street business run similar, I imagine, to that of gangs or the mafia. Like these "businesses," papping has its rules, but as in theirs, no police or unbiased authority steps in to mediate. Thus, street politics—intimidation and power—enforce the rules of our games. Now that I understand pap rules, mostly I adhere to them, and mostly I succeed. But I still get hurt.

When Abbey sees the commotion, she runs over and jams her elbow into Sid's dinosaur ribs. "Get the fuck away from her," commands little-bitty Abbey. She doesn't know the details of our argument, but she doesn't need to know. She doesn't care about pap-rules. She doesn't care about Sid. She's loyal, and I'm her friend.

Sid backs down—he would never hit a girl—and leaves. I get out of my car and lift the doll-size video-pap off the ground in a hug as tears leak out. Those tears arrive not because of Sid's attack, but because my new friend Abbey—this woman I've known only a couple of weeks—is the only pap, after a year in the business, to *ever* stick up for me.

"Put me down!" she directs. "We got each other's back."

★ ★ ★

Speaking of doll-size, you know Hannah Montana, don't you? Born Destiny Hope Cyrus, her dad called her Smiley when she was a baby, which became Miley. Miley is fifteen right now, barely old enough for the tabloids to buy her. And as with Zac and Vanessa before her, no one older than a tween knew who she was last month.

Just ten minutes from my house down the 101, Miley lives at home with her parents in Studio City. I'd hate to live in the Valley—it's suburbia at its finest—but work-wise it's a pleasant break from the city. Besides, a decent group of paps work Miley regularly, and her family's not so bad either. (Interestingly, I find that "parents" rarely have a problem with us. And why would they? For years, they've been working toward this, possibly even more than their kid.)

Last week, Miley's look-alike mom Tish got everyone out of parking tickets when a puffed-up cop spotted us waiting in an alley. "Oh, Officer," said Tish. "They're being so respectful. I don't think they need tickets. We're leaving now anyway."

Miley's responsible for our good behavior. She and her dad have established the rules.

One afternoon, Billy Ray came outside to have a talk with us. "What happened yesterday was unacceptable," he said. "I can't have you using vocabulary like that around my Miley. [F-bombs being dropped by us were what he was referring to.] And this rushing up on her, getting in her face to take a picture, it has to stop."

We all nodded in agreement. And we meant it. Rules make our job easy: they tell us how everyone else is going to operate.

A few days later, we followed Miley to the Coffee Bean where she smiled and waved to all of us on our long lenses. Once she was inside, Sam, a burly Aussie with two black holes where his two front teeth used to be, turned to a non-regular Miley pap who had decided to join us that day, and in a flat, stern voice said, "We do NOT use language like that in front of Miley."

The guy was speechless. After all, "f—k" said in the normal course of business is standard operating procedure. (At this point, it's important to note that paps loved Miley Cyrus, and more importantly, we loved the shots she was giving us—we were all making great money on her picture sales—so the last thing we wanted to do was stop those pictures. Also, I think that a lot of us respected that Miley was young and still innocent, and it was not our place to taint her.)

Later that morning, a Sunday, Billy Ray invited us all to church. "Don't think y'all can bring the cameras inside," he said. "But you're welcome to join us."

No one took him up on the offer, but it went to show what a pleasant environment we were working in. Like I said, no one wanted things to change.

★ ★ ★

When we photograph Hollywood's fountain of youth—stars like Miley, Zac, and Vanessa—the mags snap up the stills and video. Sixteen is usually the bottom age limit: you can be sexy at sixteen, but much younger borders on gross, even for the tabloids. Miley Cyrus, Zac and Vanessa, Ashley Tisdale, Selena Gomez, Hilary Duff, the Jonas Brothers, and most of the teenage celebs that live with their parents in Studio City (all these peeps, at this time, live within walking distance of one another) began to see paps when they turned of age. (Notably absent from this list is Justin Bieber. He is a bit younger than this crowd and won't become "adult-famous" for a few years. Besides, at this time, he doesn't live in L.A.)

For at least the first few months, the teenagers all love it. Even I, a pap, think it would be pretty cool to be papped in high school. They are fun for us to work on too. They "perform." They can't seem to help themselves. They pose and smile, take direction well, and they love props. Vanessa, for instance, once walked out of her house cuddling a teddy bear for no other reason than a photo-op. And for me specifically, Zac put quarters in his meter three times—three "takes"—until I assured him I got the shot. The teens are smart too, and intuitive. Maybe because they've engaged in hide-and-seek games more recently than we "grown-ups" have, these kids figure out our tricks much quicker than their adult counterparts usually do.

But always, after a few months, something happens. Like trees on their street, we become part of the neighborhood landscape. At the same time, agents and producers whisper in the up-and-coming teenager's ear: "You're so wonderful and talented. You don't need the paparazzi. Don't give them any pictures. You're a king or queen already." Some of the teenagers will listen to their PR people. They will get coy and stupid. And, they will find *as quickly as we arrived, we will go*. The young celebrity might find his picture—and his prominence—just disappears. *Poof.*

But some—the smart and the confident, I notice—will work it (at least for a bit) and we will watch them climb, climb, climb the popularity ladder. At a young age, they will *establish* their celebrity. And for better or worse, they often need us to do that.

By giving it up, "kids" like Miley Cyrus and Zac Efron SKYROCKETED into adult money, fame, and power. In a season, they went from being famous to tweens and their parents to being famous to *everyone*. And in this business, name recognition equals more opportunities and more choices. Who doesn't want that?

How to Get Famous

Speaking of fame, like gravity, Hollywood operates predictably. And if you recognize and understand the laws of fame that govern this town, then you as a celeb have much power. You can influence how often you are worked, how frequently you are in the tabloids, how much name recognition you have, and how your "celebrity" is defined. It is *your* choice if you want more photos or if you desire peace—*you* hold the controls. But beware: it's diamonds—not stars—that last forever.

Hot Buttons

Besides the baseline criterion—being a beautiful Hollywood woman under forty (or better, under twenty)[14]—there are specific things that make someone temporarily *hot*:

---

14. These rules apply to women. Very few men get famous via the tabloids. If you're a beautiful Hollywood *man* under forty (or maybe forty-five, if you get better with age), generally no one cares. The exceptions: men will sell with babies, bathing suits, and balloons, or if they are young, stylish pretty boys like Zac Efron. But the general rule is *Men Don't Sell*. The reason is that women mostly read tabloids, and women like to look at other women. We want to see what female celebrities are wearing, how they've done their hair, who they're dating, what their bodies look like, and how they compare to *us*.

- **If you are pregnant.** We love to see you grow and glow. And yes, you are beautiful. Just go with it.

- **If you are somewhere with young children or dogs.** No one can resist animals and babies.

- **If you are currently relevant to Hollywood,** i.e., you're a sought after movie star or are in a hot TV show. Extra hot-button points if you are a spectacular dresser—good or bad.

- **If you are new to the scene.** Mostly these are the under-twenty girls, but occasionally, as in the case of the "Desperate Housewives," they can be near forty.

- **If you are involved in a scandal or story:** a bad breakup, a drug or alcohol addiction, a new movie, a new romance, or a loss or gain of weight. As soon as the news hits, *that afternoon*, we're on you. In a few days, you'll get accustomed to the multitudes outside your door. After a week, you may stop coming out, thinking we'll never leave. *But we will.* Unless you actively work it, work us, unless you do something to *keep us interested*, then you probably have a *hot* (salable) window of a few weeks, i.e., two tabloid cycles. (Except for getting fat. If you become fat, we like to look at you as often as possible.)

- **If you are involved with another celebrity, romantically or just as friends.** One plus one is MUCH greater than two.

- **If you make yourself interesting by "performing" for the paparazzi and change it up.** Reality show people are great examples. Also, young stars like Zac and Miley, as discussed.

When you do the same thing over and over, the mags will get bored. Madonna once said, "I wore this [outfit] many days in a row so paparazzi would stop photographing me."[15] And that's how it works: make yourself a non-story, make yourself rote, and you live pap-free. But make yourself a story, and...*bam*!

- **If you are in the right location.** If you want to be seen (photographed), hang out where we do. If you don't, move to Pasadena, deep in the Valley, south of Venice Beach, or out of L.A. altogether. You'll rarely be worth the trip. Case in point: the cast of *Lost*. Because they lived in Hawaii and weren't accessible to paps during the show's seasons, they never got tabloid-huge and most were quickly forgotten after *Lost* ended. Now, if a Hawaiian pap had made a conscious decision to work, say, Evangeline Lilly (the brunette heroine), and she were amenable to it, then the two of them could have made her tabloid-hot in no time.

In summary, there are a few celebrities—for example, those with young children (Jennifer Garner, Reese Witherspoon, Heidi Klum), those who dress colorfully and smile (Gwen Stefani), those who are a mess (the usual suspects)—who can effortlessly stay *hot*. There are also those who are consistently fashion-savvy (Kate Bosworth, Sarah Jessica Parker), stylized (Katy Perry, Lady Gaga), awful dressers (the Olsen twins, Drew Barrymore), or practically naked dressers (Matthew McConaughey, David Beckham), and they will always sell too. But for most celebs, staying salable takes effort.

★ ★ ★

15. Madonna, "My Worst Outfits Ever," *Us Weekly*, April 28, 2008.

And speaking of David Beckham (which we were…sorta), when people ask me my favorite paparazzi story, this is the one I tell.

Claudia and I start the day as partners. We arrive at the Beckhams' at 7:30 a.m. David has a game this weekend, and ever-prompt Claudia saw him leave early the previous morning, presumably on his way to practice. Generally paps don't follow him to soccer practice—there's rarely a shot—but Claudia and I are both having profitable months and we're up for a challenge.

At 7:55 a.m., David pulls out of his driveway in his DB-monogrammed convertible Porsche. Kitschy, but he's not to blame: he and Victoria received his-and-hers cars as a "Welcome to America" gift from TomKat Cruise; it would be rude not to drive them.

Claudia and I decided in advance that I would follow David and she would stay at the house and wait for the lovely Posh Spice to appear. I fall in behind two security cars which trail him and his nine-year-old son Brooklyn. We stop first at Brooklyn's private elementary school, the Curtis School, and David pulls down the drive to the entrance. I take my cue from security and pull over beside their two cars on the shoulder of Mulholland.

One security guard who looks a little like David and is wearing a suit and a small earpiece comes up to my car and knocks on the window. Except for limo drivers and Oscar attendees, no one wears suits in L.A.

"Hello, Miss. May I have your card, please?" His accent is formal, refined British, and he's intimidating—reminds me of airport security or the Secret Intelligence Service. I'm still amazed at the power that mere "people" can command when they just look the part (*Dukes of Hazzard* Larry). I've figured that out, though, so I just smile politely and respond, "Mmm. No, I'd rather not."

"We just like to know who we're working with, ma'am," he tries again.

"I'm Jennifer." I offer up, and put out my hand to shake Security's.

"He's just going to practice."

"I know. You think he might stop for coffee?"

"I doubt it."

"OK. No worries."

Security doesn't push it further and walks back to his car. About ten minutes more go by before the Porsche exits the school. David gets on the 405 South and drives at a moderate speed. He has his hand out the window and is playing with the wind. The traffic is light, it's a relaxed follow, and I'm enjoying being out this early—the Southern California spring morning is crisp and cool with plenty of sunshine.

Before today, I've only seen David once in real life, and only through the lens. I had gotten a tip and had shot the Beckhams around midnight leaving a restaurant with no fewer than ten security guards. One guard had pushed my camera into my face. It was the most violence I'd ever incurred from a celebrity or his entourage. I guess, like Aaron said, if video's not rolling, the Brits aren't afraid to scuffle. (I did manage a few decent shots that night—exclusive too—and when I was in Thailand over the holidays, I ran across a two-page spread of my photos while thumbing through *Heat,* a British magazine. That was wild.)

Like in his photos, David is, in person, undeniably one of the finest specimens of a human being who has ever walked the earth. Desiring to smell the rose that God put in my path this morning, I casually pass the two security cars and pull up in the adjacent freeway lane beside David.

I glance over and suck in my breath. No question, he is the David that Michelangelo sculpted.

I roll down my passenger window, and before long he looks over. I raise the cup of coffee I have in my hand and mouth "Coffee?" hoping he'll realize that I'm the photographer following him and that I'm asking him to stop for a picture. This morning is on his terms; I knew that going in.

David's head rolls back slightly as he smiles at me—and sends me spinning toward heaven.

I drop back behind security (who's swerving all around now and clearly in distress that I'm so close to his boss) and keep my distance until we hit the Long Beach exit where the Galaxy, DB's soccer team, practice.

Just after leaving the freeway, David pulls into Starbucks.

My heart skips a beat. *Is he doing that for me?*

David goes directly to the drive-through lane, and both security cars pull into parking spaces to wait. I pull in behind David. The drive-through makes a tight curve, such that David's head and my head are less than ten feet apart even though we're both in our cars. Our windows are rolled down.

"Hi," I say, feeling my face get flush.

He looks right at me, sunglass-less. His eyes twinkle and he flashes his signature smile, the one that looks like he's kind of bashful.

"Do you think I could have a picture?" I ask respectfully.

There's not a shot unless David allows it. He can easily tuck back into his car or put his hand up and avoid being photographed. And if I get out of my car, he will just turn his head and roll up his window until security escorts me out of the way.

"Ohhh…no, I don't think so," he says gently, almost like he's sorry.

"OK. Are you sure?" I persist, though am conscious not to grovel. Usually I will sacrifice my dignity for a picture, but today is different. I prefer an angelic encounter with or without the shot.

"I'm sure you'll have another opportunity," he says politely. David seems to be enjoying the interaction too, leaving his window down, his body language giving no indication he doesn't want to converse.

Good-looking Security has finally noticed us talking and rushes over. Casually, David waves him away.

"Hmmm…" I start. "Well, how about tickets? I'm dying to see you play."

"Yeah? You should come to a game."

"Yeah, I should." I pause. "*Good* tickets would be nice. You know, like, your box."

"Well, I generally give my tickets to my family." He puts me down softly. It even looks like he's blushing.

"Oh, of course you do. That makes sense."

Pause. He keeps his head a bit out the window. We're both *engaged* in this conversation.

"You know, David, maybe it's best I can't photograph you. I'm shaking so much I don't think I could hold the camera."

Another award-winning David Beckham smile, dead into my eyes mere feet away.

I love you.

I try to think of something clever to say, but can't.

"Sooooo. What now? No pictures, no tickets. I'm just a nice American girl. You're sure, yeah?"

He smiles again. Then, he slowly reaches into his car, grasps his aviators, and slides them over his perfect nose.

Is he doing that for me?

"Yeah?" I question. Putting his sunglasses on, I think, means that I can have a picture, but I want to be sure. "I...I can have a picture?"

Ever so slightly, he nods. I bring my camera up—shaking as fiercely as I suspected—and fire away for about fifteen seconds while David takes his cup of coffee from the girl at the window and glances back at me.

He pulls his Porsche forward into the street. I wave at the Starbucks employee with the jaw-dropped expression as I pass the drive-through window without ordering. Then David turns right toward soccer practice and I turn left to get back on the freeway. I "thank-you" honk my horn, and he sticks his hand out the window and waves.

If I died now, my life would be perfect.

★ ★ ★

Bartlet is the first call I make on my drive back to town. He thinks I'm joking. It doesn't happen that way, not with a star like David Beckham.

Claudia had stayed at the Beckhams' house, but since we'd committed the day together we'll split the sales. I'll get 30 percent, Claudia will get half her staff cut, and CXN's three owners will make over 50 percent. David's shot often—not by paps, but by official sports photographers—and as no real story is associated with my pictures, they aren't super valuable. (To anyone other than me, that is.) I'll get respect points in the pap world, but I'll be lucky to make more than a couple grand from the set.

Still, today wasn't about the money. (Although, I will be disappointed if they don't sell—*what's pleasure if it can't be shared?*) And, David's random act of kindness *will* take a little skin off his back. He's an experienced enough celebrity to know that by giving it up, more paparazzi action will perpetuate. Paps will see these shots and may choose to work on him because they will wonder *will he give it up again?* But, despite the inconvenience, David did it anyway.

He made my day and will make my tomorrow and my weekend. I won't kid myself and think that I made his day, but I do wonder if his random act of kindness for little ole me maybe, possibly, made his morning. We all know it feels *beckham* to give than to receive.

The MAMMOTH Celebrity

The Beckhams are one in, quite literally, a billion. At any given time, there are only a handful of MAMMOTH celebrities in the world. Right now, that's stars like Brad and Angelina, Tom Cruise, Jennifer Lopez, and Madonna. These celebrities operate with security *fleets*, they are almost always in private jets and cars, and they are rarely photographed *not* on their terms. Paps may doorstep them when we know they're in town, but we're typically successful only when the mammoth celebrity chooses to give it up. They are rarely our targets because we can rarely get them. These celebrity elite definitely must change the way they operate in this world, but that's as much about the public as it is the paparazzi. And with their fame comes enormous power. With so much money and so much security, they are able to control a good part of the world around them.

Chapter 18

*B*ack to reality. I've often wondered what makes some of us desire kids so strongly and others not want them at all. For me, there wasn't a time when I didn't want kids. Even in my twenties, I knew I'd have three. And with them, of course, a healthy husband.

Conversely: I always knew I didn't want them early. I had too much to *do*—travel, play, work. I was in no rush. Besides, guys were everywhere. At least a few years ago they were. No one told me they would go away.

Since I moved to L.A.—and aged—there's been only one short-lived boyfriend. Sure, I had prospects. OK, so maybe Adrian wasn't a *realistic* prospect. And OK, OK, maybe Aaron was a dream too. But without my Aaron dream, I would have lacked hope—hope for romance, hope for a family. So I let it stay alive longer than it should have.

But now, with no viable male and having vowed that this year, my thirty-seventh, would be the Year of the Baby, I have decided to consider the completely unnatural and awkward twenty-first-century alternative to sex: the sperm bank. Not that this idea is sitting easily with me. Sure, I am thankful that I have the option, but to be honest, I find it *very* disturbing. I mean, what will people think? "She can't even find somebody to sleep with her?" More than that, what will my "potential" kid have to deal with? "Your dad was A Sperm?" How will that affect him?

But the more I think about it, the more I warm up to it. My other option, using a friend—who at this point would have to be Aaron or Simon, the only two men with whom I feel remotely comfortable enough to sleep with but neither of whom I want to involve in the rest of my life—is not attractive to me. And since I don't sleep around (I don't even know *how* to sleep around), if I want a kid, what option do I have?

So swallowing that heavy pill of reality, I took two action steps. First, I said what I was going to do out loud. I told my mom, my sisters, and a few close friends including "the girls" that if I didn't meet a guy in the next year I would try to get pregnant with a sperm donor. Some were skeptical, some were supportive, some were judgmental, and some were empowering. The backing of my traditionally conservative mom was particularly meaningful. Second, I did some research. 'Cause in the end, if I do decide to get "artificially inseminated" (I hate this term), I want everything to be in place so that when I am ready, I can just make the appointment and say, "*Go*. Let's do it. *Now*."

Los Angeles has a huge sperm bank. Each sperm is assigned a number, about which you may see basic genetic information. But the bank offers no pictures of donors. To me, the idea of blindly picking a donor number based on height and hair color alone seems too much like driving down La Cienega, pointing my finger out the window, and picking the first XY chromosomes I land on. So I spend a big part of April on the Internet and on the phone. I research sperm banks in Scandinavia—I figure if one race is consistently beautiful, it's the Nordics! And I find a bank in Denmark, which much like Match.com, has copious personal information about each donor online. Like the L.A. bank I checked into, it has no pictures, but what it does include is personal feedback on each guy from the sperm bank staff. Since every donor is screened for physical and mental health, and hobbies and educational level are irrelevant to me, I am looking for one thing: Who's attractive? "Dane" and "Atle" (pseudonyms, not numbers—so much more personal) were clearly the staff picks for "best looking."

Next, I called the bank to see how it worked. They told me that the United States had recently instituted new restrictions which did not allow for the importation of "human tissue," so if I were serious about Dane or Atle, I could either come pick up their sperm myself (and smuggle it back into the States or spend months in Denmark till "it took"), or I could go to Mexico where they could FedEx it to me. A long trip to Denmark sounded pricey, so I got on the phone. After leaving many messages—I don't speak Spanish—a competent-sounding, English-speaking doctor in Tijuana called me back. He told me that if I could get my fallopian tubes checked out in the States, and they were passable, he would squirt me full of Viking material during each ovulation cycle.

It felt like an episode of *Sex and the City* except without the humor. *Should having a kid really entail crossing the Mexican border for Danish sperm applications? Was using a sperm donor the moral solution, or was I going against nature? Would I ever find a real daddy?* I didn't know the answer to these questions. The only thing I knew was that, for me, *not* having a child was *not* an option. I was born to be a mother.

★ ★ ★

Justified or not, lately, it felt like I was always getting the short end of the stick.

"Officer, can you tell us what happened, please?"

Officer Cregg walked up to the white board and drew a diagram. "This was Ms. Buhl's car," he said, pointing to a car he had drawn. "These were the three cars behind Ms. Buhl that she was blocking," he said, pointing to the three cars he had drawn directly behind my car.

He walked back to the podium. "Your Honor, Ms. Buhl pulled up in front of me on Beverly Boulevard to view the set of *Entourage*. I asked her three times to please move along—she was blocking traffic—or I would have to ticket her. I did not want to ticket her, Your Honor, but she refused to move, and the cars behind her couldn't move. I had no choice. She was impeding traffic."

"Thank you, Officer. You may be seated. Ms. Buhl, you may approach the podium."

I walked up.

"Would you like to ask the officer any questions about his testimony?" the judge asked.

"Yes, I would."

"Go ahead."

"Why are you lying? Why did—," I began only to be interrupted by the judge.

"Ms. Buhl, you may only ask questions to *clarify* the testimony. Would you like to do that?"

"Yes, I would."

I tried again. "Did you see my camera—"

"Ms. Buhl, you're testifying. This time is only for questions. Do you have any questions?"

"I guess not." *Damn. How is this gonna uncover truth? I need a lawyer.*

"OK. Then please tell us what happened," the judge said.

I went to the diagram and erased the three cars that Officer Cregg had drawn. "There were no cars between the traffic light and me," I said. "When I pulled to the side of Beverly, there was no one behind me within several hundred feet. And no one came up behind me for at least three minutes because the traffic light here [I pointed] was red."

I stepped back to the podium and continued, "I slowed down to look at the film set, but my car was still moving forward when Officer Cregg banged his hands on it and leaned his entire head inside my window to look around. He went like this." Here, I illustrated to the judge the officer's head movement, which to me had looked like a turtle coming out of its shell. I continued, "I feel sure he saw my camera equipment lying on the front seat and took me to be a paparazzi. He demanded that I stop—as my car was still moving at this point—and he said, 'Pull ahead, ma'am. Right there. Pull up to the curb and stop.' I stopped only because he told me to and I was obeying him. I did not want to stop. I was only rubbernecking and slowing down, and that's not illegal."

Monitoring the set of *Entourage* on the sidewalk in Beverly Hills was, I would venture to guess, the most power Officer Cregg had enjoyed in quite some time. He took his job seriously, and he was gonna show me who was boss.

Of course, there's irony here: the crew of *Entourage* loves paps.

I carried on, "The officer then told me that he was writing me a ticket because I was 'impeding traffic,' but I looked in my rearview mirror and asked, 'What are you talking about? There is no one behind me.' I pointed behind me and asked him to look. The officer refused to look, and after another sixty seconds with him writing the entire time, I appealed again, because *still* no one was behind me. 'If I leave now, I will never have impeded anyone,' I told him. But he continued writing, then handed me a ticket, and in a very sarcastic voice said, 'You can go now.' And he smiled."

"Thank you, ma'am. Is there anything further?" the judge asked.

"He's telling a bold-faced—"

"Thank you, ma'am." And in the same breath, and in the kindest tone, the judge said, "In the case of [*blah, blah, blah*], I rule in favor of Officer Cregg." Then, he hit his gavel and said, "You're dismissed."

As I walked to the courtroom exit past Officer Cregg—who hadn't looked at me the entire time—I couldn't help myself. "Fucking liar," I mumbled.

Then, I quickly corralled my closest pap friends and arranged a gang-bang outside the courthouse taking Cregg's picture and posting it on the Internet with the true story. The following week, I spotted him working as a greeter at Walmart.

Kidding! (No one shops at Walmart in L.A.!) But I wished that as I paid my ticket.

★ ★ ★

It's June 16th, the day after my thirty-seventh birthday. Summer is boiling full-steam, and I head to Malibu. What's ahead of me in the next few months will change me forever. Of course, I don't know that yet.

I'm going to Malibu to join Simon on "McC." McC is what Simon calls Matthew McConaughey because he can't pronounce "McConaughey," much less spell it. Simon's always impressed with my "big words" and math, i.e., paycheck, calculations. But where he's lacking in some areas, he's a genius in others, and you'll find no one better at making fun of celebrities.

I Nextel Simon every morning to pump me up, and unless he's in a funk, he'll get rolling on a comedy routine that would top *Chelsea Lately*.

This morning I take the scenic route through town to the Westside, then onto the PCH. The Pacific Coast Highway follows the ocean shore from southern to northern California. Surfers, seagulls, and sailboats dot the bright blue waters, and it's hard to pay attention to the road.

Simon beeps me on my way in. "Did you remember your oxygen? You're headed for the Bubble today. The air is thick out 'ere."

"The Bubble" is what Simon calls Malibu—shiny and sparkly on the outside, suffocating on the inside. "The Bu" is what the tabloids call it.

McC just moved from his Airstream trailer where he lived for months parked in a Malibu campground off the PCH into a rented home in an elite neighborhood on the north end of Malibu beach. In McC's new subdivision, the ocean—meters away—is blocked from the public's view by elephant-size homes like the one he's building. (He rents adjacent property while overseeing the construction.) Julia Roberts, her husband Danny Moder, and their three kids are also new to the neighborhood, having moved into a custom-built, eco-friendly home situated on a cliff overlooking Little Point Dume beach. I don't think there's anyone (besides maybe Bitchworth) who reviles the paparazzi like Julia Roberts. Simon "gets a giggle" when he thinks of how her "britches must'a knotted up" when she discovered Matthew would share her same chunk of sand. You see, the problem is, Matthew *adores* the paparazzi. And since he always produces an attractive salable picture with strong resale value (especially wearing a bathing suit, his most frequent attire), we love him too. Or at least we love photographing him. So now every time Julia heads down to her beach, she must "SMILE!"

About once a quarter, Simon and I split our favorite greasy *brekky*—a sausage, egg, and cheese biscuit from McDonald's. Simon is borderline manorexic, thus we always *split* any meal we eat together. Today, I'm in charge of coffee since my hour-plus commute has made me the later arrival. I buy us two cups from Micky-D's and a biscuit to share. At around nine, we eat on the dirt shoulder of McC's dead-end street and outline the day's plan.

Within a mile from Julia and Matthew's is an elite school where young kids with famous parents go, and a Vons grocery store where they—and others—shop. It's a sticky square mile, and like wildebeest crossing the African plain, a few celebs who make the journey will inevitably fall prey to the paparazzi.

Today we decide that Simon will sit on Matthew since he already has a cordial relationship with the handful of loyal McC photogs, and I will troll around looking for anyone else who can be picked off.

After parting, my first stop is around the corner at another dead-end, Julia's. Next to Julia's driveway is a small path, a three-minute hike leading down to the ocean at Point Dume, one of the best surfing spots in SoCal. Even though Little Point Dume beach, a.k.a. Hut Beach, is public, all direct paths to it are gated and bolted with prison-style locks, and the neighborhood pays a security guard to monitor *her* (Julia's) path, specifically. After a few drive-bys, I strike up conversation with a guy trimming the bushes around Julia's mailbox. "I hear Julia Roberts lives here," I say in my best tourist voice.

"Yep." He nods. "She's around."

I didn't ask if "she were around," but he seems proud to be in the loop as he shares this piece of first-rate information. No one knows she's back. The last photographs of Julia were from Rome where she filmed the starring role in the movie *Eat, Pray, Love.*

I dig more. The yardman, Gino, a jovial Mexican with an Italian nickname and at least 350 pounds on him, tells me that Julia's husband Danny surfs almost daily. Danny's not especially famous, but surfing shots are rare, and they would be hard for the mags to pass up.

Gino's full of life and light, evidently not having worked long enough in the Bubble to be asphyxiated yet by its poisonous interior. I'm drawn to him and decide to be up front: "Gino, I'll give you a hundred bucks if you call me the next time you see Danny walking down that path." This is slightly risky—I don't know if Gino is loyal to Julia, and I could get myself and my car blacklisted—but I go with my gut.

Gino's eyes light up and his smile extends. "I had a feeling you were one of them." Gino's from South Central L.A.—no dummy. "OK, sure, I'll call you."

Verbally, it seems I've found a tipster, but that means nothing. Everybody takes your number (it's easier than saying no) but only a small percentage of them ever actually tip. They either forget—find the process non-stimulating—or upon reflection find they ethically disagree with the cause. Out of at least a hundred I've propositioned, I can count on only about five calling. Tip money alone isn't enough to make someone tip; they have to want to do it for other reasons.

Lucky for me, Gino has an impetus: clipping bushes, all alone, all day long, mind and body sizzling in the sun, Gino's clearly bored. And, for a people-person like him, that's an unbearable physical state. (Believe me, I know.)

An hour after we meet, Gino calls: "I'm friends with the gate guard. I'll make this happen."

Sweet. Gino's in.

Nothing happens that first day, but with a Julia tipster in the bag, Simon and I commit the week. Each day I make the trek down to Malibu, and Gino stays in constant contact regarding the comings and goings of the Roberts-Moders. He tells me their cars, their future in-and-out of town schedule (which he finds out from the housekeeper), their beach walks, and so on. He *gets* it. He knows what information I need to know. Suddenly Gino's mind-destroying job of clipping bushes eight hours a day in Julia's front yard becomes bearable. Suddenly he's Sam Spade.

Over the week, Simon and I skirt between following and photographing Julia, unbeknownst to her hawk eyes and thanks to Gino whom we throw four hundred bucks at; Matthew and his pregnant girlfriend Camila Alves; and Tommy Lee and Pamela Anderson, who appear to be back in love once again. Pink drives by us for a nice photo-op on her motorcycle, and at the grocery store we stumble across the Red Hot Chili Peppers's Anthony Kiedis in his golf cart. (Per Gino, Anthony apparently lost his key privileges when he let a friend borrow the unlocking jewel. No doubt, Malibu is serious about protecting her Point Dume.)

Simon and I work a tag team formation as tight as the Blue Angels—it's undercover papping at its finest. One of us Nextels the other immediately upon a celeb-sighting, and the other leaves his or her station to get in second position within minutes. If I spot someone at the Mayfair Market, for instance, as often I do when grabbing lunch, I know to take the risk of trying to get valuable *in*-store shots because Simon is hidden outside backing me up. "Minnie [Driver] is on her way out. Left-hand door," I radio. I *trust* Simon. I know he's blacked-out behind his car tint and windshield visor, and he'll hose it. Simon and I make a seamless pair.

Compared to Hollywood, relatively few paps work in Malibu, and if you know what you're doing, there's the potential to make lots of money. Upon first glance, it's an ideal locale: Malibu rarely gets too hot—the breeze from the beach and the heat from the sun combine ideally; vegetation is green and luscious (thanks to sprinkler systems) and smattered with yellow and orange fruit; the ocean air, moist and salty to the skin, smells of fried fish and shrimp available from seafood shacks along the PCH; girls cross the road wearing short-shorts showing off toned beach legs, ponytails high on their heads, and fashionable flip-flops; and guys walk around shirtless with chests as hard as the surfboards they carry on their heads.

But this splendor comes with a weighty price tag. It's a far drive and a long day, especially when you spend it trolling down the beach lugging fifteen pounds of gear through thick sand. Malibu will exhaust your body. But, it's not the outside that will kill you in this beautiful little beach town, *a lovely place* with *a lovely face*. Rather, there's a beast inside, one that will slowly, but inevitably, break down your soul.

The Bubble: A rich, white (I'm not saying Malibu is prejudiced; I'm just saying that Matthew's Brazilian girlfriend Camila Alves is the darkest person on the beach), militarized zone (so it appears, with so many cops and all), which must at all costs be preserved. "A bubble so pure that the slightest drop of dust causes pandemonium," says Simon. Sound pleasant? Trust me, it's not.

The Malibu city cops give you your first indication that you are in danger if you spend too much time here. These protecting officers, given power by the residents, blanket the area in a far more oppressive fashion than even the LAPD do in Beverly Hills. For kicks, most days Simon and I play our unscientific "Count-the-Cops" game, and with one every few miles, we generally score over a dozen each day. "Code Blue in Malibu."

At the two grocery stores in town, three or four security guards are perma-stationed, and the City of Malibu is trying to contract the venerable Kenneth Starr (remember him from the Monica Lewinski days?) to work on the ironically titled "Britney Law" and come up with *more* laws for the city, specifically aimed at keeping paparazzi out (and fighting the First Amendment, which besides the freedom of speech also ensures the freedom of the press, which, yes, includes photographing public figures in public places). Starr has expressed interest in working on it "at no charge to the city." Thanks, man.

That, friends, is the Bu. Now meet the Malibu mafia.

★ ★ ★

It takes me an hour to get down to Little Point Dume/Hut Beach, where Matthew is. The route: park on the street, walk a half mile to the cliff top, amble the thorny path to the stairs, climb down hundreds of steps, traipse through soggy muck to sand, walk a half mile to where the ocean swells produce one of the best surf spots in southern California, wade through the rough waters of the treacherous "point of dume"…finally, arrive at the idyllic Hut Beach.

It is Saturday and Simon and I have been in the Bubble for a week now. Two hours ago, he and the other paps saw McC head down to the beach with his surfboard. Matthew took the gated path, which would have taken him about three minutes. Simon and the rest of the guys went in from the east, a slightly quicker route (forty-five minutes) than the one I took, but a $20 parking charge.

I sit on my beach blanket taking pictures of Matthew while he surfs. I also occasionally shoot Melissa Joan Hart, who happens to be nearby and is also watching Matthew so she doesn't notice me. (Melissa's pictures end up on the cover of *People* magazine.)

At first I am noticed by no one. I am unassuming, sitting with my camera tucked between my legs, which I pull up every once in a while to take a photograph. But eventually people react. Beachgoers, always female, walk by and comment: "You are the most disgusting form of a human I've ever seen"; "We hate you—leave our private beach"; "Get away from my umbrella—don't sit near me." I can see the confusion in their faces, though. I am tan and fit. I look good in my bikini—just like them, or their daughters. So why am I taking pictures like a paparazzi?

About one football field away, I see the other paps bunched together unobtrusively behind the boulders near the cliff's face. From that distance, they would be shooting Matthew with 300–500mm lenses. I know Simon is with them.

I watch as a massive group of people begins to gather and head toward the huddled photographers. When they get to them, commotion begins. Later, the video will show throwing sand, rocks, and fists; and throwing equipment and paparazzi into the dangerous surfing waters. Soon, "the Mob" chases the paparazzi away and everyone disappears down the beach.

Fifteen minutes more, and a rainfall of sand pours over me. I jump up quickly, shielding my camera.

"Get out of here," says an adult man who continues kicking sand at me.

"Please stop, please," I beg as I move away. "You'll ruin my camera."

He follows. "This is *our* beach. Leave."

"Look, I'm not bothering anyone." I speak calmly and politely, trying to diffuse the situation. He stops kicking.

"You're bothering *us*."

"I'm not bothering Matthew, which as you know, is why I'm here. I'll be leaving soon."

"Well, I'm the Beach Master and I want you to leave now."

"Seriously?" I say stifling a chuckle. Later I find out his name is Skylar Peak.

"Yes, I was voted in."

I laugh out loud. I don't want to rile him up, but honestly I can't help it.

I don't respond to anything more he says, but begin to gather my things. I have enough shots anyway.

Today, I will make several thousand dollars. That's why I am here. But, ultimately, I will not break even.

The next day, Sunday, I do not attend but hear it is equally vicious. Once the weekend's videos and pictures are released, local and national, celebrity and noncelebrity news is filled with the "Paparazzi vs. Surfer Turf War." Photos of the fights blanket the Internet as the media devours the salacious news story. Celebrity blog sites publish record numbers of viewer comments, though they seem to come mostly from the Malibu teenagers challenging the paps to a rematch. Both *Larry King Live* and the *Los Angeles Times* interview me.

The following Saturday, the twenty-eighth, the *L.A. Times* was there:

> *After hundreds of Internet threats and the mobilization of sheriff's deputies by air, land and sea, Saturday's much-anticipated revival of the paparazzi-surfer war in Malibu came down to this: One woman with a handwritten sign and an unflinching desire to make a point.*

Yep, that one woman was me. Me and my Sharpie-colored picket sign that read: *America's beaches should be free and accessible.* Don't get me wrong, I understood why many of them didn't like the paparazzi, but I couldn't stand by and watch this violence happen to the people I had come to see as my colleagues, especially when they had done nothing wrong but be there. In addition to the fact that paparazzi (and anyone for that matter) are legally allowed to take pictures of famous people in public places, it also infuriated me that the residents kept their *public* beach as inaccessible and private as possible. On top of that, most of the people on that beach were likely consumers (or had been at one point) of the very magazines and websites that bought our photos and published them. (I don't believe that not a single one of them had ever read *People* or PerezHilton.) All of it reeked of hypocrisy.

None of my peers joined me on the picket walk, but I could hardly blame them—most weren't Americans and couldn't afford to single themselves out with the law. Probably they didn't feel the personal disgust that I did with my countrymen either. Mostly, I imagine, their self-conceit was not as all-consuming as mine was.

Eventually a cop told me I had to leave. "But this is America. Aren't I allowed to protest?" I objected. He walkie-talkie'd his supervisor and then reported that he'd have to arrest me if I didn't go. "On what grounds?"

He checked again with his supervisor. "Inciting a riot." That was a joke since there was absolutely no mutinying anywhere. But, in the end, my "sign" was clearly not going to affect anything, and I didn't really feel like spending the night in jail having enough sleep issues as it was, so I turned back.

★ ★ ★

My contempt for the Maliboobians stayed with me for days afterward. I took it with me to CNN's studios where I was planning to photograph Christina Aguilera, a guest on *Larry King Live*. Besides myself and about thirty other paps and autograph seekers waiting for Christina was paparazzo Frank Opis Epstein, or "Opis," as he's started calling and photo-crediting himself.

Though Frank and I are both Americans—uncommon in this business—we are not friends. His tipsters come from stores like Gucci and Rolex because, as he told me the first time we met, "That's where I shop."

CNN sections off its exit area for the paparazzi. It is not a problem if we shoot, but we must stay behind the red rope. Frank and another pap, who I didn't know but was on crutches with a broken leg, stood by the section of the rope which had the most space around it. When I asked if I could squeeze in, they laughed, and to keep me out, locked their bodies together in a barricade. Just like in Malibu, I was blocked out.

I walked to the other side of the rope but still saw no available space from where to shoot. I returned to their side. When they saw me, they squeezed together again and planted their legs (and crutches) wide to take up more space. When I attempted to step in beside them, they moved their bodies sideways and shoved me. Wrath gaining momentum, I tried again, this time with my elbow. Then, as I remember it, Frank turned to face me, grabbed my camera, and pushed it toward me. I tripped backward but caught myself. With his hand, he continued pushing my camera into my face. Later, I won't recall whether he hit me with it or if it was just close, but either way, I felt like he was trying to make me fall or hit me with the lens. And, I panicked.

What occurred next was an instinctive reaction. I opened my mouth and bit into his hand, which was right there at my face. I didn't have to move to bite it.

And he didn't pull it away either, perhaps afraid he'd tear the skin, but I also didn't release my jaw right away. I actually was unable to. It was like I was watching the scene from above and couldn't move. Eventually, he had to jerk his hand away.

Frank never yelled. He didn't call security. He just calmly looked at me and said, "I *will* call the police."

I didn't respond and found a new spot as far back in the crowd as I could. For the remaining fifteen minutes of the Christina wait, I stared in a fog at the scene in front of me. Everything seemed to blur. I wasn't even sure what had happened anymore. I knew I'd bitten Frank, but how had it come to that?

I watched Frank. He acted as if nothing out of the ordinary had just happened, and even yelled, "Christina. Here!" when she came out. I didn't lift my camera. I had nothing left.

When I got home, two questions plagued me for the rest of the night: *Who am I?* and *How the hell did I become this way?* After the Frank incident, I felt as despicable as the Malibu residents whom I had judged. I knew I had reached the lowest point in my paparazzi tenure. (For f—k's sake, I bit someone!) Worse, I didn't know how I would ever find a way—much less the strength—to climb out of this situation. My career was probably ruined. But more importantly, I was ruined.

Chapter 19

B artlet called at daybreak. "Jennifer, why did you bite Frank Opis?" His voice actually sounded kind. Though he rarely acted with sensitivity, Bartlet knew I was losing it. He wasn't angry with me, but more alarmed.

"Because I thought he was going to break my camera, or hit me. And he pushed me. And I felted trapped," I said. "I think. I don't know. I can't remember." I could hear the defeat in my voice. I wished, desperately, to erase last night.

Bartlet told me that Frank went to Cedars-Sinai Medical Center—the hospital of the stars—for a tetanus shot (*Am I a dog?*), then filed a police report and got a restraining order against me.

I didn't have the energy to defend myself. "I'm taking the day off," I said and hung up.

I got back into bed and spooned Despondency and Despair. If I had somewhere to run, I would go, away from all this. Regardless of what Frank or I had done, my body couldn't take any more hate. The celebrities hated me, the paps hated me, the cops hated me, Malibu hated me. All rightfully so! I hated myself too.

If I could only call Frank and grovel and beg for his forgiveness. I was sorry. And not just sorry that I might get into trouble. Frank may be a stooge in my opinion, but I shouldn't have bitten him—*how had it come to that?*

My cup was empty, and I had nothing but that miserable pride of mine with which to combat the all-consuming hate; hate that was closing in on me from all sides. *That's* how it had come to that.

★ ★ ★

One week later, what little there was left of my relentless hubris sent me—alone again—to Little Point Dume. It was Independence Day. Like a bird fighting its reflection, slamming itself into a sliding glass window till it dies, I couldn't stop myself.

This day, there were only a few hecklers, and some were even kind. I shot exclusive bathing suit pictures of Matthew and Camila, the last before she had the baby, and I made a lot of money. But the cost to my self-respect was exorbitant. I was wronged, and I was angry about that, of course. But I was more angry at myself. The hecklers comments stung because, deep down, I knew they were true. *Why couldn't I have just let them have their beach? Who did I think I was?*

During my time on the beach, I began to wonder why I had been so hard on the residents, so full of disdain. The world often believes rich-America, like Malibu's citizens, is only concerned with greed and wealth retention. But I'm beginning to believe it's less about self-indulgence and more about fear. Sure, exclusivity is repugnant to the rest of us, but perhaps that wasn't what the beach fight was really about. These Malibu residents live in a bubble on a beautiful beach their ancestors stumbled across years ago. They love this place. It's where they socialize, exercise, network, and relieve their stress. Many of these people don't know what it's like to *not have*, and it scares the hell out of them. What would they do and where would they go without their pristine, quiet, beautiful beach? The crowded and noisy world outside is much less appealing, and although I want to tell them that on one hand, a lack of possessions actually produces a freedom like no other, on the other hand, they are right: to live without money in America is scary and, frankly, a life-threatening proposition. We have a very small social support net.

And I know all this firsthand: during my two years of travel before I moved to L.A., when all my belongings were strapped to my back, I experienced it. It was then, *out* of America, *away* from wealth, that for the first time in my life I felt real freedom—a joyous and liberating freedom where nothing tied me down. The enjoyment of people replaced the enjoyment of stuff; the love of others replaced the love of possessions. And that intimacy with my fellow man brought me a happiness that I'd never felt before.

But when I came back from my two years abroad, I was faced with another eye-opening experience: destitution. Although I'd paid thousands into our dole, I was ineligible to collect unemployment upon my return because I had quit my job by choice and left the country. Despite having a graduate degree, I couldn't find a job. In a matter of days, I moved from the top of Maslow's hierarchy of needs—self-actualization—to its bottom—food, shelter, and clothing.

So, I could see these residents' side of the story. The United States without money is frightening. Highs will always be met by lows. And without help, most can't wait out the lows, especially if we're doing our beloved art, starting new businesses, or pursuing dreams. My heart often longs to go back to that place of freedom again: a place surrounded by nothing but love. But that's nearly impossible to do here, even for the richest of us.

So as I stood there on the beach in Malibu, my rage turned to pity, even empathy. I didn't hate them anymore—not even Skylar, the Beach Master. I understood them. And, as much as I didn't want to admit it, I was one of them. Protective and possessive, but worst of all, prideful, we were all the same.

★ ★ ★

For now, I shove my professional woes under the rug and refocus on my real priority: finding a man. And I do: BMG8865. He's cute, a little dorky (which I like), and has classic features. He wears glasses (Mom thinks I should nix him for that), his hair is longish and curls on the ends, he's twenty-one and fit.

I find him through Xytex, a sperm bank in Atlanta, which—quite brilliantly—includes adult photos of their donors. Finally, someone figured out the one thing mamas like me really need to know when they're picking out baby daddy sperm: what does he look like? The office staff is informative as well: "8865 has the best skin...7430 is getting a little chubby." They tell me that most of the donors are college students, and as the bank happens to be in my college town, I bet many of its boys hail from my alma mater. This makes me smile.

And so I get a doc...in L.A., not Mexico, thankfully. She's running tests on my tubes and my hormones and everything else that accepts sperm. Just to make sure that when I'm ready—if it comes to that—it'll take.

As a baby starts seeming more plausible and more near, I am again plagued by my underlying concern: *How do you tell a child that there isn't really a father. There's only* A Sperm? *And what will he tell his friends?* I know some kids have two mamas, and some have two papas. Will the next generation have sperm donors and mamas, and egg donors and papas? Shit, growing up is hard enough.

But for now, the tight belt which has been cinching my chest has been loosened a notch. No, this is not how I dreamed of having a family. Nobody dreams of this. But at least, maybe now, I *can* have a family...even if it's not the structure I thought it would be. At thirty-seven, I'm learning that life is often not how I thought it would be.

And for the first time in years, I realize that maybe that's OK.

★ ★ ★

Growing up in the '80s meant growing up with the Brat Pack—*Sixteen Candles, The Breakfast Club, St. Elmo's Fire*. So when I read that '80s star Molly Ringwald had moved to L.A., I was ecstatic—I loved Molly Ringwald.

Spurred by a starring role in the TV show *The Secret Life of the American Teenager*, Molly relocated her family from Europe to Venice Beach and rented a modest home a few blocks off Abbot Kinney.

For three Saturdays in a row, I'm on her. It's a commitment: not only is Molly a long drive, but working her also means I have to pass up all the other celebs who are typically out and about on Saturdays. But I know she's worth it. Magazine editors are around my age, and they'll remember Molly. She'll sell.

In many beach neighborhoods, residents like Molly park in a communal alley behind their houses and can exit on one of two streets enclosing their blocks. So in order to watch both of Molly's exits—along with a potential *walk* out the front door toward the shops and beach—I need to sit in the opposing alley, uncomfortably close to her house. It's convenient to be a woman in these situations: people may find my car a nuisance, but they don't see me as menacing, as they might if a guy parked similarly. I can leave my windows and visors down, even unzip my pants if my skinny jeans are too tight, and no one's going to complain.

The first Saturday, I sit all day long with no signs of life. I don't yet know Molly's car and her garage door is down, so it's impossible to tell if she's home. I try again the next Saturday, and this time I see her. I haven't seen a picture of Molly since her old movies, and I'm pleased to report she's just as I remember she looked as little Samantha in *Sixteen Candles*: precious. She looks sick, though—hunching over as she gets out of her car, coming *home* at around 9:30 a.m. (I must have missed the departure.) She goes inside, not to resurface for the rest of the day. I get a couple of shots, but they aren't particularly becoming so I don't send them in. I want Molly's first experience back in the States to be fabulous, and I won't have the tabloids making fun of her with my help.

Finally, the third Saturday, I get to know my little redhead. And Molly Ringwald, the teenager I so wanted to be, lived up to my dreams. In her back alley drive, Molly comes out with a small video camera, and her husband and daughter come out with a bicycle-built-for-two. Molly laughs as she takes pictures of her family. My smile is bittersweet as I take pictures of a family life I so covet. Then, as if that weren't enough, the three drive to Santa Monica and buy Molly a bike. Hidden behind my tint, I watch and photograph as she test drives bikes in the shop's back parking lot until she finally settles on one—frilly and pink with a basket and horn.

Besides today, I've only ever had one other "I wish I were them" day in my life as a pap—the day I followed Justin Chambers (*Grey's Anatomy*'s Dr. Alex Karev) and his wife and their five kids as they adopted a new puppy.

Truthfully, I don't covet the life of celebrities. I don't covet their money, or their fame, or their power. (OK, maybe I covet their clothes.) Really, I want just one thing, and you know what that is. And off the top of my head, I can think of more than a dozen stars who would surely give up all their money, all their fame, and all their power for the exact same thing. We are all just human.

Chapter 20

Several weeks and several magazine sales later, I can see a break in the clouds. The Malibu thunderstorm is over, hopefully Frank Opis has "gone away," and I have a baby plan in the works. Sunshine is still in the distance, but it is bright. And as I reflect back—and ahead—I realize that although life doesn't promise me happiness, in America I'm free to pursue it. And that's big.

I put in an informal resignation with CXN. Since I'm freelance, there's no real resigning, but it's time to go. I feel sure Bartlet is going to be sad to see me leave; I am a top earner for CXN and Bartlet is a businessman. It hurts when all I get is an email: "No problem. Bring your Nextel to the office tomorrow."

It makes sense to go, not only to feel valued and appreciated, which I never have with CXN's management, but also for financial reasons. Because my reputation has grown so much in the last eighteen months—which I didn't fully realize until I started listening to offers—I find I can command 70 percent rather than the standard 60 percent, of picture sales. Doing the math, going from 60 to 70 actually means a 17 percent increase in overall pay. (Simon could never understand how that worked even when I did the fractions for him.)

After positive interviews with International PIX (iPIX) and its American owners, Will and Jimmy, I accept an offer with their agency.

Jimmy tells me later that the head of Just Jared, the largest inside industry blog, congratulated them on my hire: "You scored a coup getting Jennifer." Finally I comprehend—not conceitedly, just factually—that in a short time I have become one of the best paparazzi in Los Angeles and by default the world. And it all started less than two years ago when Paris Hilton crossed my path, and I "just knew" that this was what I was supposed to be doing.

★ ★ ★

I think if you're a female over the age of twenty and you get pregnant, you can't claim it's "completely unplanned" if you're using no birth control or using only a half-ass birth control method. Conversely, if you're thirty-seven and haven't had a boyfriend for years, it makes perfect sense to think getting knocked up is about as likely as sighting a pink panther.

So when I slept with Bo, a pot-smoking Canadian backpacker who lived in a Hollywood hostel, the ludicrous thought of getting pregnant didn't cross my mind, at least not right off. The morning after, I was concerned only that Bo—who told me immediately *after* sex that he was "probably" a sex addict, that he was into multiple-partnered sex, and that he was looking for an open relationship—might have given me any number of STDs. Fabulous. I sure know how to pick 'em.

I had met Bo at the Starbucks on Western Ave. It had been my ritual this summer to start off my mornings there. Bo asked me out, and one afternoon we went whale watching in Long Beach together. It was fun to hang out with someone who knew so little about Hollywood culture. A couple of times we went "dutch" to dinner.

It was clear right off that Bo had "issues," as the dating world likes to say, so we probably weren't meant to be together for the long term, but he kissed me on the whale-watching boat, and it felt nice, so I kept seeing him. A few dates later, the kissing turned into groping, and all of a sudden it turned into *way* more than I'd planned for.

I didn't stop it, but I didn't exactly enjoy it. I just lay there thinking, *Ummmm, THIS is what I've been missing out on for the last [insert: very large number of] years?*

To make matters worse, when our lackluster lovemaking was over, *he* started to get upset. About what, I do not remember. Never did I want someone gone more than *right then*. But we were in my bed, of course, since he lived in a bunk-bedroom with roommates. After twenty minutes, the longest amount of post-coital cuddling I could muster, I told him he had to go.

The next day I called to ask Bo to get tested, as testing myself right then would have been pointless because one of the worst STDs, AIDS, would take three to six months to show up on my test. I explained awkwardly, "I've never had casual sex. I've only slept with [insert: very small number of] boyfriends in my life…I'm sure you're fine, but I'm just scared."

The more I asked, the more angry and upset he became. "You don't trust me…You don't like me…What do you think is wrong with me?" Eventually, he hung up on me. Once again, fabulous.

Fortunately, he must have realized I really was just doing this for my own protection, because the day after that, Bo texted to say he would get tested. A few days later, he called. His test results had come back clean. Phew, I was in the clear.

Then, I ovulated. Since I've been considering a sperm donor, my doctor suggested that I monitor my ovulation cycle. For the last three months, I'd been testing my cycle. For the first two I had come up with nothing—no surge in hormones, no release of egg. My period would come, but the stick never changed. Something was wrong.

This month I'd bought four kits—twenty-eight sticks—and peed on one every single day. To my relief, about nine or ten days before my period was due (and four or five days after I'd had sex), the stick began to show a surge in hormones. According to the kit instructions, "the line" still wasn't dark enough to say I was ovulating, but at least it was turning color. Phew, I had some hormones left.

Eight days after Bo and I had sex, I went in for a pre-scheduled OB-GYN visit and told my doctor of my ovulation woes. "Oh, you have a short luteal phase," she explained, and I wondered why she didn't mention that possibility before. I had no idea what a luteal phase was, so looked it up when I got home. The second half of a woman's cycle, after ovulation, is the luteal phase, and if that time period is too short (the average length is fourteen days), then an embryo may have difficulty implanting. A luteal phase under ten days will generally not support pregnancy. The doctor also said, "We'll need to do several more tests before we try insemination, and may need to supplement with hormones." Fabulous, again.

★ ★ ★

Day 23. When they inseminate you, or if you're trying to "get pregnant fast" (by reading *Get Pregnant Fast* books), you wait till you ovulate and then have sex/squirt sperm. It seems that once your egg is loose—and she lives for two days—then the sperm, who live for up to three, have the best chance of swimming to meet her. Nobody seems to mention that having sex, letting the sperm swim aimlessly around in there, and *then* releasing the egg, also might work.

Cursed with an extremely short cycle (apparently a luteal phase issue), I get my period every twenty-three to twenty-five days. Today is Day 23 from my last period, and I did not get my period this morning. Not necessarily alarming, but JoDeane did tell me yesterday that her Internet research produced some articles saying that sperm live for up to two or three days *or more.*

Now it seems that although it's *very* unlikely I'm pregnant (I'm *sure* I ovulated four to five days after sex with Bo, and not before), it's not impossible.

★ ★ ★

Day 24. Today, instead of my period, I receive a letter from the LAPD. Signed by a "Detective Gonzalez," it asks me to call a number because the detective wants "to talk." It only gives a reference number and does not specify what the topic is. Bartlet (who I still talk to most every day) says it is obviously about the bite I gave Frank weeks ago, and if I ignore it, it will go away: "The LAPD have much bigger battles to fight than ones between two paparazzi," he says.

Not getting my period on Day 24 isn't completely unusual. Still, I don't "feel" like I'm about to get my period. Today, I feel nothing, except for an odd sense of…something.

Are you there, God? It's me, Jennifer. Where is my period?

★ ★ ★

Day 25. My period did not come this morning, and all of a sudden I have a strange sense "down there." I didn't think you could feel if you were pregnant, at least not this soon.

Around one, Claudia Nextels me. She knew I'd slept with Bo, and rumors were obviously spreading that there was an off chance I was pregnant. "Buy a pregnancy test and meet me on Robertson."

"I'm not officially late till tomorrow. I'll do it then."

"I'm gonna come get you, and we'll go to Rite Aid together if you won't go yourself."

"Fine," I say, mildly irritated. I'm not ready to deal with "results"— good or bad. Especially since, in this case, I don't even know what *good* or *bad* would be.

An hour later, after a stop at the drugstore, I arrive before Claudia at Cuvée on Robertson. I order my usual turkey and Gouda sandwich and sit down to wait. When she walks in, she shuffles me immediately toward the restroom. Right then, her Nextel goes off. It's J.R. with a Lindsay tip.

"Damn. I gotta go."

"No problem."

"You can do this without me."

"Right."

She rolls her eyes. "You wanna come?" she says, offering to share the Lohan tip.

"For sure, no. I wanna sit right here and eat. I'll call you later."

As I eat lunch, a tornado swirls through my head: *Besides eleven days ago, it has been [insert: a ridiculous number of] years since I've had sex. Bo and I slept together only once. He'd have to have had super-sperm for one to have survived till I ovulated. Besides, he's a heavy pot smoker—and marijuana kills them. How many could have been viable? I was starting to like BMG8865 and his curls.*

Regardless, I know I'm pregnant. I can feel it. Still, I don't take the test.

After lunch, Claudia hooks me up with the massive Lindsay follow, the one I didn't want to join in the first place. About five minutes later, we both lose it, quite intentionally.

"I'm done with the day," I beep. "Going home. Gonna happy hour with the girls."

"I'm ringing you first thing in the morning," Claudia responds before signing off.

JoDeane calls as I work my way east. She tells me that I'm not pregnant, but if I am, it's supposed to be, and "don't even think about" getting out of doing the pregnancy test tonight.

Georgia, Amy, and Jo are all there when I get to my apartment. "Let's go to Figaro!" I say.

"Let's do the test," Jo instructs.

"Oh, come on. I promise I'll do it after happy hour," I say hoping for a compromise as Jo pulls me into the bathroom.

"It's just a formality now," I inform her.

I pee. She yanks the stick out of my hand. I wash my face. She stares at the stick for forty-five seconds, then looks up at me.

"You're pregnant."

"I know."

Tears start immediately. But only for a minute, while JoDeane hugs me. She tells me that everything's gonna be OK, and that it is good that I am fertile and healthy. "It's supposed to be," she keeps saying.

I can tell when Amy and Georgia hear because all of sudden their conversation quits. They run in and stand at the bathroom door and stare.

Eventually, Amy says, "Congratulations!" and that makes us all laugh.

"Let's go to Fig," I say. "I need a drink…or at least some crème brûlée."

For the next two hours, we sit at a sidewalk table at our local haunt and talk about the fact that *I'm gonna have a baby*! Everybody knows it's what I've wanted for the last five years. I can't say I'm happy or sad at this moment. I'm just numb.

"I could have a miscarriage. Lots of people do," I tell them.

But I know I won't.

Georgia says what's on everyone's mind: "Let's not tell him. We don't want him involved." Then Amy adds, "And whatever you do, don't include this in your memoir because he'll read it and show up at your doorstep and you'll have to kill him!" Oops, too late.

★ ★ ★

Two days after finding out I'm pregnant, I go over to Adrian's house.

Sleep teased me the night before. It circled my body, laughing, but refused to land. The "feeling" in my groin had intensified, and with it anxiety. JoDeane, a nurse, says the mass of cells, which will form the fetus, is implanting into my uterus and some women can feel it early on. To me, it's a constant sensation somewhat like a tightening clamp in my pelvic area.

I get to his house around 9:15 a.m. It's a Saturday. I walk from the street through his yard and up to the front door, nervously, like I'm trespassing. Though I am not; he has told me to come.

We bumped into each other at San-Sui, a sushi restaurant in Los Feliz a few nights before. Georgia saw him first and nudged me. I turned and smiled. He came over to say hello. I stood and we hugged. We didn't have much to talk about, so the conversation quickly turned to our common ground.

"You never did that ride-along interview you promised. Please don't put me in your doc," I politely ordered.

"Ah, come on. You're already in it. We need you. It'll be great for you anyway."

"In what way? I have no interest in being in the movies. We had a deal. I spent three hours helping you on your documentary, and in exchange you agreed to a ride-along so I could make money. Your pictures from that day never sold by the way."

We parted, sat at nearby tables, and ate our respective dinners. He finished first, and on his way out said, "Call me. I'll do the ride-along."

"I don't have your number."

"Oh," he said, like he was surprised. "Well then, just come by. How 'bout Saturday?"

I only stared at him.

"OK? Saturday? See you then?"

"Sure."

When he left, Georgia grabbed my wrist in urgency. "*No way* you don't go to his house Saturday morning." No matter the premise, Georgia knew: you do *not* pass up an invitation to a celebrity's house. *No way.*

★ ★ ★

So it's Saturday, and I'm knocking on Adrian's door. I shake a bit from nerves and a bit from no sleep. I try to calm myself with deep breathing—I don't want him to think he impresses me. I peek in the window and see a bohemian den filled with strange antiques, musical instruments, and Buddha-like statues. His car is in the drive—he must be home.

After about five minutes with no answer, I take out a scrap of paper from my purse and scribble a note which basically calls him a flake and tells him, again, not to use me in his documentary.

As I'm figuring out where to leave the note, the door swings open.

"Hi," a girl in a bathing suit and 1970s velour cover-up says.

"Uh, hi. I'm just here…to pick up…Adrian," I stammer.

"Oh, you're the photographer," she says cheerily.

Wow. She knew I was coming. "Yes. I'm Jennifer," I say feeling a little more confident.

"I'm Robyn, Adrian's roommate," she offers with an extended hand. "Adrian's still sleeping, but I'll go wake him up. Does he have your number?"

"I'm not sure." I scribble down my number for him. *Once again.*

She doesn't invite me in, and I feel awkward standing on the stoop. I return to my car and consider leaving—I doubt Adrian will wake up for me—but just then, my phone rings. A number pops up. (An *actual* number, not an unlisted one.)

"Hello?" I answer.

"I'm just getting up."

"Adrian?" (Like everyone should recognize his voice.)

"Yeah, yeah, it's me. So, we're supposed to do that ride-along, yeah?" He has a sleepy voice, but it's upbeat.

"Well, you said for me to come get you," I respond self-consciously.

"I'm just getting up. You wanna come in? Why don't you come in?"

I walk back to the door. After one knock, he answers. He's wearing a T-shirt and blue boxers, and he's hotter than I remember him ever being. He stands in the doorframe with the door wide open, smiling. I fight my eyes in their downward pull and try to act like this is normal—*Adrian Grenier in his underwear.* I shake like the a.c. window unit in my apartment.

"Come in," he says as he escorts me through the den and into his kitchen where a housekeeper is cleaning dishes and Robyn is preparing a basket of food. Robyn's a natural host and asks me about my job and myself. Adrian watches us, not saying much, just smirking, clearly thrilled with my discomfort.

"You want to go get breakfast?" he suggests.

"Sure. But that doesn't get you out of your ride-along."

I think Adrian believes that I want to do a ride-along so that I can hang out with him and therefore if we go to breakfast, that will suffice. I think I want to do a ride-along so that I can make money off him. At this point, I'm not sure who's right.

"A ride-along will be so boring. Let's do something else," he tries to persuade me. "I know. Why don't we go for a swim? You wanna swim? I have a saltwater pool and Hilda can make us breakfast here. Do you want an egg sandwich?"

Hilda looks up and nods. A saltwater pool and full-serve brekky are the kind of mornings I love. "That sounds fun." I agree.

I keep a bathing suit in the car and walk out to get it. I inhale and exhale slowly. If only I could bang the side of my head and make my rattles stop. I quickly text Georgia: *I'm about to go swimming with Adrian!!!*

He's in his suit when I get back. "You can change at the pool house," he says, and he leads me out the back of the house and up some stairs. Turkish-style platforms and cushions are arranged in several seating areas around a large pool. The pool house has been converted into another roommate area (a la *Entourage*, there are apparently four people who live in the house), and I change inside. I walk out wearing only my new purple bikini, which I think looks pretty good.

With a fancy dive off the board, Adrian gets wet. I follow feet-first. The water is crisp but slightly heated, and it doesn't alarm my sensitive skin. I immerse under it, open my eyes, and blow bubbles. The salt water relaxes and cleans me. I love pools. I'd give anything to use Adrian's for the rest of the summer, photos or not.

He gets out first and sits on the side. Hilda brings us egg sandwiches, and we talk as we eat. I tell him more about my memoir (which he's known about), and he tells me more about his documentary. He suggests several times that instead of taking pictures of him, we work together on something more fruitful. "We could do something productive for each other," he says.

"Like what?" I question. This ride-along date has taken one year to materialize, so I'm skeptical.

Adrian responds by saying that when his documentary comes out, I should help him promote it, thereby promoting myself. And the book.

I tell him, again, that I don't want to be famous. Again, he doesn't understand.

Since we're talking, I can stare at him without it being weird, and I do. Adrian's eyes are huge and almost black, and his lashes tangle about them. His mouth curls asymmetrically like any beauty mark would. And his body is lanky, just my type. But I find, surprisingly, I don't lust for him. Our conversation is combative, and we talk over one another trying to one-up the other's accomplishments. He keeps his phone by his side and texts constantly. When we talk, his eyes don't look past me, but his mind does. Adrian is charming and charismatic, but he never *engages* me, never makes me feel like David Beckham did—like he wants to be in no other place than right here, right now, with me.

We dry off in silence, and my nerves return. "I wasted two hours and have no pictures to show for it." The words come out unfortunately whiney.

"You're welcome to take pictures, but they'll look like anybody's Facebook page and nobody'll buy them."

I know he's right, but then I also want *proof* of our swim. "I'll take some to use for my book," I say.

He gets in again, for me, and I take a half dozen pictures and one video with my point-and-shoot that's always in my purse.

Dripping wet, he gets out, grabs a towel, and nuzzles up close to me to look at the shots. He tells me to delete a couple of them, but it's a new camera and honestly I don't know how to. "They're fine," I say. "We'll just leave them."

"No." He's laughing and tries to grab the camera.

"They're fine," I say again, giggling. He wraps his half-wet body around my half-naked one and nudges me into his chest. Our four hands jumble together on the small camera. His body practically engulfs mine. After a long time, he finds the delete button, but just as he's about to push it, I yank the camera away. I like him here. He holds on and with our bodies fully entwined, we wrestle.

Eventually, I get shy about our physical proximity and pull away. He takes the camera and deletes the two pictures I'm certain he cares nothing about.

I follow him inside to change. He continues upstairs, and I can hear him singing. I feel pretty sure there's an open invite to see what's up there. But if Adrian wants me, he's gonna have to ask me. Whether it's because I'm too insecure or because I like to be pursued, I stay downstairs and change back into my clothes.

As we leave the house together, he grabs a watermelon and a guitar. He's apparently going to the beach.

"Those are good props. They'll make a salable picture," I note.

He poses without complaint, strumming the guitar gently as he leans on the back of his car, a silver Prius just like mine.

"You should come to this party I'm having tonight," I suggest. "It's my roommate's birthday."

"We aren't really friends. How can I come to your party?" His response is bordering on rude, but Adrian's human like me, so I forgive him and shrug.

Then he says. "Well, we're even now, right? You have your shots. We're even?"

"Whatever," I mumble and head toward my car before he moves toward his. As always, I'm careful not to be the last one standing.

He drives away first. As he passes my car, he leans his head out the window and says with a softer expression and his trademark smile, "Hey, maybe *we* should pull a Britney—and date?" Then he drives on without waiting for a response.

And with that, my friends, I do believe Adrian Grenier almost asked me out…!

Chapter 21

*A*m I really gonna have a baby? It seems impossible. All the worry, all the planning, then all of a sudden, I'm *just pregnant*. And I know, for me, it's better this way. I'm an obsessive planner, but I handle change just fine. Now, there's no obsession. There's no planning. I'm just pregnant.

My spirit and intuition know nothing will happen to the baby, but practically speaking, my mind tells me miscarriages are common, especially at my age. I use that as my excuse for not telling my family—or Bo—while I figure out a plan. In the meantime, I quit the pot that I've smoked many nights over the last few years as a sleep aid, and, to my surprise and delight, I find sleep becomes less antagonistic overall.

My body's changing too. Besides looking rested, in just two weeks my breasts are rounder and fuller, and my face has a warm tint. I look at my reflection in the mirror and think, *Wow, she's pretty*. And while I'm scared and lonely and not sure how any of this is gonna go, I have to admit that it makes me happy when I think of the ever-present "feeling" inside of me. For the first time in my life, I am not striving for something else, not looking around the corner for the next thing to love or to experience. I am content with me.

Bo calls. I make it clear that we are, from here on out, completely platonic. (I already have enough drama in my life!) And he agrees. He keeps calling, though, and I consent to join him at happy hour for one purpose: information gathering. The more I know about him, the better I can make my decision: to tell or not to tell.

We meet at Fig and grab an outside table. I stare at him like I imagine one would stare at a loved one in his last hour. He doesn't notice as I drink in every feature—his wide smile and perfect nose (mine sucks; hope the baby gets his), flawless skin (ditto), curly brown hair, dark eyes, a few errant moles. His body is not too large but not too small, and pretty hairless. I study his gait when he gets up to use the restroom, and I etch his expressions into my memory. I keep the drinks date going longer than it normally would, asking him questions—mostly about his relationships—to get a sense of how he might bond with a potential child. He begins with, "Sex will never control me," then tumbles out a twenty-minute tirade (which several other diners also get to hear) from a deep part within his heart. It's sad and painful and honest, and it brings up serious love and attachment issues. When he's done, I can only think to reach across the table, hold his hand and tell him *I'm so sorry.*

Bo mentions that he'll be leaving for Canada soon. When I ask him what he will do once he gets home, he says, "Make a little money, then hit the road again. I'm a wanderer, a wanderer full of wanderlust. That's just the way I gotta be."

And I realize that's what it is about Bo that I'm drawn to. In this way we are a lot alike. Of course I'm ready to settle down now and give my baby a good, stable life. That might not be Bo's cup of tea.

Though that's not what bothers me. It's the other stuff I can't shake. Bo's troubles consume me for days afterward. I believe his heart is good, but it's clear to me that he's affected by a tremendous amount of hurt, which he hasn't dealt with. As a soon-to-be mother, I am having serious doubts regarding Bo's ability to have a healthy relationship with a son or daughter—at least in the way that I would want for my child.

The few friends who know I'm pregnant all say the same thing: "You're not gonna tell him, are you?" Everyone instinctually seems to know that including him in my life—and more importantly, in my child's life— would be a bad idea. Aaron is the most adamant: "Mate, I'll break his legs first. Yours second." Only little Elif back in Turkey has a different opinion: "You must tell him. I'm sure his family is lovely people. They will be a big help for you. You may not want him, but you want his mother."

And initially, I'm inclined to agree with Elif. Besides not telling a man that he has a child—can you even do that? Not only is there the obvious ethical dilemma, but what are the legal implications? Georgia is on it: "The law's often on the mother's side," she says after a bit of research, "especially in California. The father doesn't always have a legal right to know."

"How can that be?"

"Think about it. Some fathers may be a danger to their children. Maybe not Bo. Or maybe Bo. Or, what if a mother doesn't even know who the father is? I'm sure that happens."

I'm under no misconceptions that involving Bo in raising my kid would be miserable for me. It would be like having a second child, but one I didn't want. And his lifestyle and "issues"—would they harm the child? Perhaps not physically, but possibly emotionally, mentally, spiritually? If my mama-instinct truly believed that Bo would not make a healthy father, could bringing him into our lives be worse for a baby than not having a dad at all?

Georgia and I continue to discuss the morality of my dilemma. "If a man is willing to 'put out' anywhere, as Bo apparently is, maybe he doesn't deserve to know," Georgia muses.

"OK, let's just say I don't tell him. What do I say to my child? 'I didn't tell your dad that you existed because I thought he and his issues were a potential danger to you?'" While I don't love this idea, it occurs to me that it does sound better than "Your dad was A Sperm."

"You're thinking too much, Jen. Meryl Streep did a fine job in *Mamma Mia*."

I'm still not quite convinced.

★ ★ ★

The next day, September 2, Skylar Peak, the Malibu Beach Master who lead the surfer-pap turf war, was charged.

Two Malibu Men Charged with Attacking Paparazzo

Officials on Tuesday said they charged two Malibu men for attacking a paparazzo who was snapping pictures of actor Matthew McConaughey as he was surfing in the Pacific Ocean in June. *[abridged]*

Skylar Martin Peak, 24, and Philip John Hildebrand, 30, both of Malibu, were each charged with one misdemeanor count of battery for attacking Richid Altmbareckouhammou, who was working for a French news agency, the Los Angeles District Attorney's office said.

Officials claim the two men threw Altmbareckouhammou into the water from where he was taking pictures on the beach. Each faces up to six months in jail and a $2,000 fine.

(Reporting by Bob Tourtellotte; editing by Jill Serjeant and Eric Walsh)

It took two months for charges to be filed, and I hear it was only because of pressure from the paparazzo's attorney. And while I seriously doubt it will change the way Malibu views the paparazzi, rectification is nice. And who knows, maybe someday justice will be served.[16]

Would the paper mention me soon too? I get a second note from Detective Gonzalez asking me to contact him. This time I check with Georgia, who specializes in contract law for a uniform company, but who is, these days, getting familiar with criminal law as well as family law, thanks to me. She agrees with CXN. "Ignore it. If they want you, they can get a warrant."

---

16. Two years later, Skylar does go to trial. His renowned defense attorney, Harland Braun, who has also represented many of Hollywood's other "unbecoming," was initially able to get the trial postponed, but eventually Skylar did face his peers. The trial ended in a hung jury, and a Malibu judge chose not to retry it. According to the papers, Skylar was lauded as a local hero, vocally supported by many, including his prosecuting attorney.

My initial guilt, though, has turned to anger, and my pride has resurfaced. I shouldn't have bitten Frank Opis, true, but I only did it because his nasty pap hand was by my mouth when he was pushing my camera into my face!

It's not the L.A. courts I fear. If Paris can handle community service or a few days in county jail, I can too. It's the threat of a civil suit that looms over me like the devil's cape—that's the one that would force me to get a lawyer and drain my money as fast as a tap at a UCLA keg party. And then what would be left for my baby's future?

Besides my legal woes, all I think about is this "feeling" growing inside me. I leave work early to go to the doctor's office down the street from my house. The clinic is used to walk-ins in this neighborhood, and I'm seen almost immediately. I lie on the table and pull up my shirt. The doctor squirts cold goo on my stomach and with a flat metal instrument irons my belly. Live moving pictures appear on the ultrasound machine next to the table. There are a lot of lines, then a noticeable dark dot. "That's it," he says. "It's not much more than a mass of cells right now."

Then we hear a heartbeat. The heartbeat of my baby. A gentle *lub-dub, lub-dub*. I've never heard a more beautiful sound. This is what I've been waiting for all my life.

He prints out a still shot for me. He asks when my last period was and counts my pregnancy weeks from that. Though I conceived four weeks ago, for purposes of medical counting, I'm considered six weeks pregnant.

I walk home with my photo. One black dot. Add a little food and water plus some kind of mysterious "energy" (God) and in nine months out pops a separate human being with all the complexities of *us*—something brand-new and spiritually distinct with a personality and feelings and a moral code and an ethereal heart that loves and hates and breaks. All this from a tiny bit of DNA—a microscopic sperm and egg from a man and a woman.

This is undeniably a miracle.

★ ★ ★

Less than two weeks later, eight weeks into the pregnancy, my elation has waned. There is no time to daydream about baby because all I can think about is vomiting. What feels like some awful concoction of prescription drugs—but is just mega-doses of hormones—swirls around in my head like someone turned the blender on "mutilate." Nauseous, fuzzy-eyed, and exhausted, I do not have morning sickness but all-day-long sickness. Each day, until about 3 p.m., watermelon and saltines are the only foods I can stomach. After that, I *must* have a hamburger or another large piece of red meat. My reaction and motor skills are so slow right now that I'm frightened to drive. I've hit at least five curbs and had two minor car accidents in the last week.

For the past five days, *if* I can get out of bed and go to work, I crawl to the back of my car when I get there, lie down, and float in and out of consciousness. I keep the window cracked hoping that I'll *hear* my doorstep leave, but also hoping that I won't; I don't want to move. The idea that I'm going to vomit consumes my thoughts, hour after hour, day after day, although I never actually puke. When I get home—well before six—I go directly to the sofa or the bed and don't move again.

It's a lucky thing my new company doesn't know how many sets I usually turn in, and a relief Jimmy, my new boss, doesn't call every morning like Bartlet did. Bartlet would be on to me by now for sure. I had hoped to work extra hard these first few months of pregnancy, figuring I'd probably have only about six before I must quit papping. (I will *not* be a giant preggers pap running backward down Robertson shooting Adrian Grenier or Eva Longoria while TMZ videographers record the ludicrous scene.) But now, I've barely shot a competent set in the last two weeks and that means much needed baby funds are dropping.

Money and child support (or lack thereof) and Frank Opis are stressors that I know I have to face, but right now I'm too sick to care about anything but walking straight—perhaps God's creative way of keeping my frazzled thoughts from damaging my baby.

It is a bizarre pairing: Zac Efron is with Tori Spelling and Tori's son Liam. Zac is in his Audi, and he won't let me have the shot. When they stop for gas, Zac gets out and finally gives it up after I beg him. But my camera is put together all wrong and it won't focus. Then I can't see through the lens, so I get nothing.

I wake up sweating and anxious. A nightmare.

Back when I first started papping, I'd have dreams that involved celebrities almost every night. I was friends with Madonna, and we'd hang out. Jessica Simpson got in a car accident, but I was there to rescue her. And take her picture. The dreams were unsettling and would disrupt my sleep.

As dreams often do, last night's formed from current events. During the week, I'd worked Tori with no luck. Then last night, I pulled an evening doorstep on Zac. I despise working nights, but I hadn't made it out before noon in the past ten days so felt compelled to do *something*.

We knew Zac was around, but these days he wasn't giving it up. It had been nine months since he'd hit the scene, so this came as no surprise. He didn't need us anymore. He was huge enough—at least for now—and for now, he'd had enough. "The tide recedes with the young lad," Simon warned.

But I knew Zac liked me—at least, at one time he did—and perhaps one-on-one with me, I might get him to cave. After all, when a boy is in his sexual prime, females have magical powers.

I figured I'd get Zac to myself, and I did. No other paps. He came out in his black Audi at about eight-thirty with Vanessa in the passenger seat. Even at night, he did a pap-check, driving down a lonely road adjacent to his apartment complex. He sussed me out immediately. But it didn't matter. I wasn't going to hide. I rolled down my window and turned my interior car light on so that he could see me.

As I opened my mouth to say, "Can I just have a couple shots tonight, Zac?" the words dissolved. His smile, when he looked at me, heated my heart and it skipped a beat. I took a breath and admitted, "I've missed you." And I meant it in a-bit-more-motherly-and-less-of-Mrs.-Robinson-way than I had in the past.

"Hey you," he said and laughed good-naturedly.

The last time I'd worked Zac, two months ago, I had waited outside his apartment complex one afternoon. When he'd pulled out in his Audi, I'd shown myself and he'd pulled over to say hello.

"You going anywhere interesting?" I'd inquired.

"Just the studio. I'm super excited."

"Oh, yeah? Why's that?"

"I'm gonna be on the cover of *Allure*. Isn't that cool?"

"That's awesome. Good for you." I had been genuinely excited for him. Zac's got a heart that exudes humbleness, and I don't know how you couldn't like him.

"You wouldn't have time to stop for gas on the way, would you? Or coffee? My treat." (I had asked this because I knew there would have been no shot at the studio.)

"Aw, sorry. Really, I don't."

"No worries. Catch you next time. And congratulations."

I hadn't gotten a shot that day, but as we'd waved good-bye, I'd thought, *Zac's gonna be a big, big star, and I'm glad.*

Since then, a lot has changed in Zac's relationship with the paps. Daily, he challenges them to testosterone-filled car races if they try to follow. And if he can't outrun a follow, he just covers. Zac never needs to race the paps—he's an outstanding "coverer"—but he's young and it's fun and that's why he keeps doing it.

Back to last night. The car light beaming on the head of an older woman looking for his picture wasn't what Zac expected.

"I haven't seen you in a while," he continued.

"You'll give me a couple of shots tonight, won't you? It's just me on you."

"You know, I can't. You might be my favorite paparazzi, but I just can't."

"Why not? For me? Only me. For old time's sake."

"It's out of principle. I can't do it anymore."

I reminded him that once he had promised me that if I asked, he'd always give me a shot.

"It's not like that anymore," he responded.

And I understood. If he really didn't want paparazzi, he had to set precedence. If he caved to me, he'd pay for it with an army outside his door for a solid week.

Simon thinks Leo got to him. Leonardo DiCaprio is a well-known publicity avoider: you'll often hear stories about him from regular L.A. folks who have seen him around town in a low-billed baseball cap, reluctant to make eye contact with anyone. Simon speculates Zac's getting mentored: he and Leo have been spotted together at recent Lakers games.

Zac was patient as I pushed back in argument. Like a good parent listening to his teenager, he let me talk as long as I needed—but he didn't budge. When I couldn't think of anything more to say, he drove away slowly. The look on his face was repentant.

At a light a few miles down the road, I pulled up beside him with another thought. It surprised him; he thought I'd left. We both knew that without his permission, I couldn't get anything. He was in full control. He rolled down his window, still being the good dad hearing my case. At my unexpected appearance, Vanessa giggled.

"You gave it up the other day when you were on your skateboard. We all knew that was your decision," I said. "You didn't have more paps on you the next day. No one doorstepped you. We all knew it was a one-off...You could do that with me." The story circulating was that Zac had given it up because he was so impressed that a pap had recognized him in an area of town where he wasn't normally seen.

My pap lingo flowed—*giving it up, pap, on you, doorstep*—I didn't have time to come up with layman's terms at a red light.

Zac responded, "You know, it'd be fine with me if I were never photographed again."

I am sure he believed this. He's too young to know better.

The light changed and we drove down the road unhurriedly, still conversing, our cars side-by-side. Zac *wanted* me to convince him, I could tell. But a fire truck blew its horn, and I had to move. Then Zac turned into the Warner Bros. lot. Although I'm sure he and Vanessa weren't going to the studio at that time of night, I knew this meant it was over.

As I drove home through the dark, I realized that something in me had changed, and it wasn't just in my belly. A year ago, even six months ago, it would have been exciting to have had a conversation with a big celebrity like Zac Efron. Even if I didn't get the shot, there would have been a rush. But there was no rush this time. There was only a feeling of annoyance that I'd come home empty-handed when I could have been on the sofa watching *House*.

In the beginning, the learning curve was steep, and I was challenged by the job's investigative aspects as well as the photographic skills necessary to do it well. Beyond a doubt, it was the most thrilling profession I'd ever had, and more exciting than anything else going on in my life. I remember the advice given to me in my early days as a pap: "Write it down before it stops being spectacular."

But the reality was, at this point, little about the job excited me anymore. Celebrity interactions blended together and rarely did I run across a new scenario. Like *Groundhog Day*, everything had already happened.

I touch my belly. There is no bump yet, there are no "kicks" yet, but I feel something very distinct. It's deep inside, and it's attached to me. And I know it's ready for me to move on. Remember that old vision I used to have? The one where I was on a diving board incessantly bouncing, getting height so that I could jump off. Well, I haven't had that dream in over two years, but tonight it will return. Only this time, I am not bouncing. I am airborne.

Chapter 22

*M*y all-day-long sickness is no longer car-wreck debilitating. The nausea continues 24/7, but it's all in my gut; my mind is clear. I'm about three months pregnant, and except for work, I haven't left the house in two months. I remain as still as possible on the sofa from 6 p.m. on and am in bed by nine. I sleep ten or eleven hours a night and could still use a three-hour nap. I've had no contact with Bo in weeks and haven't the energy to care. The pressing desire in my heart right now is only to be a mom. I want a husband too. Not for a lover, but so he can take care of me.

Today, I start work at noon and call it a day at four. I pop into Joan's on Third to rest and get a bite to eat before the drive home. I sit near the front window staving off vomit with a fruit bowl when Ansell, a work acquaintance, walks in. Ansell works for West Coast Wing and though we have no problems working together, I wouldn't say we're fond of one another. I haven't seen him in a while, and he stands there just staring at me. "You look really good," he finally says. It sounds like he's almost confused by this.

I can't imagine I'm looking good when all I can think about is throwing up. These days I wear only yoga pants, and I've stopped putting on makeup and fixing my hair.

"Thanks," I say, and we fall into small talk.

When he gets ready to leave, he pauses before he affirms, "I don't know what it is, but you look *so good.*"

I'm confused. Ansell's not hitting on me; I know that. So what is this?

He continues, "It's like…you're *glowing*."

And he says that word—"glowing"—like he knows.

Glowing. I'm glowing. No one has ever told me that I glowed.

I beam.

I'm pregnant, and I'm glowing, and in six months, I'm gonna have a baby!

★ ★ ★

I'm finishing the day in Studio City outside Hilary Duff's house when Claudia rocks up. I'm thrilled: competition or not, she and her smiling face are a real treat for me these solitary days in the field. I haven't made any close friends at iPIX, and now that my paparazzi days are numbered, I don't want to bother trying.

Claudia is equally excited to encounter me, and I climb into her 4Runner to visit. The light will be gone in thirty minutes, and on the off-chance that Hilary comes out before then, we agree to work together sending any photos we get to CXN but leaving my name off the caption so I won't have to explain to iPIX why CXN has my pictures. Not that I'd get "in trouble"—I'm a freelancer. It would just be frowned upon for reasons of professional loyalty. Claudia, on the other hand, could get fired if she were to send her photos elsewhere—she's staff.

Ten minutes into our catching up, Kirsten Dunst walks past my car door. She smiles at me, casually, as you would when passing a friendly stranger. (She wouldn't recognize me from our short car-to-car exchange over a year ago.) We know that Kirsten's mom lives a few doors down, between Hilary and Jennifer Love Hewitt, but Kirsten's car wasn't there, so this is very unexpected.

"Damn," says Claudia.

I sit frozen. Claudia fiddles with her car controls hoping that Kirsten won't think it odd that two girls are doing nothing in a car on the side of the road. She doesn't seem to. Two Brazilian male paps might not be as lucky.

Kirsten stops beneath a telephone pole right behind our car.

"What's she doing?" I whisper. My window is cracked, and she's close enough to hear our conversation.

On the post is a "Missing Cat" sign. Kirsten untacks the sign, puts it under her arm, then continues walking down the street.

"Oh, man. Oh, man."

To get a shot this late in the day, we really need a flash. It's Claudia who says what we're both thinking: "I'm not flashing her. Not here."

"No, me neither. It's too ugly."

"Flashing" in a suburban neighborhood feels really awkward to a pap. Basically Kirsten is "home," and there's an unspoken courtesy we normally give celebs when they are home, which includes not flashing them if they walk outside. This late in the day, we were hoping that Hilary would have left in her car, then we'd have followed her to somewhere public where flashing is copacetic.

We watch in the rearview mirror as Kirsten walks from pole to pole taking down signs. Our 70–200mm's could probably get us a grainy but salable photo, but we don't want *just a photo*. What we need is *an angle*—we gotta see Kirsten's face, and at the same time see what she's doing. We need "the story": *Found Dunst Cat.*

"Claude, not much time," I say. "We gotta do something."

"Damn," she says again.

It's an opportunity that we can't ignore—it's a great story—but we have no idea how to shoot it. What we do know is that Kirsten will not give it up easily.

Kirsten crosses the street and begins to head back toward her mom's house.

"Let's just get out, and, and...do whatever," my experienced pap-self suggests.

So, we hop out with our long lenses protruding from our jackets and fast-walk-shuffle up the opposite sidewalk to get in front of Kirsten. She is now past her mom's house moving toward more telephone poles in the opposite direction. We manage to scoot our way ahead of her.

"What now?" Claudia asks.

"Why are you looking at me?" I utter sharply. "Oh, all right. On three: one, two, three."

We turn together and pull our cameras to our faces. "Hi, Kirsten. Can we get some shots?"

Kirsten stops, stares at us—truly like we are buffoons—then turns, unhurriedly, and shakes her head as she walks away. She knows that she doesn't have to rush—there's no way we can get by her, plus move another twenty feet for a shot with our long lenses before she gets inside. Besides, she knows we want her taking down the signs, and she's now done with that. Kirsten's a smart celeb. She knows the game.

We know it too, so we don't even move.

"Bummer," says Claudia.

"We screwed that one up."

But please don't think I feel sorry for Kirsten (even if she is my celebrity look-alike). Our shots would have made her look like a caring, responsible animal owner—*to what was there to object?* We won't even bother to work her tomorrow: she lives on a bitch of a curve and will be watching for us. Anyway, the cat story was the one to get.

★ ★ ★

After seeing Claudia, my lonely routine becomes even more miserable. She reminded me that I missed CXN *a lot.* Not only do I have no pap colleagues *to see,* I have none to talk to. Even Jimmy, the boss, rarely calls. Most days I have to come up with my own stories. By contrast, Bartlet used to call me three or four times every day, and if I couldn't think of a celeb to work the following day, he'd always figure something out. Bartlet pushed me to work harder and to think harder, and he made me part of a team—an unorthodox one, yet one I really miss.

But with only a few months to go before baby, I'm gonna suck it up and stick it out with iPIX. Bartlet has and continues to refuse to give me 70 percent—it's a Tall Poppy thing—and 17 percent more in a paycheck is a lot to trade for "a team," especially now, when baby fund stockpiling is necessary.

Quite unusually, Jimmy calls today with a plan: "Why don't you work on Kristen Stewart," he suggests.

"Who's that?"

"She's the next big thing. In the new movie *Twilight*. Opens this weekend."

I look her up. Kristen fits the Hollywood criteria—unmistakably gorgeous and still a teenager. She has those delicate features, symmetrical face, and perfect skin that typify most American movie stars. But beautiful people aren't special here, and her fame will depend on two things: how well the movie does and how exciting her private life is (and how much of it she lets us see). She can get famous without us, but in order to do that, she'll have to be spectacular.

Kristen lives with her family in the heart of the Valley, the suburbs of Calabasas. Their house is a '70s-style ranch in the middle of a cul-de-sac which could be anywhere in Suburb, USA. The right side of the lawn is encircled with a dreadful twelve-foot-tall, wrought iron *Alice in Wonderland* gate. Parked in front of the house are a pickup truck and several hot-rod cars. There's also a black Mini, which I discover later that her mom, a tough-looking woman with tatted sleeves, drives. The Mini's plate reads "Mad Hatter," so we know who's responsible for the gate.

But I don't notice any of this my first time here. Rather, when I rock up this Wednesday morning, all I see is Kristen and her boyfriend. I recognize her easily from my Internet research. She's sitting on her front stoop in her pajamas, about ten feet from the curb, and she's smoking. I don't make eye contact and pretend to be chatting on the phone. I am the sole car to circle the street, but since Kristen will become a star only this week, she isn't yet savvy to what a pap or pap car looks like, and she takes no notice of me.

But if I drive around again, she might. A slight curve in the road presents itself, and I know I can shoot from around its bend. Without delay, I pull into her neighbor's drive behind two cars. The owners are probably home, but I'll be quick. Trees now shield my car, and I am sure Kristen can't see me. I drop my window, find a hole in the trees, and fire off several frames.

Frankly, I'm not too excited as I get the shots. As I've mentioned, mags don't generally like pictures featuring cigarettes. Besides, Dule, my iPIX colleague, shot Kristen and her boyfriend just a few days earlier when she was wearing a better outfit and the two of them were kissing. That set printed, but anything more of Kristen needs to be really good, at least until *Twilight* breaks and people know who she is.

After a few seconds of shooting, I zoom in on the back screen of my camera to check the frames and ensure my settings are right, as I always do if there's time. Low light and a longer-than-preferable distance have rendered the images on the grainy side, but after two years on the job, I read light quickly and usually correctly, so at least they are well exposed.

In the zoom, I also see that she is not smoking a cigarette. Rather, Kristen has a small, glass pipe that she is lighting with one hand while holding the thumb of her other over the carb (the hole) and taking a deep inhale.[17] I don't look at any more frames or fiddle with my settings. I know it doesn't take long to get high. Pulling my camera back to my eye, I continue to shoot, watching her pass the pipe to her boyfriend before they go inside. It all happens in less than a minute.

"Luck,"—according to philosopher Seneca Roman—"when opportunity meets preparation." About four times a year, a pap will get a big hit. These days that means anything over five grand in initial sales and residuals. "Opportunity" will come…if you put in the time and know what to do when it arrives. Paris Hilton will walk your way flaunting the Holy Bible, Justin Chambers will cross the street perfectly aligned with his five kids in one frame, or Jessica Alba will pose in a bathing suit on the beach for a photo shoot. My big hits weren't because I was

---

17. Later, in an interview with *Vanity Fair*, Kristen Stewart reflected on that shot and how it and *Twilight* instantly changed her life. ("Kristen Stewart on the People Who Critique Her Red Carpet Poses: 'I Don't Care About the Voracious, Starving Shit Eaters,'" *Vanity Fair*, June 5, 2012.)

"lucky" in the traditional sense of the word; rather, they were because I was prepared when opportunity crossed my path. That's the philosophy behind the daily Britney gangbangs: Rodeo2 paps will work Brit for months and months and only make a few hundred here and there. Then, the day when she shaves her head, they're there, they're ready, and they make bank.

If I had rocked up on Kristen's doorstep my first year in the business, I wouldn't have gotten the shot. I would not have known, so instinctively, how to set up my camera on this cloudy grey morning from seventy-five feet away; I would not have picked the right ISO or f-stop; I would not have chosen nor owned the right lens. And if I had not picked, by gut and experience, the correct lens and settings on that first try—*before* I checked the frames—I would have missed *the shot*. Besides, if I were in my first year as a pap, Kristen would have busted me: my car would have driven by too slowly, too suspiciously, *twice*; the small hole in between the trees, accessible only by pulling into a neighbor's driveway, wouldn't have registered on my radar as an option; and, no doubt, I would have given Kristen a solid, several-second eye-fuck alerting her to a voyeur. These things can't be taught. They must be experienced.

Eventually, as a pap you start to just know things—like which path people will walk from the store to their car; which way they'll face when they get out of their car; where they'll exit a parking structure; or where they'll stand to pump gas. You begin to know that when they check into a hotel, they will peer out their balcony or they will go for a walk on the street. Or, if they're part of a new couple, you know they will eventually kiss. And at the same time you are becoming aware of human tendencies, you come to know your camera, seeing through its eye like you see through your own. Eventually, you become a fully trained operative.

★ ★ ★

When you get something incredible—and exclusive—and nobody else knows about it, then you generally work it to death.

It's Thanksgiving week, and since Kristen's pot pictures are exclusive and there's little chance they'll get scooped, we're holding their release. During the holidays, mags basically shut down, letting a host of good, publishable pictures pile up. When pictures pile up, prices go down, and some shots and celebs get overlooked because there are too many choices.

Also, without the pictures floating around, other paps aren't alerted to her presence, so Kristen and I have the week to ourselves.

After a few days of following the teenage hippie around unnoticed, I begin to like her. She drives the pickup. It looks like my old one, not like the 1960s one she drives in *Twilight*. Kristen reminds me a lot of her seductive trailer-trashy character in the movie *Into the Wild*—a bit rough around the edges but a gem nonetheless. She's disgustingly beautiful—impossible *not* to rubberneck—but she's refreshingly *not* Hollywood. She never went to high school, dropped out before the ninth grade, and was introduced to acting because her parents were both film crew.

"Why don't we offer the shots to the studio instead of the mags?" I suggest to Jimmy one afternoon. The studio can't want a pot-smoking heroine as its image when the *Twilight* series is geared toward teenagers. It makes sense to me that they would pay more to have them in their possession, thus never released to the public.

"Can't," says Jimmy. "That would be considered extortion. Besides," he reminds me, "the studios don't protect their actors like they used to."[18]

For now, the strategy which Jimmy and Will opt for is to try to sell direct to large international publications for exclusive market buy-outs,

---

18. I've since wondered if Kristen wishes the paparazzi would have made her that offer a few years later when a paparazzo snapped her cheating on her later real-life boyfriend, Rob Pattinson, a.k.a. vampire Edward Cullen.

keeping in mind what we know about the American market: they may not buy the photos at all.

★ ★ ★

So, the Monday after Thanksgiving, just after *Twilight* comes out, iPIX releases the pot-smoking pictures. They held the set for five days. Five days is about the max an agent wants to sit on pictures. They're scared to take the risk the set might lose value. A few weeks old means old news.

As expected, few in the United States are interested. The noted exceptions are *Star Magazine,* which put a shot on its cover in the upper corner—not a full cover, but a cover nonetheless—and TMZ, which picked up the set in an exclusive online deal. (Run by lawyer Harvey Levin, TMZ may print trash, but at least it's true trash. TMZ staffers don't make up stories about breakups or hookups, and they're as "investigative" as it gets in the world of tabloid journalism. I'm a fan.) I think the *National Enquirer*—which Jimmy reads devotedly to "get the facts"—prints it too. But no other glossy mag in the United States makes mention of it.

But the real sales for a picture like this will be in Europe and Australia. The *Twilight* books are just as big in those countries, and unlike the States, the Commonwealth has no problem exposing celebrities' drug habits.

Here's what happens: Will, iPIX's seller, calls Europe and says, "We have Kristen Stewart smoking pot." And, like me, they say, "Who's that?" Turns out, *Twilight* won't be released in Europe for two more weeks—two weeks after its U.S. release, and three weeks after the shots are taken. Will has to explain that *Twilight* is about to be "the next big movie," and Kristen Stewart is about to be "the next big thing." OUCH. If European and Australian mags run the pictures pre-*Twilight* release, their readers won't be interested—they won't know Kristen either. If the mags wait to run the pictures three weeks later, after the movie's release, they'll be scandalous. But since the pictures are already on the market in the United

States, they'll also be old news. As much as Europe and Australia love the pictures, there is no place for them. Kristen-Stewart-smoking-pot-on-her-doorstep becomes a big fat non-event.[19]

★ ★ ★

The girls and I, and our extended friends and boyfriends gather for a gastronomic Thanksgiving. We celebrate a week late for scheduling reasons, but the turkey is just as good and a hell of a lot cheaper. Right after supper, Alexandra suggests, "Let's go find out the sex!"

The five of us—Alex, Jo, Georgia, Amy, and I—hop in the car and drive ten minutes to Treasured Moments Ultrasound, the 4D video sonographer in Glendale. I pay $49 and for ten minutes, we watch my tiny four-month-old baby *boy* wiggle around in my growing womb. Yes, I said *boy*. Finally I was going to have a permanent man in my life—albeit a teeny tiny one—who I would love unconditionally. His nose seems a bit squished (like mine), but besides that, he is perfect. Lullaby music plays in the background, and we goo and gaa over this miniature version of me.

---

19. Had we held the set longer, I might have made twenty or thirty grand. As it was, I made about five or six. But expecting iPIX to sit on pictures for three weeks without alerting anyone of their existence would be like getting a starving dog to ignore his Kibbles 'n Bits breakfast to wait for a T-bone steak dinner: it just wasn't gonna happen. On another note, the "KStew" set is a great example of one of those "ugly" stories that I told you the magazines fear. It's a story that people often hear and talk about, but one they don't ever actually see. Everyone believes it's true—enough people have seen it online or heard about it on the radio—but the hard proof is missing. American magazines are just not interested. Another example: Kate Middleton's topless photos. We all heard about them, but unless we concertedly Google searched, few of us ever saw them. (The photographer of these photos would have made boatloads more had Kate been in a bathing suit.) To be clear, "ugly" photogs (like drug, topless, and infidelity exposures) are available—the Internet has far fewer inhibitions—but in the current media environment, they don't print in many magazines nor on reputable blog sites (i.e., those which actually pay us), and in turn they are not all that valuable.

Oh my goodness, he's a boy. I haven't thought of boy names. I was so sure he was gonna be a girl. What do I know about boys?

"Baby boys need daddies," I cry to JoDeane.

"And someday he'll have one," she reassures me.

★ ★ ★

My body is entering the a-little-overweight-and-frumpy stage. My stomach pooches out just enough that my pants won't fasten, and since maternity outfits would give my condition away to the paps, those are not an option. (After my rocky start in the business, I still don't trust most of the paparazzi so I attempt to keep my personal life as private as possible. Just like many of the celebs, I suppose.) I live in baggy clothes. The 24/7 nausea has finally lifted, and although the level of fatigue I experience is still astounding, it's manageable as long as I get ten hours of sleep each night. Work's not so bad these days, and I even join my friends for dinner occasionally.

Last week, I broke the news to my family and everyone else except for the paps (and Bo). While my family members uttered the obligatory congratulations, Mom was the only one who was truly excited. As I had feared, I could hear everyone's thoughts: *How the hell is she gonna pull this off? I hope she's not looking for money.* That hurt; I won't pretend it didn't.

It also made me feel guilty. Yes, it's true, I am alone in this world. Is it fair for me to bring in another, a child loved unconditionally but raised by only one person?

JoDeane's husband Andy reassured me, "That's more than a lot of kids have. He's gonna be just fine, Jen. You're gonna love him more than most moms and dads combined."

Andy's right. For years now, I've craved a baby like an addict craves a hit. Now, I'm just worried I'll love him too much.

Year 3

Chapter 23

*I*n the paparazzi world, as with Thanksgiving, little happens over Christmas. Mags take a break and lay out stock stories in advance. Most celebs are out of town. It's a good time to not work. I spend the holidays at home in Atlanta showing the family my baby bump and trying to figure out whether spending time at home, post-baby, is an option. (To my delight, it turns out, it is. Everyone's softening.) I drag a suitcase full of hand-me-down baby clothes back to L.A. with me.

By early January, I'm almost six months pregnant. If I don't share the news with the paparazzi myself, someone will do it for me. Anyway, now is the perfect time: *I am gorgeous.* My new wardrobe full of tight-fitting tank tops accentuates a stunning yet still petite baby bump protruding from an otherwise lean body. (And at five-foot-nine, I've never had anything petite in my life!) I find often that both men and women stare at me and smile to themselves. Femininity, something I haven't felt since becoming a pap, blankets me like a dusting of baby powder. And, let's not forget, *I glow!*

Simon, Aaron, and Claudia, my closest pap friends, already know. (No, Bo still doesn't; I haven't decided whether I'm telling him yet.) It's only appropriate my agency find out next. After making sure Jimmy is in the office one late afternoon, I pop by to show him the bump. "Spread the word," I tell him. "I don't wanna have to do it."

By the next morning all of iPIX knows, and by the afternoon, all of CXN. Of course, Bartlet calls, sore that he wasn't in the loop earlier. He loves gossip, and his questions and comments keep coming: "So, who's the baby's daddy?…You're gonna use that guy—suck support out of him, right?…With baby baggage, you can forget about ever finding a husband…." Suddenly, I am a Tall Poppy in all its glory! It frustrates Bartlet that I'm so happy about becoming a single mom, and he's very annoyed that he can't get the dad's name out of me: "I know it's not Simon," he says. "Simon's too smart for that." (He doesn't even posture that it could be Aaron. Our "liaisons" will be news to him, and he'll hate that he never knew.)

When I tell Jimmy about my conversation, he rolls his eyes. He doesn't know why I still talk to Bartlet, but I tell him it's Bartlet's way of showing he's still looking out for me. If he didn't care, he wouldn't call.

Over the next several weeks, I run into many who have yet to hear. When they see my bump, a few question my ability to work, to which I just respond, "I'm going to work till I can't work anymore." Frankly, with the hormones subsiding, the job's getting easier. Maybe I'll keep at it longer than I expected.

And when any of them ask who the dad is, I just say, "Not a pap," and leave it at that.

★ ★ ★

Again and again, it's said that Jennifer Love Hewitt is the nicest celebrity in Hollywood. And I'd agree—Jennifer's right up there in the elite company of Gwen Stefani, Jerry O'Connell, Selma Blair, and Miley Cyrus. All of whom, at this moment at least, are wonderful.

And I would know. Daily, I watch the stars interact with life. I see how they treat their friends, lovers, strangers, coworkers, and *us*. Don't get me wrong, being "nice" or being respectful to paps doesn't mean always being willing to give it up. Jennifer Love Hewitt doesn't always want to be photographed—she'll cover sometimes—but regardless of her mood, respect and humility bubble up from her person like carbonation in a fresh bottle of Coca-Cola.

I was sad to read about Jennifer and her fiancé Ross McCall breaking up. Claudia and I had taken the first engagement photos of the couple; I'd spotted them one day while sitting a few houses down on Duff.

Working breakups is not quite as awful as working about-to-die stories, though thankfully I've never actually had to work the latter. (Nor would I ever. I couldn't do that to myself or anybody else.) Still, breakups are no fun. Nobody wants you there, and you don't want to be there. As a freelancer, I can say "no" to these kinds of stories and usually do. But today, quite by accident, I end up in Jennifer's neighborhood after losing Ryan Gosling, who *by the way* drives like a maniac in his Prius even when he doesn't know anyone's on him.

Although there is no way to tell if Jennifer is home—her garage door is down, no car is in the drive, and I know she often works in a studio all day—I sit on her anyway.

When you sit on Jen, you've got to sit right on her house as she can exit one of two ways. She's pap-savvy too, so there's no hiding.

Ravens circle all afternoon. Some leave right away. Some stop and wait for a bit, but not long. Jen has already been photographed post-breakup, and frankly, there isn't much to see but a bare ring finger.

Lucky for me, all the blackbirds have scattered when she does come out. I give her lots of space on the road and follow her to a Taco Bell. There, she motions with her hand out the window for me to come forward.

"You're not in the mood, are you?" I say with empathy as I pull up beside her. I decide immediately that I won't photograph her if she doesn't want it. Apparently, the pregnancy hormones are making me soft.

"Things are hard right now," Jen says. "Would it be all right if I give you some shots over there [she points to the sidewalk], but you don't take me going into Taco Bell?"

"Of course," I say.

Not that I have a choice. Paps are never in a position to turn down "free shots," even if we know that the real shot is the only one that will sell, as in this case. Jennifer-standing-on-a-random-sidewalk will be lucky to fetch a hundred. But, Jennifer-carrying-Taco-Bell, now that's a nice story.

But Jen could always cover, go home, and give me nothing. Acceding to her request is really my only option.

"Thanks." she says. "I just don't need it right now. You know what they'll say."

I do. Jennifer and Ross had gotten engaged right around the same time some unflattering "butt" shots came out of her in a bikini on a Hawaiian beach. Since then, she's been a tabloid staple—the present size of her derrière always a fascinating topic of discussion for whatever reason. With Taco Bell pictures, the tabloids would say something like: *Jen Turns to Fast Food to Curb Breakup Woes. Soon Her Ass Will Be* Muy Grande *Again.* Or, *Jen Beefs Up after Breakup.* Or, *Devastated, Jen Cows Down.* The idea is frankly disgusting.

The tabloids would also say, "We'll take it for a grand." Ah, well.

Jen walks up and down the sidewalk, smiling in her grey and blue sweats. It all looks so boring, I don't even get out of my car, just shoot from the window.

"Thanks, Jen," I say after I've gotten enough of the same thing. "And hey, I was bummed to read about you and Ross. I'm sorry."

"Thanks," she says. Then goes in for her comfort food, and I pull out of the lot. As I'm exiting, I pass a suspicious looking car with a thug inside: a jump.

Now 'tis true, I don't want him to ruin my exclusive—pitiful as it is—but more than that, I don't want Jennifer to get screwed. Like I said, Jen's one of the nicest celebrities in Hollywood, and on the several occasions that I've photographed her, she has been *particularly* nice to me. Which has contributed to me making good money on her pretty, happy pictures. You better believe, I'm gonna jump at the chance to pay Jennifer back.

I pull back in, park, and walk into the restaurant. She's ordering at the counter.

"Jennifer," I say, feeling a bit funny about addressing her so familiarly. Though paps always address celebrities by their first names (we do not call them Ms. Hewitt or Mr. Pitt, for example—that would be weird), it still feels awkward when I'm not holding a camera. Without a camera, it's like we're "the same," and why would I know her name when she doesn't know mine? "Another paparazzi just pulled up," I say. "What should we do?"

After a quick discussion, we decide that she should walk out close behind me and I will block her. And I will carry her Taco Bell bag. She makes it clear that she's very appreciative that I told her.

I've never blocked for a celebrity before, but I've seen it done by plenty of "heroes." As we walk to the car, I stand tall and Jen crouches behind me. The jumper just watches, not bothering to raise his camera. He can't say much anyway since it's my story he's jumped.

My shots of Jen never sell, not even for a hundred. But, no matter, for baby and me, the good energy pays off loads more than cash ever will.

★ ★ ★

Unfortunately, that good energy is short-lived. The next day, a notice from the city attorney's office comes in the mail. A complaint has been filed against me for the charge of battery against Frank Opis Epstein. It seems I should have called Detective Gonzalez back.

I call Georgia first. She wants to help but doesn't think she has the expertise. "You're gonna have to get a criminal defense attorney," she says apologetically. "But I'm gonna do research for you."

She assures me that I'll get off, but it will cost me. She refers to Frank as "The Asshole" during the whole conversation. "I can't believe The Asshole's doing this to you," she says. "The Asshole's a mean, mean person."

Georgia may hate The Asshole even more than I do. I love her for that.

Next I call Mom, who is notably more excited than sympathetic or worried for her daughter: "Jenny, it's just like Barbara Walters. [Mom's reading Walters's eighty-year-long autobiography.] Legal problems are great for autobiographies."

Fantastic, I'll publish my book and Frank will get all the profits. That's just great, Mom.

I get several attorney recommendations. I settle on Beverly Hills's Josiah Seaborn and leave a message with his office.

Josiah calls me back promptly (at $500 an hour, no surprise) and listens in silence to my story in which I insert the word "self-defense" at least twelve times. When I'm done, he says with grim condolence, "This is very serious [huff, sigh, five-second J.R.-long pause here], but I think we can win."

He tells me that the complaint notice means that charges haven't been filed but that the courts are investigating whether or not they will file. Josiah says (several times) that it is very important not to have a misdemeanor or felony charged against you in the state of California. Although he doesn't say why.

But I know why. I know a lot about the California justice system. Remember, this "justice" system put Paris Hilton, of all people, behind bars. Maybe you thought that was funny, but note this blond felon was jailed for *twenty-three days* for nothing more than driving with a suspended license—something, in all likelihood, one of your friends has done. Also, remember Officer Cregg of the LAPD? "I asked [Ms. Buhl] three times to please move along or I would have to ticket her. I did not want to ticket her, Your Honor, but she refused to move." Yeah, not how I remember it.

No, Josiah is right, the State of California is *not* where I want a charge filed against me. This state would relish using *La Paparazza* as an example for others. They'd slap me with one of my California "three strikes" and chuck me into a cold, hard cell.

★ ★ ★

Five days later, Josiah and I meet for our first $500-an-hour session. He asks me to put together some character references from fellow paparazzi: letters that will explain how I've never assaulted anyone, talk about how scary the business is, and how I might feel threatened working in it.

You find out who your friends are when you need them to do something uncomfortable. Only Aaron will do it. Simon, Claudia, and even Bartlet sympathize with my plight—they can't stand Frank Opis either—but they don't want to get involved.

Claudia defends her decision with this: "I've heard you get quite mad, Jen."

I try to reason with her: "Do you really think I'd chomp down on Frank just because he blocked my shot? Yelling at paps in the field is wholly different from going after someone physically."

"Of course it is," she confirms. "I'd just rather not write a letter."

Maybe Simon's been right all along: I've got no friends in this business—or at least none that will go to bat for me in a serious pinch. *It's past time I got the hell out of here.*

★ ★ ★

Frank Opis boasted to Simon that money isn't a problem because his family attorney is kept on retainer. He also told him, "Jennifer needs to learn a lesson."

Dressed in a suit for the first time in years, I arrive in the lobby of the Biltmore hotel down the street from the L.A. courthouse. Josiah and I have arranged to meet here an hour in advance of the hearing to review the details.

He is twenty minutes late, and when he does arrive, he stays on his cell phone for another twenty minutes. When he finally gets off, he begins to text. *Really, dude?*

I interrupt, "Do you think we could go over the case again? I'd really like to come up with a game plan." I'm sure this is old-hat for Josiah, but this is my first time facing criminal courts and I'm *petrified!*

"Oh, yeah. Just a sec." He continues to text.

Five minutes later, still pecking at his phone, he mumbles, "I don't think you should go in. I'll speak on your behalf."

"Don't you think it'd be good if they heard from me? I was kinda hoping to speak."

"I think it's better if I speak for you."

This is not looking good. I wonder if Josiah remembers anything about my case. It's been a month since we met. I pull out my notes and rattle the paper in the useless hope of getting his attention.

Ten minutes before the hearing, he finally puts down his phone. I quickly re-explain the details and review my defense, which I've been forming over the last few weeks. It feels like I'm the lawyer briefing the witness.

"I've learned more about Frank," I say. "A few months ago, he gave Hilary Duff a $1,000 gift certificate to a hair salon to try to bribe her into being his 'personal celebrity.'"

Josiah raises his eyebrows.

"Do you know who Hilary Duff is?" I say. Josiah's about sixty. I feel sure he doesn't know who Hilary Duff is.

"Yeah. Of course."

"This business doesn't work like that. That's creepy," I tell Josiah. "Hilary's bodyguard was so worked up about it that he came out to the street the next day to question other paps about Frank, to figure out how concerned he needed to be."

"Hmmm. That's good," Josiah says, scribbling some notes.

I remind him that Frank will probably have a very different version of events than I do. "Maybe he'll say that I ran up to him, grabbed his hand, and bit him. What else can he say, after all? He can't say that he threatened me and pushed my camera into my face."

"So, your camera did hit you? You weren't sure of that last time."

"Oh, I'm quite sure of it now. It definitely hit me."

"Yes. Good. I don't doubt it."

"I was in a crowd. I couldn't run," I continue. "My camera was attached to me with a strap around my neck. Here." I present my "evidence" and show Josiah how entangling a camera strap can be.

Josiah recaps. "So Mr. Epstein was using a weapon which hit you, which was attached to your neck, which you couldn't release."

"Yes. I couldn't run. I was trapped in my camera."

"And, where would you go anyway? You were in a crowd."

"Yes. And even if I had been able to undo myself from the camera, it would have fallen to the ground or Frank might have dropped it. Thousands of dollars crushed on the cement."

"That's your livelihood!" he says a bit loudly.

"Yes! How would I work?"

OK, so it seems my lawyer is pretty awesome after all.

★ ★ ★

We don't have to wait long before we're called. A short, soft-spoken court officer whose job it is to make recommendations to the court greets us. The officer smiles and smiles as if he's welcoming us to his dinner party and asks me if it's all right that he speak with my lawyer in the other room. He finds the softest chair for me to sit my very pregnant self in while I wait.

After fifteen minutes of active prayer on my end, the two men return and the court officer addresses me again. "Your lawyer has spoken on your behalf, and he doesn't want you to speak because of your Fifth Amendment right, and that's OK." He speaks as a gentle third-grade teacher would to the class. He offers another big smile. Then he shakes my hand heartily before we depart.

Josiah walks me to *his* car and tells me what happened. Frank didn't show, nor did his lawyer, which is in my favor because he was requested to show (however, he wasn't *required* to show because he'd already made a statement in the police report). Frank's statement, according to Josiah, is that I came up and hit him in the back, then grabbed his hand and bit it. To me, this statement sounds positive for us because it sounds so ludicrous to me versus my recollection of what happened.

Josiah also discovered that Frank has three witnesses. A bit worrisome that he has so many, but I'm skeptical they'll actually help. One of them is probably Crutch, the nighttime pap who was with Frank at CNN. Crutch's broken leg, I found out, was due to a fight he got in with "B-list-Hollywood," another nighttime pap. That can't be good for credibility, can it? Anyhow, if I can't get my best pap friends to write a simple letter on my behalf, I'm not confident Frank's gonna get his acquaintances to show up in court.

Josiah tells me, further, that the court officer will call Frank to get a follow-up statement before deciding what he will recommend to the courts, i.e., whether he will recommend pressing charges against me, or not. Overall, my lawyer is "hopeful"—*Hopefully not hopeful that I will continue to have to pay him $500 an hour*—and says he'll follow up with the court in a week.

★ ★ ★

I am meeting the girls at the Alcove for our habitual Sunday morning girl's breakfast. JoDeane arrives first and hustles back outside to wait for me.

"Bo is inside," she warns when I arrive. "And he's moving back to Canada next week."

With no thought of my belly, I walk in. But he's already gone.

Though I haven't verbalized it much, JoDeane knows I've gone back and forth on "whether to tell," and she knows instantly that I need to see him again. "I think he was on his way to work," she says when I come back out. "Go!"

My stomach cinches and I drive the two miles to the Starbucks where we first met. I don't know what I'm going to say. Over the months, I have defended my decision "not to tell"—many times, both to myself and others—each time increasingly confident in my reasoning. The more I devour child-rearing books, the more I want to take my chances at finding a different kind of father, someone who will love my son and teach this boy what it means to be a man—and a good one at that. The idea that (if I told Bo) he might *not* want to be involved (and I'd have to tell my son that his dad didn't want him) absolutely devastates me. But the idea that (if I told Bo) he might actually *want* to be involved sounds equally dreadful, given my concerns about his lifestyle, issues, etc. Like most parents, I want the best for my kid and I am determined to do whatever I can to give it to him, even if it means making a choice that he might hate me for someday.

And of course, I can't predict if I'll find a husband for myself, let alone a father for my baby. I mean, I haven't in thirty-seven years; why should that change now? But I am choosing that as my goal during my time off—after mothering my son, of course. And, it feels less like a desperate desire and more like a natural one to be proud of, proclaimed and honored: *I want a man! I need a man! Match.com, here I come!*

Except for in the belly, I still don't look pregnant, and with a billowy scarf covering the bump I walk in Starbucks assuming he won't notice. Then I see him. In a moment, all my reasoning falls away like blocks in a game of Jenga. Bo is inside of me. Part of me. Forever. He should know.

He greets me softly—he always gives me an endearing, guilty-kid kind of look—and starts pulling me a free shot of espresso. He asks me how I've been; tells me how nice I look. He doesn't seem to notice the bump; maybe he just thinks I've gained weight. We talk about Canada. He says he's moving back to Montreal, selling his car and hitchhiking his way home.

After about five minutes, I turn to go, this time concertedly protecting my belly with the scarf. After my initial wavering, my resolve has returned. I am sad, but less sad than when I walked in, and more sure than ever that this is the right choice. No, Bo isn't the man to father my child. And no, at least for the moment, he doesn't need to know. For now, until next time, *au revoir* my baby's daddy.

★ ★ ★

No one can say that Frank's not cunningly smart. Or patient. He went to the hospital; he accumulated witnesses; he visited the police. He made an effort to build the strongest case he could. I can't speak to his motive, but if he wanted to bury me, he may have gotten his wish.

Then I get the call: "Hi, Jennifer. It's Frank. I believe congratulations are in order. I've just heard."

"Thanks," I mumble bitterly.

He continues. "Children strike a soft spot in my heart."

Does he have one? I can't say anything nice so stay silent.

"I'm sure you know why I'm calling," he says.

"Not really." I figure it has something to do with his case against me, but my hands are tethered to his whims, so I have no other response.

"Well, I know you understand that I have a rock-solid case against you…"

I want to hear him out, so I keep my mouth shut. Red flames would shoot out if it opened.

He goes on to tell me that because I'm pregnant and he's a "nice guy," he's willing to settle. Frank says that if I pay his several-hundred-dollar-medical bill—outrageous, in my opinion, for a simple tetanus shot, but no surprise from the elite Cedar-Sinai hospital he went to that night—he will stop legal action against me and tell the courts that we came to a settlement. Several hundred, several thousand, or more, it didn't matter. I would never have enough money to fight a battle with such hate. A settlement would save me thousands, and more importantly, my sanity.

Georgia finds a friend who draws up a settlement agreement for me in an hour. For free.

A few days later, I meet Frank in the parking lot of Bristol Farms grocery. He signs, I give him a check, and it's over. That darkness that has oft resided in my heart this year is one shade lighter this afternoon. Maybe it is in Frank's too.

Chapter 24

*G*eorgia nudges me: "Jen, look. It's your 'friend.'"

It's nine-thirty at night, and Georgia, Alexandra, and I have met up for an after-dinner coffee and dessert at Fig. Katherine Heigl is now standing behind me trying to get a table.

I lumber up slowly—with six weeks to go, I'm big now—and say hello. Katie wraps me in a bear hug and lets her congratulations flow. "Josh said that you were pregnant!" (I happened to be pumping gas beside Heigl's husband at the Chevron last week.)

Katie and I chat about babies and life, like old friends, until she's seated. I return to my table.

As always, when celebrities are present, I find it difficult to concentrate. *Should I be calling someone giving out a tip? Should I take the picture myself? Should I stay cool and not do anything, since at the moment, we're all on level social ground?*

To add to my angst, Katherine is with both Josh and Justin Chambers, her co-star on *Grey's*, who surprisingly sells quite well. Any shot I take now would be posed and not hugely valuable, but regardless, it would still be one worth taking.

I'm in this business to make money, I remind myself, not for my pride. I know Katherine won't mind if I ask them for a shot, and I know she'll say yes.

Georgia can tell what I'm thinking. With regard to my profession, she has always been my Most Supportive Friend. She's practical about the business as a lawyer would be, and she doesn't think that anyone is better than anyone else, including celebrities. So when we pay our bill, Georgia walks toward their table so I can't chicken out. She's already given me the words to say: "Ask them something like, 'Would you like to contribute one last picture to the baby fund?' That'll make 'em laugh."

I swallow my hubris and pop the question. The trio responds with a resounding "Of course!" so excitedly that I wonder which number Fig is on their bar-hop.

At least I don't have to pull out the giant SLR. With the small point-and-shoot I keep in my purse, I point and say, "One, two, three."

The group must pose without moving for a second because of the delay in the consumer camera. Then Josh insists that I get in the picture too. He grabs my camera and takes one of Katie holding my baby bump.

After we're done with pictures, I make introductions. "This is Katie, Josh, and Justin," I say to Georgia and Alex, like what's going on is normal, the way it always is.

Katie, bubbly with a drink in her hand, keeps up a lively conversation with me, while Georgia and Alex stand awkwardly to the side until about ten minutes later when I notice they're seated and in animated banter with Justin. Apparently they accepted his third invitation to join the table.

I might as well sit too.

"Please," Justin says as he pulls out a chair for me. He buys a round for everyone—sparkling water for me—while we visit for more than an hour. We talk about the business, the neighborhood, *Grey's* plots, everyday industry stuff really. We're all good conversationalists.

I tell Justin that my favorite set ever is one I took of him and his family. He knows right away which I'm talking about, and grins. "With the kids. On Sunset. I love those pictures."

I explain that it's rare to get a picture where five kids and celebrity are all in one tight frame, so the residuals do fantastic. "I think I've made more money on that shot than any other," I tell him. Then I specify, "Six or seven thousand," to put it in perspective. He raises his eyebrows as if impressed. I want to laugh. He probably makes double that every day.

I tell him about one of the shots in the set that never printed. "You have a guitar swung over your shoulder. Your wife, kids, and new dog are behind you, and you're walking up the steep hill from Sunset Junction. I love that shot. It reminds me of the *Sound of Music*."

"I'd love to see it."

"I can print it for you."

Then Justin asks if I would ever consider coming to his home to do family portraits. Now, let's be clear, I would LOVE to be The Family Photographer to the Stars, but this is a very unorthodox idea. And I'm pretty skeptical about it, especially because Justin doesn't know me at all. Realistically, no celebrity is gonna invite a paparazzi into their home unless they are really sure of that person (like Adrian did, for example). I wouldn't even do that.

This evening, though, it sounds like a great idea. "That'd be fun," I say and give him my card.

I stopped working on Katie when she became an everyday gangbang target, maybe a year ago. But that day in the nail salon long ago, I had mentioned to her that I was writing a book, and I'd been hoping for another opportunity to remind her about it. Katie's the kind of celebrity "friend" who would pose for a pap shot with my book in her hand, or maybe even write a blurb for the back.

When I bring it up, she immediately seems to recall my project. "I love the idea!" she exclaims, and with a mischievous rise of the brows says, "Hmmm...You. Now that's a role I'd like to play."

"You'd be perfect," I tell her. And she would. "But you'll probably need to play yourself."

Josh likes the idea too. He implies some embellishing would naturally occur in the book.

"Actually," I respond with a laugh, "no need. Real life's got it all."

Josh and I fall into conversation about our home state of Georgia. He's the son of a doctor and grew up in Augusta.

Katie leans in when she hears our discussion. "I'm filming a movie in Atlanta in May. Why don't you come and shoot it?"

Great idea, Katie! But Katherine Heigl is no Lindsay Lohan, and I just don't see her texting me each morning with the location whereabouts. (Same way I don't see Justin calling me for the Chambers' family photos.)

"It's with Ashton *Koocher*," she informs me.

"*Koocher*? As in *koochy*?" Josh says. He and I both laugh.

"*Kutcher*, honey. Ashton *Kutcher*." Josh lovingly corrects his wife who can't quite pronounce the name of her super famous co-star.

Our table wraps up at about eleven-thirty. Katie asks for my card, saying she'd like to get me "a little something for the baby" and invite me to "game nights" at their house. Her intentions are genuine, but somehow, like the Atlanta idea—and the invite to her honeymoon—I question the follow-through.

Don't get me wrong; she isn't being disingenuous or flaky. It's just that I imagine she has encounters like these all the time, and it's impossible to remember or follow through on every single one. Regardless, I've always believed that paps can tell a lot about these people we follow around day after day. Having worked Katie, Josh, and Justin a number of times during my pap tenure, I can honestly say that each of them tonight was as lovely as I would have expected.

And, for a brief starry night, I felt like a star myself.

★ ★ ★

Spring is just around the corner, and I haven't seen Adrian for several months—not since the swimming pool day when I was only a few days pregnant and he suggested we "date." He's been out of town, which I've noticed since his car has been parked in the same spot all winter.

At about 4 p.m. this lucky Friday the thirteenth, hearing that Adrian has recently returned to L.A., I swing by his house.

He's pulling out of his drive, and he sees me before I see him.

"Hey. What's up?" he calls over.

"Hey. Long time no see," I say, stopping my car.

"How are you?"

We're side by side in our matching silver Priuses.

"Well…I'll show you."

I pull to the curb and get out. I'm wearing a tight baby blue tank top that shows off my bump and my boobs.

"Wow," he says, raising his furry eyebrows. "You're pregnant."

"I am."

"I didn't know you had a…were seeing anyone?" Adrian remembers my relationship status. And that's his first thought.

"I'm…not. Not anymore."

"Oh really? What happened?"

"Well, I guess it'd…I'd…it'd…been so long since I'd had sex that I didn't really realize how easy it was to get pregnant."

"Really? How long?"

I love that he ignores the fact that it was easy for me to get pregnant and focuses, instead, on the sex part.

"I'm not saying," I reply, getting red. I wouldn't mind Adrian thinking I'm a good girl, but I don't want him to think I'm completely chaste.

"No, really. How long?"

He's flirting now. I can tell it in his voice and by his cheeky look. I love that his head's in the gutter, and he wants to know.

"A long, long time," I respond.

"How long?" he persists.

"Let's just say years."

He smirks. "Well, if I'd known that, I coulda helped you out."

Sigh. And as much as I wish I could say that Adrian was staring long-ingly into my eyes as he said these words, his beautiful eyes were instead turned to his phone. Constant texting: what an awful communication crutch we have in this century.

"All right, so it's been a couple of years since you had sex…" he contin-ues, still looking at his phone.

"Yeah." I don't add anything. Adrian still makes me nervous; it's best I say as little as possible.

"And, so you got pregnant. And not keeping it wasn't your thing."

"Right." I laugh at the sheer ludicrous nature of this conversation.

Adrian seems undeterred. "Boy? Girl?"

"Boy."

"Adrian's a good name," he suggests.

I laugh again. Adrian's not arrogant—or alone—in recommending his own name. No joke, I can think of only one guy, Dule, who didn't suggest his moniker for my little one when he heard it was going to be a boy sans dad. And that's only because Dule hates his name since no one can pronounce it. I guess, guys need to have a male heir. I mean, if I were having a girl, no woman would ever think to suggest her name.

"So, how did it happen exactly?"

Just like a typical dude, Adrian gets back to the sex of it all.

"The timing was…improbable," I stammer out, still nervous, "based on the day of the month and other things. I actually was much more worried about STDs since just after sex, the guy told me he was looking for a bisexual girl in an open relationship. I wasn't really thinking about getting pregnant."

"And I assume you're all-OK there?" Adrian, again, seems unfazed by his words.

"Yes, no diseases. Just pregnant." *Does he really need to know?*

He grills me for a while about the identity of the dad, but I stay strong—plenty of times I've seen Adrian at the Starbucks on Western Ave., Bo's employer.

I'm still standing outside his car, the sun is setting, and it's getting cooler. My getting-ready-to-nurse nipples are poking through my shirt and I feel self-conscious. My roommate jokingly calls them "Bo Derek nipples" and says I should be proud. Simon calls them "bear's noses" when they suddenly appear under my shirt, and I don't think that's a compliment.

"I'm freezing," I say. "Can you back up into the sun?"

"Get in," he says. "I'm not going anywhere. Just pulled out for my mom."

Sure enough, his mom backs out just at that moment. She has an older man in the passenger seat.

"Bye, Mom," Adrian calls out. "See you guys. I love you."

The man hollers "I love you" back.

We continue to chat in his car. Adrian continues to text. I pull down the visor mirror to get something out of my eye.

"I look awful," I say. And I do. After last night with my other celebrity neighbors, the tap dancers in my head wouldn't let me rest.

"I think you look really good," he says.

"Ugh," I groan. "I have no makeup on, and I barely slept." I'm not fishing for a compliment either. I just want him to know I generally look better.

"Maybe that's why I think you look so good," he replies.

Now, I'm totally flustered, regardless of his texting. Adrian just said I looked good, and he was serious.

I stare at his mouth, longingly. He has a little chip in his tooth, the left front one, which I've never noticed before. *Has it always been chipped?*

There are a few seconds of uncomfortable silence, but nice-uncomfortable. I don't know if he notices since he's still texting.

"You know, you're interesting," he comments.

I wait for him to continue.

"I mean, not having sex for…but then…" he trails off. I know he's struggling with the juxtaposition of my life—how can I be a good, moral girl who doesn't have sex for years, yet one who is also an in-your-face paparazza? I know he's not thinking about having sex with me, but he is thinking about *sex* and *me*.

"Just like L.A.," I offer with a smile. "In so many ways good. In so many ways not."

We talk for about ten more minutes. Then I hop out of his car to get a magazine clipping from my trunk. It's one of "our" pictures, which printed from the day at the pool. (As promised, I never sold the backyard shots to the magazines.) This is one of him leaning on his Prius with his guitar. I have two copies, which I've carried around for months: one for him to sign for me, and one for me to sign for him.

He signs first. *Good luck being a single mom. Adrian.*

"What kind of note is that?" I question as my heart sinks. He knows what I'm thinking too: my boy needs a dad.

He shrugs.

Adrian's documentary, *Shot in the Dark*, tells of his upbringing and being raised by a single mom. Adrian never knew his dad growing up.

He's getting kind of aloof now and has pulled back into his drive and put his cell phone away. It signifies our time is coming to an end.

Thanks for the shot. (Heart) *Jennifer.* I sign his more personal.

"Well, good luck," Adrian says, then just stares at me.

"Thanks," I say, turning toward my car, always wanting to be the first to go. "See ya around."

★ ★ ★

Later that evening, my roommate and I watch a rerun of *House*. Like many people, I watch TV to forget about life for a while. But like many paps, I struggle to find things to watch. The *Grey's Anatomy* folks appear in my days way too often to want to spend my evenings with them; the same for the *Desperate Housewives*. *Ugly Betty* is out because America Ferrara's "a bitch." And *Entourage*—no way—I definitely can't watch that.

Mostly I watch *House*. In its plethora of reruns—currently three shows in a row, four nights a week on the USA Network—it's a great combo: fantastic writing and mindless entertainment. All the episodes end in the same feel-good way; it's a respite for the senses. The main reason I watch *House*, though, is because of "House," a sexy doctor I've never worked, who still makes me dream and forget about life.

"Too bad our lives don't tie up in a bow each night with music and cozy resolutions," Amy notes.

I ponder lives. They don't really come to happy *or* sad endings. In fact, they don't come to endings at all. Even when you die, your life is not fully resolved. Or if it is, you've probably lived a lonely last few years.

I've often wondered how my story would end. And I've come to realize that while life doesn't end, it is a chain of seasons. And seasons do end. This season of my life is ending. A baby is coming, and for me that means no more papping and no more celebrities. My friends and activities will also change as my life refocuses. As well—and this is big—I'm finally ready to be called "a woman." That's right. At thirty-seven-and-one-half, I'm not a girl anymore. My ambitions and prayers have even changed. I pray for peace instead of adventure, for wisdom instead of winning, and for happiness instead of exhilaration. I continue to beg God for love.

Chapter 25

*M*y hormones command: *You gotta get ready for baby.* Like many nesting moms-to-be, I obsessively clean my house and my car, for which Simon, the ultimate clean freak, has bought me a paintbrush so I can dust!

Sleep comes easily whenever I have time for it. I still desire ten to eleven hours a night, and upon waking it takes me several minutes to get out of bed as an invisible, twenty-pound, lead blanket seems to cover me.

The need to make as much money as I can before my child arrives haunts me, though I now loathe every split second of being a pap. When Claudia told me long ago that everything in her nature went against this job, I didn't get it until now. "Pregnant pap" is an oxymoron. The constant adrenaline—the "why" Aaron gave as the reason, two and a half years ago, we do the job—simply doesn't work for me anymore. My baby *hates* it. So now, as I drive, I divert my eyes in an attempt *not* to spot celebrities on the road. I'm thankful when my doorsteps *don't* leave, and if they do, I hope to lose them. If I don't, I pray they hurry home without getting out of their car. Rarely do I exit my car: besides being sloth-slow, a pregnant paparazza is most unattractive. No matter how beautiful the mommy-to-be, she exudes pure ugliness when walking backward with squatted knees, her eight-month swollen bump bulging in front of a random celeb.

For these reasons, at least three times a week, I spend my day—which now goes from about one to five—at the West Hollywood Whole Foods. I feel fortunate to have found this comfortable sit in the heart of celebrity neighborhoods. I secure one of two tables where I can see all the checkout lanes. Then I write or work on the Internet, eat salad, and drink smoothies. Pap "friends" pop in and out all day to say hi. Sometimes one of the security guards will come over to tell me if a celeb has walked in. Even if they don't, I'll always catch the star checking out. If I don't think they'll cover, I'll go for interior cash-register shots (rare, good money), then head outside and shoot them carrying their groceries to the car. If I think they may not oblige, I'll leave the store, go hide in my Prius, and nail the exit shots.

Already, I've shot Leonardo DiCaprio with his current girlfriend Bar Refaeli (his hat was pulled low but you could see his eyes—score!), *Grey's Anatomy's* Ellen Pompeo (reliably, she comes every Friday), Christina Ricci (the *Addams Family's* Wednesday), T.R. Knight (George O'Malley on *Grey's* and Heigl's real life BFF), and Dita Von Teese (the burlesque dancer and Marilyn Manson's ex-wife). Not always huge celebs, but grocery-store shots, so full of colorful bananas and broccoli peeking from the bags, always sell. (They're much more interesting than just a celebrity walking down the street. They show the stars actually shop for their own groceries—"Just like *Us!*") And the start to finish—spotting to shooting—is so swift that only moderate amounts of adrenaline toxins seep into my pregnant body. All in all, it's not a bad way to wind down my career shooting stars.

★ ★ ★

My weekends, at this point, are pretty stress-free too. Mostly I spend them in front of the TV. As previously mentioned, I've never watched *Entourage*. Intentionally. Besides the show offering me no escape from my reality—they write it right I'm told, and much as it happens in Hollywood—I never wanted to elevate Adrian to any sort of exalted celebrity status in my head. Moreover, if the possibility existed for us to "get together" (a faint fantasy of mine still), wouldn't it be better if we just merged as a guy and a girl?

Plus, I don't have HBO.

Three days after our car talk, I'd explored every foreseeable Adrian Grenier sex scene in my head. I had exhausted all of the possibilities, and then I let them go. But I started to miss them. Without an active crush— and being that *House* wasn't on over the weekend—life felt listless again until the arrival of *el bebe*. I caved and rented the first season of *Entourage*.

Snap! Adrian plays himself on TV. I'd suspected this all along but never imagined the degree to which similarities exist. Like Adrian, Vincent Chase in *Entourage* is a pretty face with an easygoing personality. Vincent is also an actor whose goal in life is just like Adrian's: to enjoy himself. Vincent, like Adrian, has loads of roommates "just for fun," and the girls, in both lives, are endless.

I could not believe it. *It was Adrian.* They just call him "Vince" on the show, and Vince somehow seems weirdly taller, but Adrian and Vince are exactly the same guy.

Watching Vince gave me insight into my real-life movie star. Adrian/ Vince doesn't hit on girls; they hit on him. Adrian/Vince effortlessly connects with any beautiful woman he wants, but without any work. Maybe Adrian and I have never kissed because I've never made the first move, and he doesn't know how to make the first move because he's never had to. Unfortunately for Adrian/Vince, this inexperience with "the chase" has produced a sort of natural apathy toward pursuing women, which is not so attractive on- or off-screen. At least not to me.

Even so, Adrian's a successful, attractive guy in his early thirties with a good head on his shoulders, and that's about as hard to find here as snow. So as I watch, I find it hard to shake my longtime crush on him.

"No wonder you like him," my roommate says when she sees the wanton look on my face. "How many guys are there like that in L.A.?"

"I've never met one," I concede.

And therein lies the problem. The issue, as Amy and I discuss, is that other than paparazzi, Adrian is pretty much the only single guy over the age of thirty that I've spoken to, much less flirted with, since Bo. Eight long months have been filled with paps, nosy neighbors, and West Hollywood metrosexuals. No wonder I'm still pining for Adrian. Simply put: thirty-something, healthy, manly-men are so precious and lauded because they do *not* grow on trees. Added to the L.A. conundrum is, of course, the massive quantity of crazy but hot women who move to this city to act, realize that they cannot act, and in an out-of-character moment of clarity, recognize that their only hope for survival is to harvest themselves one of the few eligible and solvent heterosexual man-fruits.

That doesn't leave much Adrian to go around.

But that's kind of OK. I'm ready for a change anyway. More than the obvious new baby change, I mean. Soon, I'll be finished with papping; I have no reason I *must* stay in L.A. Three of the girls—Georgia, Alex, and JoDeane—are transitioning back to their homes in Michigan; and while I don't see myself in the South, where my family is, maybe a new city's in order for me too.

Not that I wouldn't miss it here. L.A. is *so much* that I would miss. L.A. is energy, culture, passion, influence, sunshine…like I've never seen it anywhere else in the world. I adore this city full of beautiful, talented young people all with a drive to make their dreams come true. But I'm getting older, and the only dream I want to come true is the dream of a family. And while I've had the experience of my life here, I'm just not sure L.A.'s the place to make that happen.

★ ★ ★

Jimmy calls on Sunday while I'm watching *Entourage*. "I don't want you to go into labor," he says, "but if you're interested, I got Katy Perry's address for you. She'll probably be exclusive too."

For a while now, Katy's been a big star in the music world, but she's up-and-coming to the pap scene and few have her address. iPIX is usually the first to get new celebrity addresses. Most of our info comes from limo companies—who iPIX pays well—and celebrities love limos.

I'm thrilled for a "new address" and arrive at Katy's bright and early at 9 a.m. Monday morning. There are no other paps, so I park, exit my car, and stroll up and down the street. Walking makes baby happy. I alternate between sitting and pacing for the next three hours, careful not to venture too far from my car. At around noon, I see Katy pull out of her garage in the standard silver Prius. She's driving slowly and her car has no tint. My assumption is that Katy's been followed only a couple of times in her life, if that, so she doesn't check for me as I leisurely file in behind. (No doubt, in a few months when she starts dating and eventually marries Russell Brand—then divorces Russell Brand—things will be different.) Katy picks up a girlfriend and the two drive to a small outdoor shopping mall off Sunset, one where outside shots are feasible and paps don't usually loiter. Katy's wearing a typical fantastic outfit; everything's clicking along splendidly.

She parks her Prius in the underground deck. I park mine nearby and watch. The two girls head to the elevator. I should too—they'll never suspect that I'm a pap—but I hate riding elevators with celebs. Since that shameful day with Cameron, I've come to realize what appropriate elevator-pap protocol is; and while it's not completely against the rules to get in the elevator with them, it *is* the last option you want to take. If there's another way—up or down stairs, for instance—the pap should definitely go that route. If there isn't, however, and you, the pap, do end up in the elevator with the celeb (assuming the celeb knows you're a pap, which in this case, Katy wouldn't), this is what you do: First and foremost, Do Not Shoot. No mag will buy a shot if it looks as if you've cornered the celeb. (Which in fact you have.) Rather, put down your camera, stare at the ceiling or the floor, and wait until the door reopens. Once it does, and importantly, once you, the pap, are off the elevator (even if the celeb is not—she can be "getting off the elevator," and that will make a fine shot), then and only then may you turn around and shoot. I once rode the elevator at LAX with five paps and Ben Affleck and Jennifer Garner, and that's exactly what happened. Riding up, everyone was silent; cameras and pap heads were down. Jen didn't cover (she didn't need to), and when the elevator reopened, Jen ducked behind Ben and the action restarted.

Today, I take the stairs. I know the elevator exits on one of three levels so feel fairly confident letting Katy ride alone. Each level is a circular ring, and when I climb to the first, I stop and wait. I watch the three elevator openings…and wait…and wait…and wait. *Where did she go?* Either Katy didn't get off, or she was exceptionally quick and had already gotten off before I got to the first floor. I assume that's what it was, and begin searching. I walk in every store and restaurant on all three levels. I even buy a ticket to check the movie theater.

After twenty minutes, I've hit every location in the mall and haven't found Katy and her friend. I decide to go back to the car and wait—I've missed the shot here, but maybe they'll go somewhere else. When I get to the garage, Katy's car is gone. *Arg!* I hate screwing up easy jobs. Easy job, easy money: a year's supply of Pampers up in flames.

That night on the blogs, there's a shot of Katy and her friend eating ice cream at the Grove. They must have turned around immediately and decided to go there instead, something I would have known had I been in that damn elevator. Man, I can't believe I still wimp out.

★ ★ ★

But when I get someone in my head, I'm stubborn. I really want her picture. According to Katy's tour schedule, she's out of town for the next six weeks. I'll have the baby in four, so today is my last shot at Katy Perry.

I'm at her house by nine. Her New York–style apartment, a historic high-rise with oversized windows and city character, is where I'd love to live. Few apartments like this exist in L.A.

At around ten, Katy comes home. That's OK. I bet she leaves again.

And at around noon, she does. I follow her to Chateau Marmont. *Merde.* This is not a good place to pap. I'm extremely familiar with the little hotel—celebs always meet here—but everyone knows you can't shoot inside.

Though I've never actually tried. I park on the street, set my camera for inside shooting, and slide it into an obscure bag, a long H&M purse with lots of handy pockets. Then I walk in.

It's not hard to locate someone inside the Chateau (assuming they're not in a guest room, of course). When you enter the hotel through the garage, you climb one flight of stairs and basically you're there. A small lobby and check-in area is connected to a cozy den filled with antique furniture and oversized sofas, a room like you might find in a Cotswold inn or *un château en France*. The den area is where many celebrities have drinks and meetings, and from there, you can look through an old square-paned window-wall onto an outside patio, another spot where dining and deals are done.

Immediately, the hostess greets me: "You're here for the baby shower?"

"Ah…no, I'm meeting a friend. I'm a little early, though." *But thanks for the info.*

"No problem. Would you like a drink while you wait?"

I order a coffee, which gives me something to do versus just lurk, and sit down on one of the sofas. When the coffee comes, I pay immediately; I'll likely drink and run.

Katy's easy to spot through the window-wall. She's outside on the patio and is wearing a marvelous blue hat with a white bow on it. She's put a "Katy" name tag on too, and altogether looks like she should be at an English baby shower versus an American one.

As many times as I've been to the Chateau—checking for people inside, then waiting outside to pick up the follow—I'm at a loss of how to shoot inside. I ponder options. *What if I go to the patio to shoot?* The patio is small, and I'm not sure I'd even manage a full-length with my 70–200mm. Besides, there's nothing to hide behind. I'd be as obvious as a hunter in a burned down forest staring at Katy, hand-cocked, waiting for the right moment. Even if I could pull off a shot before I was escorted out, an unintentional body might easily ruin it. No, shooting on the patio doesn't seem like the way to go.

I'll just wait, I tell myself, *for opportunity to cross my path.* I stand up, sit down, pace, pee, fidget, try to figure out a plan, sit back down, and just watch.

Directly outside the multi-paned windows, the staff sets a long wooden

table and eventually the women sit down. Katy sits near the center, looking into the Chateau. I wonder if there is a glare, or if she can see me as
clearly as I can see her.

I drink my coffee while keeping an eye on her hat. I determine that I
must shoot from the inside out, so I discretely reach into my purse and
adjust my settings. I pull down the ISO to 800—although the picnic
table is under an awning, there's a healthy amount of light outside and
with a wide open aperture at f2.8, I think I can get a clean shot at the
corresponding shutter speed.

Aaron gave me advice the first week on the job: "Be an actor," he said.
"Pretend you're someone else. That's the only way to do what we do."
And it comes to me: Angelina Jolie in any one of her movies: badass, sexy
bank robber/CIA operative-type. Perfect! *I'm well trained and stocked with
the tools to pull off a multimillion-dollar diamond heist. My cover—eight
months preggo—couldn't be more brilliant. The audience is on my side.*

Besides the staff circling about, my current audience at the Chateau
includes two groups of people. There is one table of four. I'll be shooting
directly over their heads if I photograph Katy through the window. The other
is a group of six who are standing in the back of the den. Two of the women
from that company keep looking at me. *See, they're rootin' for ya, Jen.*

For about twenty minutes more, I pace, change seats, pee again, and
envision myself as Angelina. I play out the scene in my head, dressed
in a skin-tight black leather outfit and tall boots. (I'm really wearing
maternity jeans and a tank top. At least I'm not wearing sweats.) Mostly,
I'm worried about the staff; the guests can't really do anything. I figure
I'll burn it in one chance, so I must take the picture at exactly the right
moment. I watch the way the staff moves in and out. I notice that about
once every three or four minutes, there is a ten-second break when no
staff is in the den.

Katy is facing the window, but as she talks she looks from side to side.
Though it's not a full-length, with the *beau chapeau*, the "Katy" name tag,
and the setting, it will make an admirable shot—*if* I can get Katy face-on,
or nearly. But to avoid the heads at the table of four and the panes around

the glass window-wall, there is only one square foot from where I can get a face shot. I'll need to shoot from a random spot in the room—just kind of "out there" in the middle.

I have my plan. I know how I am going to execute. So now I wait. I sit and sip my lukewarm coffee. I breathe. I relax. *Je suis* Angelina. *Je suis jolie.* There will be a lull in the staff, I know. If Katy is looking up at that time, I will stand and shoot. If not, I will wait for the lull to happen again.

My camera is in my bag and both my hands are on it. My right hand is on the shutter button, and my left is wrapped around the lens in the shooting position. I am a crouched tigress waiting to pounce. I am strong and warm and powerful and beautiful, like Angelina. No one around me knows what's about to happen.

It is five minutes before no staff is in the den again. When I look outside, Katy is gazing up not talking to anyone. It's now. I stand, move to my mark, let the bag fall to the ground, bring my camera to my face, and with my arms pulled tightly to my chest for steadiness, take one precise shot. I can hear how slowly my shutter moves—the "open" and "close" both audible. I hold my breath to become even more still, refocus, and take two more shots. My adrenaline makes that easy; my control is complete.

After the three shots, Katy looks away. Just as calmly as I began, I finish. I pick up my bag and reinsert my camera. When I look around to see who's seen me, to see if I'm about to be escorted out, the maître d' is suddenly there, facing me.

"Would you like more coffee?"

"No, thanks. I'm good."

I notice one of the well-dressed women from the far side of the den is staring at me. She looks to be about fifty. I raise my eyebrows slightly in acknowledgment, and at that, her awed expression breaks and the words "Oh my God" form on her lips. I nod, crisply and confidently.

Katy stares at me through the window, and I see her motion to a waiter. I should hurry. I gulp down the rest of my coffee and walk out before anyone has a chance to close in.

As I make my way to my Prius, I can't stop smiling. I rocked it. Nobody shoots in the Chateau.

When I check my shots, I discover that the first has Katy's eyes shut, the second has camera shake, and the third…is perfect.

I only need one.

★ ★ ★

The ensuing follow will be tricky since I'm pretty sure Katy is onto me. A professional perk with iPIX is that the agency offers me "free" staff backup, i.e., they'll loan me a staff guy for an hour or two and my percentage doesn't get cut. Rarely do I need it, but today I'll take it. I call Jimmy.

Meanwhile, I move my car from the street and park across from the Chateau in the lot of a Mexican restaurant. Though it's difficult to watch from this spot, I need to do everything possible to prevent being jumped. Too many paps drive down Sunset every hour and check for their compatriots outside the Chateau. Katy may go somewhere else when she leaves; I don't need stragglers.

Malheureusement…before my backup arrives, a blacked-out SUV pulls up to the curb directly outside the Chateau. This pap position is a dead giveaway to any celeb, and it's possible for a pap to get an exit shot. But today it's not a shot I'm worried about—it's too far away and too dark of a shot to scoop mine—as far as I'm concerned, the jumper can stay there. The follow, however, is another matter. As much as I don't like to block, preserving both my exclusive and Katy's address is hugely important. I want today's picture to sell for as long as possible, so it's in my best interest that she has few current shots on the market. As well, it's iPIX's address, and the agency deserves to use it alone. The jumper probably got an inside tip, so according to pap protocol, he's legitimately there (versus if he had just seen me, and jumped). In this case, blocking is a bit "rude"; regardless, I worked hard for this shot, and I'm not giving it up easily.

My backup arrives. It's Fitz, a Filipino-American guy in his mid-thirties.

We coordinate positions over the Nextel and I explain to him that I have shots, so my chief concern is "protecting" them and Katy's address. "It's OK if we lose her," I say. "Just don't let the jumper stay with her."

I sense right away that Fitz doesn't like being told what to do by a woman. Besides, I'm sure he's annoyed that he's just been *pulled off* his cushy Michael Jackson sit only to block. Fitz is assigned to Michael most days, which usually involves two to four weeks of sitting for every two hours of action.

As a bit of an aside: Fitz is the guy who, in three months, will see an ambulance come to Michael's Beverly Hills home. He will call Jimmy, and Jimmy will commandeer his five staffers from various posts around town to meet at Michael's within the half hour. When the ambulance leaves the estate—and because Jimmy has worked as "Michael's pap" for over ten years and has been a pap for even longer, he has prepared for this moment with thousands of celebrity photos—"opportunity" will cross his path, *and he will be ready.*

As the ambulance pulls out of the driveway, the guys take shots. One shot—*the shot*, and in this case *the multimillion-dollar shot,* a price unheard of in decades or perhaps forever—will expose the inside of the ambulance where Michael is. Jimmy, through coordinating his staff, will get the last shot of Michael Jackson for his soon-to-be-heartbroken fans before he's pronounced dead.

Back to today's story. At this moment, my focus is as sharp as my Canon in bright daylight, and when Katy pulls out, I fall in straight behind her. A few cars go in between, then Fitz, then the jumper. The jumper doesn't know he's about to be blocked, so he's not immediately concerned about his position. We're going east on Sunset.

Katy drives erratically from the get-go. No question she knows we're here. I'm glad, though; she'll help in the block.

I beep Fitz at Crescent Heights, our first red light. "We should be able to block here," I say.

When the light turns green, Katy turns right, but I stay put on Sunset, all cars except the jumper's wondering why I don't move. The jumper clues in quickly, and I can see his car trying to move into another lane to get by Fitz and me in our standstill lane.

"It's CXN. The jumper is Leo," Fitz beeps.

Leo is a guy I like well enough, but he is fairly new from across the pond so I never worked with him at CXN. But I know CXN is dying to get Katy's address, and if it does, Bartlet will remind me for the next year that I was the reason CXN got it.

"He got around me," Fitz beeps a few seconds later, and obviously couldn't care less.

"How did that happen?" I respond curtly. This happens to the best of us occasionally and the worst of us frequently. In this case, I suspect Fitz let him go around. Since I said we were not aiming for additional shots, Fitz has no incentive to care.

We all turn right—Katy's direction—and now Leo is in the lead.

We see Katy's car far ahead. She clears the next light, but none of us is even close when that light turns red. It's a long red, and by the time we start again, she's nowhere to be seen. CXN and I continue down the road just in case we bump into her. Fitz turns off immediately, his duty done.

"No hard feelings," I say, pulling up next to Leo in my car. Both our windows are rolled down. "I know y'all need her address. I had to block."

"I hear ya, mate," he says. "Did you get some pictures at least?"

"I did. Inside even."

"Nice one. Didn't know you could do that."

"Me neither."

My Nextel goes off. It's Fitz, and I roll up the window so Leo can't hear. "Go ahead."

"I've got her," says Fitz.

This is incredibly good "luck" and only fair that it falls the way of the paps every once in a while. *I lost them*, Katy must have been thinking. *How the heck did they find me here?*

Luck.

Katy had stopped at a gas station a few blocks over, and on his way back to Michael's, Fitz recognized her Prius (the plate, of course, since everyone has a Prius). Even if Fitz can't block (or didn't care to), he certainly can shoot. He nailed several admirable full-lengths as Katy walked in and out of a food mart. Besides the hat, Katy wore a fur-collared coat, a lip-print skirt, and multi-colored nails. And since I'll make 70 percent on those sales too, that's a year's worth of diapers for sure!

A job well executed, no screw-ups, and a little luck. Days like today are what I'll miss.

★ ★ ★

Four weeks go by with little more than Whole Foods action.

In that time, and in a large part due to the efforts of Ashton "Koocher," Twitter is now a phenomenon. We're not even sure, yet, if the stars realize how many sets we've gotten from their tweets telling us exactly where they are going, what they are doing, and when.

"I'm gonna go workout this afternoon," tweets Ashley Tisdale.

Cool. We'll catch you at the gym.

"Be so nice to get back to L.A. tonight!" tweets Mandy Moore.

Sweet. We'll see you in the morning.

"Swam my way out of a strong current today. Not many could do the same," tweets Matthew McConaughey (or someone pretending to be).

Of course you did.

I get Twitter… if you are in high school. I get it if you're a new celeb and building fan support. I get it if you're John Mayer, a quirky singer-songwriter looking for inspiration. But an established celebrity—what in the world, other than self-love, inspires you to muse all day long about your home habits to people you don't know?[20]

---

20. By 2014, *celebrities* have become the paparazzi's biggest competitors. By posting photos of themselves on sites like Twitter and Instagram, stars often scoop pap shots with photos of their choosing. The mags get pictures for free and the celebrities have more control over their public images. It's a win-win for everybody but the paps.

Regardless, we are your followers. (And your personal assistants' followers and your film crews' followers…)

And so, we know Dakota Fanning is home. Dakota's fourteen, just hitting puberty and thus the tabloid pages. She's too young to be a great seller, but her role in *Twilight* has put her on the "adult" map. Anyway, on this sunny day, I'm not looking for a pot of gold. A few hundred and an easy follow would be just fine.

I bank that a high schooler will sleep later than me, but when I get to her house in Studio City, her dad is pulling out, and an hour later, her mom leaves. This is unfortunate since Dakota is too young to drive. Having no Plan B, I follow the mom. She takes me to Griffith Park. We park the cars and I make a loose follow on foot through the playground, around the carousel, until—voilà—we reach Dakota. She's with her sister Elle, and they're attending what appears to be an organized club event. *'Appy days.*

Even with a nine-month baby belly, it feels creepy watching young kids at a park. I don't see anything to shoot behind, so I go back to my car to hide in its cover and post up in the one spot where I can see and shoot in the dark behind my tint. I notice another blacked-out vehicle with the driver inside, car windows rolled up and visor down. He must be annoyed. I'm sure he didn't expect me when I wasn't on the follow this morning.

A few uninteresting shots later, the girls and mom leave. The other pap and I make a stealth follow and watch as Dakota gets dropped off at a friend's house. I remember when I was fourteen and got dropped at a friend's house: I'd play all day, then go home for dinner or maybe spend the night. My instinct says that Dakota won't leave again—there won't be a shot—so I wave "good luck" to the other pap and quit for the day.

It's just four when I get home, but I'm exhausted. Alexandra encourages me to listen to my body. "Take a nap," she says. "Maybe it needs to prepare for something later." But my due date is still two days away, and first babies are always late.

After my nap, I meet up with the girls for dinner at Elf in Echo Park, our favorite vegetarian restaurant. People often queue an hour before the restaurant opens to get one of the six tables inside—which we didn't do—so we wait. We stand outside on Sunset and watch the traffic stream by. The air is a perfect temperature, maybe seventy-eight, and I'm happy. I look around: dingy streets, rooted-up sidewalks, fine dining establishments, Mexican fruit stands, high-end boutiques, Laundromats, stray cats—it's all here. And I think, I love L.A.

I don't remember the sky that night, but later I learn it's the new moon. In a new moon, the moon is directly between the earth and the sun. It starts in shadow, then as the night goes on, a thin crescent appears and a cycle of brightness begins.

I eat only half of my splendidly rich chickpea-and-spinach crepe with goat cheese butter. I take the rest home in a doggie bag, watch a little TV, and get into bed just before midnight.

★ ★ ★

I can't fall asleep. I think I need to use the bathroom. At 1 a.m., I am out of bed and on the toilet. Soon, I'm curled up in a ball on my black-and-white retro-tiled bathroom floor with my belly cramping. Excitement fills my blood. *This is it, Jenny. You're gonna meet your baby.*

At 1:15 a.m., I throw up the crepe. At 1:30 a.m., I puke out my remaining dinner, and at 1:45, I retch out all that's left. Apparently, this isn't uncommon. I go back and forth from the toilet to the tub to the cold, tile floor.

I decided in advance that I would let Amy sleep till I really needed her—first-time labor can last as long as a whole day—but my moans are loud and impossible to stifle. My roommate comes in at 2 a.m. and tries to make me breathe in rhythm and do the exercises we learned in class. With each contraction, however, all I can do is sit on the toilet, tense every muscle, and make dying noises. Soon Amy starts to time the contractions, and by 3 a.m.—just two hours after labor began—they are only one and a half minutes apart. Every fifteen minutes or so, I feel the baby "drop"—a bizarre sensation.

313

Amy and I talked about my birth plan in advance. I didn't want go to the hospital too early because I wanted to avoid unnecessary intervention. But like my conception, my labor wasn't going by the book. It was going significantly faster…and with no letup.

"I think he's coming soon," I say to Amy. "Maybe we should go."

She agrees, gathers my hospital bag, and helps me to the car. On the way through the back alley to the garage, another contraction starts, my knees buckle, and in writhing pain, I attempt to pull off my clothes. Amy stops me. Our car ride to the hospital is without a doubt the most painful ten minutes of my life. It doesn't feel like the contractions ever stop, and I'm surprised I don't black out. Amy insists that I keep my clothes on, but I claw at them mightily—every single fiber scrapes me like switchblades.

Since it's the middle of the night, we pull right up to the hospital door. I wait for a contraction to pass before trying to walk in, but when I do, another starts. I fall to the floor unfortunately without clearing the automatic door. For the duration of that contraction, the door opens and closes, opens and closes, opens and closes—as if someone is not only monkey-wrenching my belly, but slapping my ears at the same time. Amy is laughing, but there's nothing she can do.

By 4 a.m., I am in a hospital bed at the Glendale Adventist Medical Center, and my contractions are thirty seconds apart. I am close to the most intense stage of labor. It's called "transition," happens right before birth, and generally lasts anywhere from thirty minutes to two hours. Although I planned to go natural, i.e., no meds, the ball of fire in my womb screams, "*YES!*" when the nurse asks if I want an epidural.

"How long will it take? Can you do it now?" I holler.

"It may take an hour," she advises.

"An hour! No, please. I can't wait that long."

Amy, knowing that this wasn't my plan, inserts, "Are you sure this is what you want?"

"*YES!*" I scream once more. She doesn't ask again.

Because my labor is going so fast, my mind can't get ahead of the pain to cope with it. Not that I wish it was taking longer: I want this baby *out*!

The nurse calls the anesthesiologist but warns again that it may take thirty minutes for her to get here, then another thirty to administer the epidural.

I don't know how I get through the next hour. The pain short-circuits my brain, and I don't remember the time. When the epidural takes effect, I am dilated to 9 cm, about through transition, and ready to push. The nurse puts me in a side-fetal position to slow down the baby until the doctor arrives. On average, first babies take twelve to sixteen hours; my labor began just four hours ago. "I'd prefer if Dr. Wu delivered this baby," the nurse says. "I've already delivered one tonight."

I'm fine with that. The pain has stopped, the baby is low in the birth canal, and I should need no further medical intervention. And, oh nelly, *I'm about to meet him!*

I'm suddenly starved, and Amy and I discuss breakfast. As soon as I deliver, she'll get me a sausage, egg, and cheese biscuit from McDonald's. I call my mom, who is three hours ahead on Eastern Standard Time and has just gotten up.

When Dr. Wu arrives and is washing up, the nurse returns to my room and I begin to push, blissfully and pain-free thanks to the epidural. This is even fun. The epidural and side-fetal position apparently stunted the labor, so I push on-and-off for over an hour, each time peeing on the hands of Amy and the nurse. "I don't know why the catheter didn't work," the nurse keeps saying.

"I can see his head!" Amy finally yells.

Dr. Wu is called in for the finale, and a few minutes later, baby slides out into his arms. The doctor places him immediately on my chest.

Wide-eyed and beautiful, baby doesn't cry, only stares at all the bright things in the room. We dim the lights. He stares at me. I talk to him. He works his way to my breast and takes his first feeding. We cuddle for almost an hour before the nurse takes him for his baby check, and then brings him back to my arms.

One chapter back, I wrote that the only thing missing at the end of my story was love. And in the end, it's true; I still haven't found a husband or even a lover. But at 7:35 a.m. on Sunday, April 26, 2009, without a camera in sight, I met the love of my life…Charlie.

Postscript

Five years later…

Simon still paps. He and I have become *real* friends.

Aaron still paps. He settled on a nice American girl, married her, and is as *broody* (British for "wanting kids") as ever. He'll make a great daddy soon.

Claudia still paps. She and I have continued our friendship, and I hope she forgives me for my early indiscretions with her former on-and-off-again boyfriend. She is also writing a book—paparazzi fiction based on truth.

Bartlet still runs CXN. We talk every few weeks, and he always asks when I'm coming back to work for him. He still refuses to give me 70 percent.

Donna and **Brian** get married. They have a full Vegas-style wedding in the City of Sin, complete with a dead Elvis and several of their personal paparazzi.

Elif returned to the textile business once she moved back to Turkey. She found herself an amazing husband and has twins, a boy and a girl.

Georgia, **Alexandra**, and **JoDeane** all moved back to Michigan. Georgia works remotely and is still a lawyer for the same uniform company; Alex just got married to her longtime boyfriend AJ, who we always loved, and she works as a nutritionist. JoDeane and Andy have two kids now, and she's still a nurse. We all remain very close friends.

Amy married a musician, and the two of them live next door to our old apartment in the same Lyman Village Los Feliz complex. Amy is still an actor.

Adrian and I never hook up, but we keep in touch. He invited Charlie and me to his poolside birthday party when baby was just two months old. Charlie was a popular guest but considerably upstaged by Adrian's date—a beautiful girl who swam and mingled through the party in her undies and nothing else. (Were they filming *Entourage* and we didn't know it?) After *Entourage* ended, Adrian moved to Brooklyn, the closest thing to Los Feliz on the East Coast.

Bo moved back to Canada and we lost touch. I never told him. Of course, my life is no secret, especially now and especially for Charlie, and I'll keep reassessing "whether to tell" as my baby grows up. And I know if and when I decide to, people—like celebrities—are just not that hard to find.

Charlie and I stayed in L.A. for the first three months of his life and the best three *ever* of mine. He was the ultimate pap-cover in his stroller when he helped me shoot an undercover job at just one month old. I shot Demi and Ashton (who were still together) and Bruce Willis at their daughter's graduation and made $1,400. After that, I retired my camera except for baby pictures…and the occasional celebrity who happened to cross my path.

The next six months—equally perfect—were spent at home in the South with family and friends. Then, Charlie and I moved to Colorado where I lived frugally off savings and residuals, loved my baby, and wrote this story. It's raw and leaves me open to judgment, but how could I not share it with the world? Hopefully you've gotten a glimpse into what it's like to shoot the stars.

And what about a man? Well, that's in the next book.

Oh, and **Kate Bosworth** got married. Simon says she still hates us, but I think I've forgiven her.

Glossary of Paparazzi Terms

Bitch– *noun*

[slang] a celebrity who "makes" getting his or her photograph very difficult. [In my opinion a derogatory term, but what does my opinion matter.]

Usage: Celebs who are bitches too often, we leave alone.

Block– *verb,* block-ed, block-ing

to prevent the shot of a pap using any object, commonly one's hand or body. Valets, security, boyfriends, and the like can block very effectively; paps often cannot since the blocker generally wants to shoot too. Always an act done *for* someone; one cannot block oneself. See *cover.*

Usage: "I was blocking Jennifer [so she could not get any shots] and that's why I was unable to take any pictures of Rihanna."

to prevent a pap from following a vehicle by using another vehicle.

Usage: There is no point in following Victoria; Beckham's security will just block.

Blow– *verb,* blew, blow-ing

[slang] to ditch.

Usage: Jessica blew me at the first intersection.

Bottom feeding– *verb phrase*

to troll around attempting to "pick off" (shoot) B-,C-, and D-list celebrities, whom no one really cares much about.

Usage: After Kristen "went bust," late day bottom feeding was our only option.

Burn it– *verb phrase,* burn-ed, burn-ing

to intentionally—usually because of lack of a better choice—get busted when shooting.

Usage: We knew we'd burn it on the first shot, so we got ready to run.

[The] Chase– *noun phrase*

[slang] the act of following a celebrity once he or she leaves a location. This term is typically, yet inappropriately, used by novice paps, as paps don't "chase"; they "follow" (except on Britney).

Usage: Carlos got a flat on the Britney chase yesterday.

Chirp– *verb,* chirp-ed, chirp-ing

the cricket-like sound a Nextel makes when connecting to another Nextel; the act of Nextelling.

Usage: Chirp/beep/Nextel me when you're moving.

[The] City– *noun phrase*

also *town.* the cities of West Hollywood and Beverly Hills, a hubbub of celebrity action; more or less east of Santa Monica Boulevard where it hits the Beverly Hilton hotel, west of Fairfax Avenue at about the Grove, north of Wilshire Boulevard if in Beverly Hills or north of 3rd Street if in West Hollywood, and south of the Hollywood Hills and Sunset Boulevard.

Usage: J.R.: "You in the city? McC's at Bristol Farms." Me: "I'm in town. I can make it."

Cover– *verb,* cover-ed, cover-ing

to prevent the shot of oneself by blocking one's face with one's hand or with an item held by oneself. Not to be confused with *blocking*, an act done by someone other than a celebrity-self.

Usage: Never try to outrun a pap. Just cover.

Doorstep– *noun*

near to the exterior of a celebrity's location, typically the celebrity's house, from where he or she will naturally depart.

Usage: Pink's [or just "Pink"] is a pleasant doorstep because there is always shade and never any traffic.

Verb, doorstep-ped, doorstep-ping

the act of sitting outside a celebrity's house (or office, or a similar "home base") waiting for the celebrity to leave in order to either follow or get an immediate shot.

Usage: I doorstepped Isla [Fisher] from two to five, but she never came out.

Down the barrel– *Adverb phrase*

into the lens of the camera.

Usage: Tabloids love it when celebs are staring down the barrel—it's like they're smiling just for us.

Flash– *noun*

[formal] the light affixed to the top of the camera which produces a sudden and brief burst when taking a picture.

Usage: I have a Canon 580 flash

Verb, flash-ed, flash-ing

to photograph with the use of the camera flash.

Usage: I had to flash Garner. Hate that. It's so boorish when she's with her kids.

[The] Follow– *noun phrase*

the act of trailing a celebrity once he or she leaves a location, typically by car but also possible on foot.

Usage: Did you pick up the follow?

Gangbang– *noun*

a large group of paparazzi photographing a celebrity at the same time.

Usage: When Rodeo2 arrived, it turned into a gangbang.

Get– *noun*

the one to photograph.
Usage: Of the former TomKat, Tom was the harder get.
Verb, got, get-ting
to shoot and nail the shot.
Usage: I got Ryan Gosling today. SNAP!

Give it up– *verb phrase, gave, giv-ing*

to allow one's picture to be taken.
Usage: Does Natalie Portman give it up?

Hero– *noun*

an individual who takes it upon him- or herself to block or otherwise "protect" a celebrity.
Usage: A hero got in the way of my shot.

Hose– *verb,* hos-ed, hos-ing

to take copious photographs of a celebrity.
Usage: I hosed Selena on Melrose.

In the bag– *interjection*

[British slang] An expression used when you are certain of success and often relaxed about the outcome.
Usage: Simon: "Rest easy, luv. Pics are in the bag."

Job– *noun*

the story or celebrity a pap is working on.
Usage: "I'll fuck you up if you jump my job," said Hooper from LMN.

Jump– *verb,* jump-ed, jump-ing

to join another photographer who is already working on a story/celebrity, usually without permission.
Usage: Rodeo2 will always jump your job.

Leave it– *verb phrase, left, leav-ing*
to depart from a celebrity (a *story*) while that celebrity is still out.
Usage: J-Lo turned into a gangbang so we left it.

Local– *noun*
[British] a neighborhood pub, typically within walking distance to one's home.
Usage: The British paps met for a beer at their local.

Long– *noun*
[informal] a lens, long in length.
Usage: "My long's in my rugsack," says Aaron.
Adj.
[formal] a description of the length of a lens. On the high end, generally over 50mm and up to 600mm or more.
Usage: The 70–200mm is the pap's go-to long lens.
Adverb
[informal] a way of shooting, using a long lens.
Usage: Are we going short or long?

Nail it– *verb phrase, nail-ed, nail-ing*
to get the shot just right, artistically and technically, for publication.
Usage: They kissed, and I nailed it.

Nextel– *noun*
a Sprint walkie-talkie–type cell phone that most paps use to chat on and coordinate with. It makes a chipper, high-pitched "beep" before establishing a talk connection, and an ugly, low-pitched "beep" when the line is occupied.
Usage: "Who you been talking to? I've been trying to get through to your Nextel all morning."

Pick up– *verb phrase,* pick-ed up, pick-ing up
to run across and then join a celebrity (or the follow of a celebrity), either by spotting the celebrity (often in the car) or getting a tip.

Usage: I picked up Cameron on Melrose and followed her to the Chateau; Pick up the follow when it leaves Jamba Juice.

Post up— *verb phrase*, post-ed up, post-ing up

to go somewhere and get ready to shoot.

Usage: He posted up behind the mannequins at Barneys.

Pull off— *verb phrase*, pull-ed off, pull-ing off

to leave the location of a celebrity, or to intentionally let the celebrity go without following.

Usage: I pulled off the Lohan follow. With over twenty vehicles, it was too dangerous.

Reccy— *noun*

[British slang] reconnaissance.

Usage: Aaron's been doing drive-by reccys of Sandra's house every day because he wants to be the first to work her when she's back in town.

Savage— *noun*

a bad-mannered paparazzi who prefers gangbang short-and-flash style shooting to long-lens stealth operations.

Usage: "With ten savages waiting outside Barneys, I couldn't be bothered," says Simon.

Verb, savag-ed, savag-ing

to work a celebrity (usually in daily gangbangs) to the point of his or her exhaustion.

Usage: A celeb can be savaged for three months, four max, then it's done. No one can put up with more than that.

Short— *noun*

[informal] a lens, short in length.

Usage: Ideally a pap should have two camera bodies set up and ready for immediate use: a short and a long.

Adj.

[formal] a description of the length of a lens. On the low end, generally between 16mm and 28mm.

Usage: My short Tameron lens zooms down to twenty-eight [28mm] and doesn't cause distortion; though in a gangbang I can't compete with a sixteen or seventeen [16mm, 17mm] for a full-length.

Adverb

[informal] a way of shooting, using a short lens.

Usage: We tried to stay long, but when Rodeo2 got there, everyone went short.

Short-and-flash– *noun*

[informal] a short lens with an attached flash.

Usage: You always use short-and-flash at gangbangs.

Adverb

[informal] a way of shooting, using a short lens and a flash.

Usage: Simon says we shouldn't be too hard on Rodeo-ers because they don't know how to shoot any other way but short-and-flash.

Sit– *noun*

a period of sitting.

Usage: Britney's [doorstep] is always a long, hot sit.

Verb, sat, sit-ting

to wait on a celebrity, generally at his or her doorstep.

Usage: I sat on Julia all day.

Stealth– *noun*

[formal] a clandestine act of moving without detection.

Usage: The stealth of our movements prevented us from being seen.

Adj.

[formal] covert; secret.

Usage: A stealth follow is hard to pull off.

Adverb

[informal] stealthily.

Usage: We follow stealth, not stealthily, because we like to think of ourselves as fighter pilots.

Story– *noun*

the celebrity herself; or the tabloid occasion for working on a particular job/celebrity.

Usage: It's an out-of-town story in Mexico—super dangerous but could really pay off; "J-Lo is my story—I'm warning you, I'll block you if you don't leave."

Troll– *verb*, troll-ed, troll-ing

British: trawl

to circle around (by car or foot) looking for celebrities.

Usage: My doorstep went to pot. I'm going to the city to troll.

Web– *noun*

a location formed by strategic weaving, and one in which a pap, like a spider, will wait for her prey.

Usage: "I prefer they come to me: Me web is sticky," Simon says.

Work [on]– *verb, verb phrase*, work-ed, work-ing

to pursue shooting a celebrity, eventually to the point of understanding his or her habits.

Usage: It's hard to make any money on Miley since the Brazilians work her every day; "Hope you don't mind how much I work on you, Katherine"; I like working Fergie—she usually goes out and always gives it up.

Acknowledgments

$\mathcal{M}$y life as a paparazza and my journey to this point has been such a wild, exciting, and wonderful ride, but I never would have been able to come this far alone. It's hard to know where to begin thanking everyone who has supported, guided, and encouraged me along the way, and inevitably I'll draw a total blank on someone (sorry in advance and please know I still love you all the same!). But I do want to acknowledge a number of special people without whom this memoir would be a very different story.

Thank you to Stephanie Bowen, my superstar editor at Sourcebooks, and Andy Ross, my rockstar agent, for immediately "getting me," and not chucking this book straight in the trash 'cause *everybody knows everybody hates the paparazzi*. It has been such a blast working with both of you, and this book is a reality because you believed in it and believed in me. I can't thank you both enough.

Thank you Elizabeth Zack and the "Evil Editor," for your edits on my early drafts, particularly recommending limits to my digressions on the LAPD, the lack of free healthcare, and similar "poor-Jen" pity parties. Thank you Julie Pappas, my sister, who made sure this was (fairly) family-friendly, and thank you Melissa Thibodeau, my friend and celebrity connoisseur, who wanted even more stories than the ridiculous number she proofread. Thank you Mom, for making me your grammar protégé, for a lifetime of gentle syntax corrections and for helping me read between the lines. Thank you Susan Gilmore for teaching me how to write in college, and showing me that I *could*. Thank you Simon, Elif, and Donna (you know who you are) for your encouragement, advice, and comradeship—without you I would never have succeeded in this profession. Thank you Amy for listening to my stories every night and keeping me as positive as possible. Thank you JoDeane, Rhea, and Alexandra for loving me just the way I was, am, and will be. Thank you Charlie, for changing my life. And thank you God for Your incredible sense of humor. I will never grow tired of the adventure you put in front of us all.

About the Author

*J*ennifer Buhl was a top-earning *paparazza* in Los Angeles for three years, where she photographed hundreds of A-list celebrities. Her work appeared frequently in publications such as *People, Us Weekly,* the United Kingdom's *The Guardian*, TMZ, and E! Online. Prior to photography, Jennifer worked in journalism at CNN, and at television networks abroad in New Zealand and Australia. She now lives in Colorado where she owns a "celebrity-style" family photography business.

Braden Gunem Photography